Lived Experience from the Inside Out

LIVED EXPERIENCE
from the inside out

Social and Political Philosophy in Edith Stein

ANTONIO CALCAGNO

DUQUESNE UNIVERSITY PRESS
Pittsburgh, Pennsylvania

Copyright © 2014 Duquesne University Press
All rights reserved

Published in the United States of America by
DUQUESNE UNIVERSITY PRESS
600 Forbes Avenue
Pittsburgh, Pennsylvania 15282

No part of this book may be used or reproduced,
in any manner or form whatsoever,
without the written permission of the publisher,
except in the case of short quotations
in critical articles or reviews.

Library of Congress Cataloging-in-Publication Data

Calcagno, Antonio, 1969–
 Lived experience from the inside out : social and political philosophy in Edith Stein / Antonio Calcagno.
   pages cm
 Includes bibliographical references and index.
 Summary: "Focusing on significant texts from Edith Stein's early philosophical work, this book explicates rich sources of social and political insight, with Stein's particular focus on individual consciousness as the entry point: how we understand and live, always from our own interiorities, the phenomenal experiences of self, others, the masses, society, community, and the state"—Provided by publisher.
 ISBN 978-0-8207-0478-4 (pbk. : alk. paper)
 1. Stein, Edith, Saint, 1891–1942. I. Title.

BX4705.S814C35 2014
193—dc23

2014027369

∞ Printed on acid-free paper

For Fadi Abou-Rihan and Joyce Avrech Berkman

Interior intimo meo...
— Augustine of Hippo

Contents

List of Abbreviations of Edith Stein's Works ix
Acknowledgments xi
Preface xiii

Chapter 1. Situating Stein's Early Social and Political Philosophy 1
    Situating Stein's Work Today 1
    The Development of Stein's Early Social and Political Philosophy 9
    Other Roots of Stein's Social and Political Philosophy 20

Chapter 2. Empathy and the Beginnings of a Social and Political Philosophy .. 27
    What Is Empathy? 32
    Empathy Debates Today 44
    Empathy and the Constitution of Selves and Individuals 51
    Pre-Empathic Givens Acquired through Inner Experience 53
    The Lived-Body Pre-Empathy 57
    Transition to the Foreign Individual 68
    The Importance of Reiterated Empathy 75
    Empathy and the Understanding of the Spiritual Person 90

Chapter 3. The Move from Individuals to Superindividual Social Realities 109
    The Phenomenological Experience of the Social World 110
    The Essence of the Lived Experience of Intersubjective Life 112
    Stein and Contemporary Social Ontology 127
    The Psychic and Logical Foundations of the *Überindividuelle* World 130
    The Ontic Structure of the Community 145
    Critical Commentary 154

Chapter 4. Edith Stein's Political Philosophy 161
    Situating Stein's Treatise on the State 161
    Interpreting Stein's Concept of the Political 171
    Critical Assessment 190

Conclusion	*195*
Notes	*199*
Bibliography	*215*
Index	*225*

List of Abbreviations of Edith Stein's Works

FEB   *Finite and Eternal Being.* Translated by K. F. Reinhardt. Washington, DC: ICS Publications, 2002.

EP   *Einführung in die Philosophie.* Edited by H. B. Gerl-Falkovitz and C. M. Wulf. Freiburg, Germany: Herder, 2004.

E   *On the Problem of Empathy.* Translated by W. Stein. Washington, DC: ICS Publications, 1988.

PP   *Philosophy of Psychology and the Humanities.* Translated by M. C. Baseheart and M. Sawicki. Washington, DC: ICS Publications, 2000.

US   *Eine Untersuchung über den Staat.* In *Jarhrbuch für Philosophie und phänomenologische Forschung.* Vol. 7. Edited by Edmund Husserl, 1–123. Halle, Germany: Niemeyer, 1925.

IS   *An Investigation Concerning the State.* Translated by Marianne Sawicki. Washington, DC: ICS Publications, 2006.

Acknowledgments

This book would not have been possible without the generous financial support of the Social Sciences and Humanities Research Council of Canada. I am also grateful to King's University College in London, Ontario, for providing me with grants that helped fund the research that went into this volume. K. Daymond looked at initial drafts of chapters as they unfolded and was generous with comments and editorial suggestions. Joyce Avrech Berkman, a dear friend and fellow Stein scholar, always offered inspiration, encouragement, and insight about various issues in Stein's philosophy and life. I have benefitted from discussions with and from reading the work of Angela Ales Bello: her studies of Stein, Husserl, and phenomenology have taught me much. I also thank Diane Enns for her friendship and philosophical conversation. I am grateful for the support of Susan Wadsworth-Booth, Kathy Meyer, and the team at Duquesne University Press. Finally, I am blessed with the love and support of Fadi Abou-Rihan. His acuity and encouragement, as well as deep insight, are gifts.

Preface

While more has been written about Edith Stein's work on empathy, as well as her later philosophy, her early phenomenological work remains largely understudied. In this book I argue that Stein's early phenomenological works, including *On the Problem of Empathy, Philosophy of Psychology and the Humanities (Beiträge)*, and *An Investigation Concerning the State*, can be read together as an original and developed social-political theory. Questions concerning the nature of the social and the political were of significant concern to early phenomenologists, including Adolf Reinach, Max Scheler, Dietrich von Hildebrand, Gerhart Husserl, Gerda Walther, and Edith Stein. These figures addressed such topics as the nature of the law and its connections to society, community, and the state; the nature and role of the state; the constitution of social bonds; and the structure of rights. By focusing on Edith Stein's social and political phenomenology, I hope to bring to light the nature and relevance of her contributions.

Chapter 1 situates Stein's social and political project, explaining the central and crucial distinction between her earlier and later works. The main thesis guiding my project is introduced here: Stein's phenomenology, and it is *her* phenomenology, which draws from Husserl, Scheler, Reinach, Conrad-Martius, and many others, presents a rich discussion of what it is for the human individual to experience formative social bonds like the mass, society, community, and the state. Stein develops a theory of the internal political and the social: she presents a theory of how it is possible for minds to live "from within," in "inner experience," the experience of complex social objectivities. In order to do this, Stein starts with the problem of empathy.

In chapter 2, I argue that Steinian empathy, contrary to prevailing scholarly readings, is a means of self-understanding or self-knowledge, that, in turn, subsequently gives the subject a more general and encompassing comprehension of what it is to be a human person by comparing herself with others. As human persons, we all share a similar structure and, likewise, we can grasp the sense of what it is to be and live as a human person, namely, an embodied psycho-spiritual unity. Traditional scholarly readings of Steinian empathy focus on the intersubjective aspect of the work, and while this is crucial for Stein, as empathy certainly yields some understanding of other minds, the other serves as a test: the other is the focal point of eidetic variation, which allows the I to verify what it experiences not only at the level of personal experience but also at the more general and encompassing level of essence, ultimately yielding the essence or constitutive sense of what is to be a human person. Stein's account of empathy, then, justifies the claim that there is an essence that we all share, namely, we are all human persons. It is not only a way of knowing other minds.

As human persons, we are marked by a rich, complex social and political life. The social and the political dimensions of reality are important for who we are. For Stein, we primarily experience the social in two ways: internally and externally. In the case of the latter, Stein draws from sociology, economics, geography, political science, and history to show how other sciences can describe the "ontic" structures that certainly help constitute the lived experience of the social and the political. For example, Stein says that Renaissance history and economics deeply informed Renaissance sensibilities concerning art and culture. Yet we also live social and political realities from "within" consciousness; they vivify themselves within our minds, and our inner experience of these objectivities is unique and replete with sense. Stein's phenomenology aims at uncovering the sense and structures that make possible our inner lived experience of the social and political.

After establishing our shared structure as human persons, I show how Stein argues that our lived experience of the social world is dependent upon the nature of our social psychology as well as our phenomenological experience of certain social bonds. Chapter 3 focuses on explaining how certain psychological structures, which she considers as belonging to the realm of physical nature and natural causality (as opposed to motivation), make possible phenomenological experience. The first part of her *Beiträge* explains how it is that we possess certain synthesizing and communalizing capacities: sense perception, categorial acts, positional acts, dispositions, common sense, etc. The psyche gives us the tools with which we can phenomenologically experience the higher, more complex sense of social bonds like the mass, society, and community. The mass is lived as a naïve interchange, what Stein calls psychic contagion, with minimal reflection and awareness, whereas a bond between human persons that is directed toward an external goal marks the experience of society. An example of the mass would be babies crying because they hear other babies crying, even though there is no apparent reason for the distress. An example of a society would be a corporation: all members of the corporation work and share some kind of associative bond insofar as all the members are working together to help generate profit for the shareholders. This is the end goal of the corporation. A community is marked by a deep lived experience of solidarity, where one lives in the experience of the other: there is what Stein calls an "*ineinandergreifen*." Steinian intersubjectivity does not end with empathy, but must be understood within the larger discussion of the lived experience of social relations like the mass, society, and the community.

The final chapter explores Stein's theory of the state. I argue in this chapter that though Stein employs phenomenological insights in her treatise on the state, one must not read this work as a strict phenomenology, as most scholars tend to do. The text is also marked by her own political sensibilities, as well as her own phenomenological insights. I show how she argues that the state must be understood as a community of lawgivers and demonstrate the limitations of this view of the state, as it undermines what a societal or contractual model of the state purports to achieve. Stein's text demonstrates an urgent need for some kind of central political stability and order at the time she wrote it in post-World War I Weimar Germany: Stein's work on the state reflects her desire for genuine political reform. In many ways, however, her treatise poses problems for Stein's own desire for a lived political experience that would preserve difference and make space for its political expression and inclusion in our everyday lives, especially for minorities like the Jews and for women, who up until Stein's day had largely been excluded from occupying certain public positions, including philosophy professorships. This is the case because Stein has a very strong a priori notion of sovereignty, which comes to define the essence of the state.

Ultimately, with this book I try to achieve three things. First, I present a cohesive and systematic account of Stein's early social and political phenomenology. Second, I explain how Stein's contribution lies in her phenomenological account of how we live and share internally the important senses of social and political objectivities. Finally, I offer a critical appraisal of Stein's project as well as of the various scholarly interventions on Stein's social and political work. My hope in writing this book is that we can continue to discuss and contemplate the profound philosophical social and political interventions of one of the phenomenological movement's central but understudied figures.

CHAPTER 1

Situating Stein's Early Social and Political Philosophy

SITUATING STEIN'S WORK TODAY

The philosophy of Edith Stein has garnered some important philosophical attention during the past decade or so.[1] Notable philosophers, such as Alasdair MacIntyre,[2] have devoted considerable effort to situating Stein's work within her historical context as well as to grappling with the richness of her thought. It would not be an exaggeration to claim that Stein's philosophy has come to prominence in large part because of her elevation to Christian sainthood as well as her designation as Co-Patroness of Europe by Pope John Paul II.[3] She thus became the first phenomenologist-saint. Traditionally, Stein's life has been divided into her pre-Christian period and Christian period.[4] This division is described as marking a move from Husserlian phenomenology to Christian philosophy. Though one sees a consistency of themes throughout both periods, including a strong emphasis on subjectivity, intersubjectivity, and the notion of the person, most scholars tend to concentrate on Stein's later philosophical works. Why?

Philosophers and scholars tend to focus on Stein's later work for numerous reasons.[5] First is Stein's well-known frustration with Edmund Husserl, both as a phenomenologist and as a friend-mentor, which is documented in her letters,[6] and her eventual break

1

with Husserl and conversion to Roman Catholicism. She went to Göttingen to study with Husserl and followed him to Freiburg when he was named chair of philosophy there. She completed her doctorate under him and served as his first private assistant. Editing and preparing for publication important works such as the second and third volumes of Husserl's *Ideas Pertaining to a Pure Phenomenology and to a Phenomenological Philosophy*, as well as *On the Phenomenology of the Consciousness of Internal Time*, Stein conceived of her work with Husserl as a "collaboration."[7] After her departure from Husserl, and following her conversion, Stein's philosophy took a very different focus. Along with Hedwig Conrad-Martius, she participated in meetings of the Bergzabern circle of philosophers and trained herself in the classics of Christian philosophy, including Thomas Aquinas, Augustine of Hippo, and Duns Scotus. Immersing herself in the profound legacy of early and late medieval Scholastic thought, she produced three very important texts: *Potency and Act, Finite and Eternal Being,* and her translation of Thomas Aquinas's *Quaestiones disputatae de veritate*.[8]

Her first text was written as an *Habilitationsschrift*, a text required by the German state in order to gain an appointment to a university teaching position. Failing to gain such a position, Stein undertook the revision and expansion of this early work, which resulted in the text later known as *Finite and Eternal Being*. Describing this work as her "magnum opus,"[9] she marked this text as the high point of her philosophy, which was steeped in Christian philosophy. An enormous tome, the book attempts to uncover the various senses of being, moving from lower forms of being to the highest form of being, namely, God. She does this by employing the notion of form; beginning with the distinction between matter and form, she discusses prime matter (*hylé*) and moves toward the union of matter and form, ending with a discussion of pure form, which is the triune God. Especially at the beginning of the text, she draws upon phenomenological insights, but even there she reads them in light of thinkers such as Augustine and Aquinas. It would be wrong to say that there is a complete rupture between phenomenology and Christian philosophy in Stein's work; her later texts, particularly her Münster lectures, draw heavily from her early phenomenological treatises, including *Einführung in die Philosophie*.[10] Moreover, it is important to remember that Stein's later project was to synthesize Christian philosophy with phenomenology. Indeed, the novelty of Stein's project consisted in this very synthesis—a project that, to this day, remains popular with thinkers such as Jean-Luc Marion.[11]

In short, Stein's characterization of her later philosophy, understood as the attempt to reconcile Christian philosophy (Augustine of Hippo, Thomas Aquinas, and Duns Scotus) with phenomenology (Edmund Husserl, Martin Heidegger, and Hedwig Conrad-Martius), as the "great work" of her life created the impression that the work of this later period properly constitutes Stein's legacy, and this has resulted in a lack of consideration of her earlier work in phenomenology. This impression has been reinforced by the fact that Stein is an important contemporary thinker for Christian philosophy and theology. Her work is used to explain various contemporary problems within feminism and philosophical anthropology.[12] Edith Stein, Sister Teresia Benedicta a Cruce, is now an official saint of the Roman Catholic Church. John Paul II urged Christians to read her work, especially her Christian work, not only as a model of Christian thought but also in order to glean insights into the profound theological and philosophical mysteries of the Christ event.[13]

The second reason Stein's later works draw more attention than her earlier, more strictly Husserlian-inspired works has to do with events, circumstances, and personalities within the phenomenological community itself. Three constitutive considerations come into play here: first, the intense philosophical tension between eidetic and transcendental phenomenology and the roles they play vis-à-vis the sciences; second, the relationship between Husserl, Heidegger, and Stein; third, sexism and racism. These factors combined to set Stein apart from the early phenomenological tradition, yielding an image of her as a Christian philosopher, not a phenomenologist. In the eyes of certain phenomenologists, Stein's early work is seen to be more proto-Christian than strictly Husserlian.[14]

Turning to the first consideration, Stein went to study with Husserl after reading the first volume of the *Logical Investigations*.[15] She was inspired by the realism of Husserl's approach and the claim that one could know the essence of things themselves. His philosophy offered an alternative to the positivist and empirical views of experimental psychology and the sciences that then dominated German universities, especially the University of Breslau, where Stein had first gone to school. Traveling to Göttingen to meet with Husserl and study with his assistant, the philosopher Adolf Reinach, Stein was swept up in the enthusiasm and passion that pervaded phenomenological circles. The Göttingen Philosophical Society provided a rich and lively place of friendship and deep philosophical discussion. Stein also attended Husserl's lectures and eventually completed her doctorate under his supervision, now published as *On the Problem of Empathy*.[16] The Husserl that Stein admired and followed was the philosopher of the (first version of the) *Logical Investigations*, who believed that consciousness could grant us access to the meaning or objective sense of real things and states of affairs in the world. By the time Stein began to collaborate with Husserl as his private assistant, Husserl had become increasingly dissatisfied with this eidetic phenomenology as laid out in his earlier version of the *Logical Investigations*. He thought his philosophy was not sufficiently rigorous, and, inspired by his famous *Logos* article, "Philosophy as a Rigorous Science," Husserl began to develop his transcendental philosophy, which he saw as grounding the very condition for the possibility of science.[17] He thus moved from what, in the *Logical Investigations*, he calls psychological description, to a transcendental phenomenology in the *Ideas*. In the latter project, it was Husserl's extreme philosophical claim concerning the *Weltvernichtung*, or annihilation of the world, that caused Stein the most grief. In the first edition of *Ideas I*,[18] and drawing from mathematics, Husserl maintained that even if one were to suspend or cancel the given existence of the world, one could nonetheless know the meaning of it. The world need not exist in order to know and understand what it is. In short, meaning does not wholly depend upon the actual existence of the world. Husserl, of course, later changed this view, arguing in the *Cartesian Meditations* that the world and other subjects are co-given *originaliter* with oneself; self, other, and world are actual givens and are necessary for consciousness to make sense of them. But at the time of Stein's work with Husserl, she would sit in his office trying to convince him of the error of his thesis.[19] Stein was frustrated with Husserl's extreme form of transcendental idealism, which he eventually tempered as he continued to write. Stein was also frustrated with Husserl's move away from the eidetic phenomenology she so admired. This growing philosophical rift, which, in part, was why Stein decided to quit as Husserl's assistant, can be read as Stein's rejection of phenomenology or, at least, as having caused an irreconcilable cleavage between the Stein of phenomenology and the Stein of Christian philosophy.

Let us turn now to the second consideration. As Husserl's assistant, Stein was charged with preparing for publication various manuscripts that had been written in shorthand on scraps of paper; these scraps were not well organized. Stein worked tirelessly to prepare the texts, but Husserl was never satisfied with what she produced. It must be said that his dissatisfaction was not with Stein's work proper, but came from his sense that his own ideas and philosophy needed to be further developed. For example, Stein worked long and hard to prepare what is now Husserl's *On the Phenomenology of the Consciousness of Internal Time (1893–1917)*.[20] She edited and assembled Husserl's texts, supplementing them as she saw fit. She was able to do this because she knew Husserl's thought intimately and had privileged access to his vast notes and lectures. After completing her work on the *Ideas* Stein showed it to Husserl, but, becoming distracted, he put it aside. Stein was frustrated once again. It was only after Husserl had read and published Heidegger's *Being and Time* in his *Jahrbuch für Philosophie und phänomenologische Forschung* that he returned to the manuscript, presenting it to Heidegger and asking him for his assessment of it. Heidegger thought the text brilliant and urged Husserl to publish it. In fact, Heidegger agreed to edit it for publication. When the book appeared in 1928–29 in Husserl's *Jahrbuch*,[21] Heidegger, claiming that he had edited the work, thanked Fräulein Stein for her help in transcribing the manuscript. Upon closer examination, it was discovered that Heidegger had simply published Stein's version without making substantial changes. He presented her work as his own, failing to give Stein credit for her collaborative efforts. Fortunately, this fact has been recognised in the Meiner edition of Husserl's original German text. Rudolf Bernet, the editor of the volume, discusses Heidegger's misappropriation of the text.[22]

Husserl's constant failure to recognize what Stein regarded as her "collaboration"[23] with him, combined with Heidegger's failure to acknowledge Stein as Husserl's collaborator on the *Internal Time* manuscript, rendered Stein marginal. She never received public credit for the work of preparing and editing Husserl's material for publication. Husserl's and Heidegger's lack of recognition served to reduce Stein's contribution to that of a mere secretary, obscuring her contribution as a philosopher and phenomenologist in her own right. Her subsequent turn to Christianity, in Husserl's and Heidegger's eyes, severed her even further from the phenomenological tradition. Commenting on Stein's later work, Husserl observed almost with disappointment that Stein is more a religious thinker than a phenomenologist.[24] Later in life, Husserl lamented that none of his students followed him, instead pursuing their own interpretations of and interests in phenomenology; as he aged, he felt increasingly isolated. And when Stein went to visit Heidegger at Freiburg about the possibility of securing *Habilitation* in 1930–31, he promptly escorted her to the door, directing her to the Catholic philosopher Martin Honecker. Both Heidegger and Husserl regarded Stein not only as a secretarial assistant but also as a religious thinker, establishing a persistent philosophical stereotype of Stein that endures today.

The third and final consideration relating to the dismissal of Stein as a phenomenologist has to do with plain, old-fashioned sexism and racism. As we have seen, neither Husserl nor Heidegger regarded Stein as an equal, as a philosophical collaborator. In fact, when Stein asked Husserl for a letter of recommendation for her *Habilitation*, he wrote that if ever *Habilitation* in philosophy in the German university should become possible for women, he would certainly recommend Stein.[25] Husserl's qualified recommendation equivocated: he acknowledged her not as a philosopher but as a *female* philosopher. Husserl never advocated that the rules for *Habilitation* be changed to permit women to hold chairs in philosophy. Indeed, the only university position Stein ever held was as *Privatdozent* at Münster's German Institute for Scientific Pedagogy, where she was commissioned to give lectures in Catholic philosophical anthropology. It was there, in 1933, that her teaching and public philosophical career ended. Forbidden to teach or publish by Hitler's anti-Jewish laws, she was fired from the institute. Furthermore, one might speculate that, given Heidegger's record on Jewish academics,[26] he had no patience for the Catholic and Jewish Stein, which might account for his curt dismissal of her from his home and his refusal to advocate on her behalf for *Habilitation* at Freiburg. Sexism and racism combined to frustrate Stein's philosophical ambitions. Furthermore, her more explicitly Christian thinking and her involvement with the Christian intellectual scene were more appreciated by her various audiences. She traveled and gave public lectures while teaching, translating, and researching, earning quite the public reputation through speaking tours and radio addresses.[27] Stein was highly regarded in the Catholic world and was in contact with eminent Catholic intellectuals of her day, including Gertrud von le Fort, Jacques Maritain, Dietrich von Hildebrand, and Erich Przywara. This recognition, along with her spiritual legacy, have helped bring Stein to prominence today as a religious thinker as well as a mystic, but her early work in phenomenology remains largely underexamined and undervalued.

I focus on Stein's early social and political phenomenology in order, first, to provide a systematic reading of this early work and, second, to give a particular reading to the several constitutive moments of this work, including the treatment of empathy, psychology, theory of community, and the state. My particular interpretation of these aspects of Stein's writings will be taken up in greater detail in subsequent chapters. I know of no such work in the English language that has undertaken the aforementioned tasks. This book, then, is a critical exposition of and engagement with a little-known but powerful period in Stein's philosophy.

Two distinct but interrelated social ontologies define Stein's thought. The first refers to Stein's early philosophical period, developed from about 1913 to 1925, which includes her more Husserlian-inspired works: *On the Problem of Empathy, Philosophy of Psychology and the Humanities, An Investigation concerning the State,* and *Introduction to Philosophy* (*Einführung in die Philosophie*). This last work consists of the lectures that Stein gave when she returned to Breslau after leaving Husserl and while attempting to secure *Habilitation* for the first time at Kiel and Hamburg. Also important is the fact that this work marks the beginning of Stein's interest in and development of more explicitly religious themes—themes that would shape and define her later Christian philosophy. While it is true that Stein was always concerned with the nature of personhood, the way she defines and approaches it shifts from a more phenomenological framework to one supplemented by Christian notions of personhood and faith; she will discuss God's role in shaping the human person (*EP* 171–72). The second stage of Stein's social ontology was developed through her encounter with early medieval thinking (Augustine and Dionysius the Areopagite), Scholastic philosophy (Thomas Aquinas and Duns Scotus), and Christian philosophy (Jacques Maritain, Erich Przywara, and Martin Grabmann). It is marked by an acute attunement to the revealed truths of Roman Catholicism as well as by a highly developed Christian anthropology. Much has been, and continues to be, written about this Christian theological social ontology, which is rooted in a thick sense of the human person and his or her relation to God.

Focusing on Stein's early social and political phenomenology, this book will not substantially take up her more explicitly religious views. This being said, Stein's later social philosophy does not exclude certain earlier phenomenological insights and conclusions, but these remain distinct from her later period, following her conversion to Roman Catholicism in 1922. For example, absent in Stein's earlier account is the intimate relation she postulates between the three divine persons of the Trinity and our own created personhood as developed in *Finite and Eternal Being* (*FEB* 352–54). Scholars such as Sawicki and Guilead argue that the two periods are separate, but because there are profound meditations on the role of the ego, consciousness, and the person in both her earlier and later thought, it would be artificial to irreconcilably separate Stein's thought into preconversion and postconversion thought, with the two realms having nothing to say to one another. As indicated above, this has, up until now, been a serious problem. In the end, I regard these two periods as distinct but related. The need to investigate Stein's early social and political phenomenology and philosophy stems from the fact that attention to this work has largely been restricted to her well-known text on empathy or has been underinvestigated, especially for English-speaking readers. English translations of the texts of this period have only recently become available, and Stein's *Introduction to Philosophy* is not yet available, but these texts are difficult to follow as they require a complete understanding of the background and philosophical landscape that Stein inhabited.

The Development of Stein's Early Social and Political Philosophy

There are fine works that trace the background and philosophical context of Stein's social and political framework.[28] One also finds excellent biographical and historical works on the life of Edith Stein that nicely explain how Stein's own life was shaped and formed by her various experiences of the social and political world. Here, the works of Joyce Avrech Berkman and Sister Josephine Koeppel, OCD, as well as the work of Angela Ales Bello, Alasdair MacIntyre, and Beate Beckmann-Zöller and Hanna-Barbara Gerl-Falkovitz are particularly informative.[29] I do not wish to rehearse what others have done so formidably well; rather, I wish to focus on Stein's texts in order to show that when we approach her social and political philosophy, we must distinguish between her preconversion and postconversion texts. I argue that, though there is a continuation of some themes through these texts, there are substantial differences between them that make necessary a distinction between the two periods.

Stein went to study with Husserl in 1913 after reading his *Logical Investigations,* which raised serious questions about the very foundations of science, especially the psychology she was then studying at Breslau with William Stern. Husserl had severely critiqued the psychologism and positivism that was dominant in both the faculties of philosophy and psychology. There, all phenomena to be investigated were reduced to some kind of psychological fact that emphasized a rather mechanistic and/or positivistic view of causality. Stein decided to write her doctoral thesis under Husserl, focusing on the problem of empathy, as Husserl had indicated that it needed further elaboration. In his lectures *Natur und Geist* (Nature and spirit), Husserl discussed the problem of empathy, but he recognized that his treatment up to that point had been insufficient. Indeed, if we look throughout the *Nachlass* volumes on intersubjectivity, we see that Husserl devotes a considerable amount of time to empathy, its different forms, and the problems it poses for his own philosophy.[30] By the time Stein arrived in Göttingen, Husserl had already moved from the logical realism of the *Logical Investigations* to his more idealist, transcendental period, marked by the publication of *Ideas Pertaining to a Pure Phenomenology and to a Phenomenological Philosophy.* Stein was thus caught between Husserl's earlier realism and his later idealism. Stein was deeply influenced by other remarkable phenomenologists who were members of the Göttingen Circle, including Adolf Reinach, Max Scheler (a frequent visitor to the group), Jean Hering, Alexandre Koyré, Hedwig Conrad-Martius, and Roman Ingarden. Of all these thinkers, Stein was most influenced by Reinach,[31] who taught her the phenomenological method and how to apply it "to the things themselves," and by Husserl, who uncovered for her the deep underlying structures of knowledge and science.

In fact, in order to understand Stein's peculiar intervention in phenomenology, one must not view it as strictly Husserlian or Reinachian. The long-standing tradition of reading Stein as a student of Husserl has resulted in a large body of scholarship focusing on the relation between the two philosophers. Studies by Steinians and Husserlians show how each borrowed from and misinterpreted the other. There is, however, a tendency to privilege Husserl as the "father of phenomenology" and Stein's interpretations are often read as *mis*interpretations of Husserl's project. Given that phenomenology was never a monolithic movement and that each thinker, as Spiegelberg[32] rightly comments, advanced his or her own version of phenomenology, though always with some degree of fidelity to the things themselves, we should read Stein, too, as following this trajectory. She was not merely a student of Husserl and Reinach; she had her own unique phenomenological voice—a voice that took shape in her earliest work on empathy. Stein's doctoral dissertation and first book exhibit her own view of phenomenology as a synthesis of both the logical (e.g., whole and parts, expression, judgment, etc.) and even transcendental structures of the mind (e.g., person, the other) that make knowledge possible (in the case of her doctoral dissertation, knowledge of other minds), as well as the object investigated by the very knowledge in question. Here, that object is the nature of the human person in general, or the knowing subject.

Stein's doctoral dissertation (or, more precisely, what remains of it, as the first part, which treats the history of the problem, is no longer extant) is structured along three lines. First is the description of empathy as an act of mind. Stein explains what empathy is and how it operates, ultimately distinguishing it from other mental acts, such as remembering, imagining, and perceiving. Second, she discusses the objects of empathy, that is, self-knowledge and the approximate knowledge of other minds that is always subject to revision and greater precision. What is uncovered here is a general structure that Stein calls "person." Her description of the person is based in a purely eidetic (early) phenomenological perspective, and the description yields a picture of what it is to be a person, or subject, in general. More will be said about this later. The essential description of the person has an intentional correlate, namely, real persons that exist in the world and in the natural attitude, but the primacy of the being, or existential aspect, of the person as foundational and created by God comes later in Stein's Christian philosophy.[33] Finally, unlike Husserl in his early published work, Stein believed that the foundation of all science lay not only in the logical or ideal, transcendental structures of the mind as outlined in Husserl's *Logical Investigations* and *Ideas I*, but in a phenomenology that also studies the natural aspects of the psychic (*psychisch*), sometimes translated as the sentient, as well as the structures of the larger social and political world. For Stein, the social sciences (e.g., history, literature, and psychology) had a great deal to offer, especially when set in their proper phenomenological context. Stein's *Beiträge* can be read in this light. There, science is an extension of the human—the individual as well as the collective, both of which have essential structures that condition the very practice of the science in question. In fact, the phenomenology of the human person, for Stein, grounds and guides the other sciences, especially history, the social sciences, and psychology. This has been a constant claim of Stein's phenomenology,[34] a claim that also guides the way we live in terms of our religion and ethics. Husserl would certainly agree, in part, with this claim.

If we closely examine these three moments of Stein's dissertation, we see not only her unique view of phenomenology but her peculiar response to the larger questions that phenomenology was struggling with at the time, especially the crisis in science and philosophy and the attempts to delineate their respective proper fields of inquiry. Stein agreed with Husserl that one must understand certain basic starting points if one is to undertake any rigorous philosophical inquiry, including inquiry into the structure of consciousness, the centrality of the I, meaning, and the possibility of understanding what is represented in the mind. As Reinach largely formed and educated her in the phenomenological method, Stein drew her method as well as the focus of her inquiry from him. Reinach understood Husserl's rallying cry—"To the things themselves!"—to mean that phenomenology could yield ideal essences, and hence ideal understanding, of things in the world. So Reinach devoted himself to various kinds of inquiries, including investigations of the natures of civil law, of essences, and states of affairs, as well as of negative judgments.[35] Husserl was more concerned with uncovering the conditions, either logical or transcendental, that make knowledge or sense (*Sinn*) possible in the first place, whereas Reinach was interested in using the method to inquire into various kinds of phenomenological objects. By the time Stein arrived at Göttingen, the split between Husserlian transcendental phenomenology or idealism and Reinachian mundane, *real* phenomenology was apparent. Stein negotiated both of these worlds by accepting the Husserlian analysis of consciousness as constituting the sense of objects of consciousness, and by focusing on specific acts and objects of consciousness, namely, empathy (in which Husserl, too, was interested) and the person. The particular Steinian intervention in this earlier period of phenomenology consisted of two things: First, following thinkers such as Scheler,[36] she accepted the fundamental role of the human person as a central structure in phenomenology. But knowledge of what a person is cannot be established simply by inner self-reflection. Knowledge of oneself as a person is earned through empathy and an awareness of other minds. Self-knowledge comes to its fullest sense only through empathy and the awareness of oneself created by placing oneself in relief against another mind. Scheler was critical of empathy as a means of knowing other minds: he argued that it is almost impossible for one to be sure of what another is actually thinking. The claim that phenomenology can give us knowledge of other minds is precarious because such knowledge remains rooted in an egological structure (at least as far as empathy is understood in the works of Theodor Lipps, Stein, and John Stuart Mill).

Second, for Stein, the ground of the sciences was not to be found exclusively in either the logical or transcendental structures of the mind, as Husserl argued, or in the possibility of ideal essences and judgments, as Reinach maintained; rather, she saw science as rooted in the complex life of persons, as they experience and live themselves, either as individuals or as collectivities in communities or societies. We see this sentiment expressed in Stein's edit of Husserl's *Ideas III*, a text with which Husserl was never satisfied and that he refused to publish in his lifetime. Stein carried this argument through into her *Beiträge*, where she criticized Hugo Münsterberg's approach to psychology and his attempts to psychologize the human sciences. I will say more about this later.

In sum, Stein's early view of phenomenology drew from Husserl and various members of the Göttingen Circle, including Reinach and Scheler. But she distinguished her particular understanding of empathy as yielding knowledge of oneself as a person by arguing that the person and his or her individual and collective life provide the grounds for all philosophical and scientific inquiry, thereby attacking both a psychologistic and positivist approach to science and philosophy. Stein's treatment of the state, the third work of her earlier philosophical period, is an extension of her social ontology, and it presents challenges to both phenomenology and political theory in general. I will take up these arguments in chapter 4. Unlike Scheler, Stein gave empathy a central role in her phenomenology and, unlike Husserl, she grounded all science in an understanding of the human person and human nature rather than in phenomenology per se, a phenomenology that Husserl understood as the foundation of all science and as itself a rigorous science. But Stein also drew from Husserl: the place of nature in her phenomenology, though uniquely her own, was nonetheless influenced by Husserl. We know that Husserl constantly revised and reworked his philosophy; hence, most of his published works feature the subtitle "Introduction." Stein's time with Husserl—a time of great change for him—was particularly fraught: Husserl was at a crossroads, moving from a more eidetic science to a transcendental grounding for all sciences. Despite the changes in Stein's own early phenomenology, which evolved from a descriptive eidetic analysis to a formal ontology in the *Introduction to Philosophy,* the notion of sense (*Sinn*) is consistent. Attending Husserl's lectures and with access to his unpublished notes and manuscripts, Stein was deeply influenced by his ideas. Husserl insisted that sense was acquired through the correspondence between meaning-intention and meaning-fulfillment, or the constitutive accord between noesis and noema. Writing to Ingarden while she was editing and transcribing Husserl's *Ideas II* and *III,* Stein described herself as a heretic and chided Husserl for failing to account for the role of "nature," or physical reality, which is, presumably, both constitutive of and prior to consciousness.[37] Stein includes physical nature, understood as the lived body and psyche, in her analysis of the human person in her text on empathy. Husserl shared this view of nature, as evidenced by his unpublished notes on intersubjectivity, which Stein reread, and his lectures on "Nature and Spirit," which she attended. But in his published texts Husserl never accords to physical reality or nature a constitutive role. Stein wanted to bring this aspect of Husserl's thought forward, but her attempts to persuade Husserl to produce a thicker or deeper account of nature and the world in sense-making and constitution failed; Husserl never acceded to Stein's arguments and appeals. Both Stein and Husserl believed that physical reality, nature, was important for phenomenology and sense-making, or sense-bestowal. Stein, however, developed and published her analysis of the connection between sense-making and nature, whereas Husserl confined his ideas about nature to his *Nachlass*. Husserlians remain divided between those who maintain that we must read and take as central what Husserl wanted and chose to publish, and those who wish to make sense of the whole Husserlian corpus, published and unpublished.

Stein's view of nature can be found in her treatment of the body and the psyche, both experienced through a physical body or physical causality (i.e., the structure of the psyche), and I will treat both of these in the chapters that follow. For example, Stein maintains that any understanding or sense we have of experience begins in a physical or natural experience of sensation and feeling. The first locus of sense-making is thus the lived body. Insofar as perception and feeling are experienced as physical, as opposed to spiritual (*geistlich*) phenomena, the lived body is part of the natural world. Adopting the early language of Husserl, which he later abandoned, Stein argues that in order to have something like empathy and the understanding or sense it delivers about self-understanding and something like the human person or human being in general, understood in an eidetic sense, we must examine the body from the perspectives of inner and outer perception. Inner perception makes one aware that one's body occupies space and relates to itself in space; one experiences one's body as occupying and moving within a certain space. Also, inner perception makes us aware of how we affect ourselves, what phenomenologists call auto-affection. Outer perception makes present the fact that the body is constantly being impressed upon; it receives *Empfindungen* (sense impressions or sensations) from the outside world. Moreover, these impressions cause us to take note of them; we perceive them. Depending upon the impression we receive, various senses work together to presentify (*Vergegenwärtigung*) to consciousness what we have experienced. The lived experience of sensations and impressions makes us aware that our body is a locus of sentience. Inner experience gives us the lived experience of having a body, whereas outer experience allows us to understand the sense of that body as a locus of impression or sentience. We acquire a sense that we are feeling beings, that we are capable of feeling the outside. In order to have anything like experience, we need a body, we need to be able to perceive and bear impressions and feelings. Stein writes:

> As an instance of the supreme category of "experience," sensations are among the real constituents of consciousness, of this domain impossible to cancel. The sensation of pressure or pain or cold is just as absolutely given as the experience of judging, willing, perceiving, etc. Yet, in contrast with these acts, sensation is peculiarly characterized. It does not issue from the pure "I" as they do, and it never takes on the form of the "cogito" in which the "I" turns toward an object. Since sensation is always spatially localized "somewhere" at a distance from the "I" (perhaps very near to it but never in it), I can never find the "I" in it by reflection. And this "somewhere" is not an empty point in space, but something filling up space. All of these unities, the unity of my living body, and they are themselves places in the living body. (*E* 42)

The sense of a lived body as a unity, as a locus of sensation, as having both an inner and outer aspect, is fundamental for higher acts of consciousness, which Stein, along with Descartes and Husserl, ascribes to the *cogito*.

Having sketched *grosso modo* some very basic aspects of Stein's unique early phenomenology, I would like to summarize how this early phenomenology can be distinguished from her later philosophy.

I see four principal differences. First, though Stein's understanding of the structure of the person continues to occupy a central role in her later Christian philosophy, the later view of the person acquires a theological aspect. Whereas in the earlier text empathy leads us to an understanding of ourselves as persons, capable of acting, speaking, valuing, and knowing, in the later texts the person is an extension of the creator God, who is Himself tri-personal. As creatures of God, we bear the mark of this divine personal structure and continue to bear traces of the effect of His creation. In the later texts, one encounters God in the core of the person, or *Persönlichkeitskern,* whereas in the earlier texts, this personal core can simply be understood as the personality, namely, that which makes us singular, which individuates us, one from the other.

Second, the notion of the person, which is set in a largely linguistic-epistemological, even valuing, framework in her early phenomenology, is subsequently placed within the framework of being. Stein's conception of the person as grounding both the natural and human sciences continued to have purchase, especially in her Münster lectures on philosophical anthropology, but it is the very being of the person, not consciousness or knowledge, as in the earlier texts, that motivates inquiry. In short, we can say that the person, understood as foundational for any kind of scientific undertaking, at first acquired its motivating force by what we know and how we know it and, later, by who and what we are.

Third, except for a few small references to it, empathy all but disappears in Stein's later work. It is no longer seen as yielding the possibility of self-awareness or awareness of other minds. Again, the later works are marked by a distinctive metaphysical turn, in which the nature of being itself makes evident what we are, both as individuals and as collectivities. Here, we see the profound effects of the medieval revival of the concept of being, especially in thinkers such as Erich Przywara, Étienne Gilson, Jacques Maritain, and Martin Grabmann—all of them influential for Stein—who took up medieval thinkers such as Thomas Aquinas, Duns Scotus, and Dionysus the Areopagite. But we must not underestimate the significant influence that Heidegger had on Stein's thought. She claimed that reading his *Being and Time* deeply impressed her. She had studied four of Heidegger's early works and saw in them profound ways of rethinking time, care, questioning, and the role of death in our existence.[38] Heidegger helped Stein to see the existential implications of her own thinking, as the inclusion of her essay on Heidegger as an appendix to *Finite and Eternal Being* makes clear.

Finally, the way in which phenomenology itself is viewed undergoes a shift in Stein's later work. Stein's earlier phenomenology, as previously mentioned, lay within the contextualizing poles of Husserl's and Reinach's thought. Though she draws upon phenomenology in her later thought—for example, at the beginning of *Endliches und ewiges Sein* or at various points in her Münster lectures—her employment of the phenomenological method becomes more loosely descriptive and less eidetic. There, she used phenomenology to describe experience, especially the most basic points of existence, such as the undeniability of the Augustinian "I am, I live, I think," but it yields no deeper or conditioning structure as it did in her earlier texts. Empathy was a deep structure of the mind that afforded all kinds of epistemological and linguistic possibilities of knowing self and other, as well as the general essence of the human person, but in the later texts, phenomenology became a merely descriptive psychology that affirms certain indubitable facts about the existence of the I or the flow of consciousness, as asserted in the first chapter of *Finite and Eternal Being*.

Though the sense that dominates Stein's earlier work is certainly rooted in consciousness, and a consciousness that is intimately tied to real things, the unified sense of being that she presents in her later writings places consciousness within a deeper ontological structure of being, diminishing the primacy of consciousness established in her earlier work. There, Stein argues that the phenomenological sense of a community or, more precisely, the lived experience of community (*Gemeinschaftserlebnis*) is, in part, constituted by "solidarity"—a particular form of consciousness whereby one lives in the experience of the other, for and with the other. In order to achieve this awareness of solidarity, deep bodily, psychic, and *geistlich,* or spiritual, structures are required. In *Finite and Eternal Being*, Stein again takes up the theme of community, but from an ontological perspective. The primacy of the phenomenological mind, which constitutes the essence of, or gives sense to, our experience of community, is here replaced by a more fundamental account in which the being of the individual entity is seen to belong to the whole, or "all," of a larger being. Stein postulates a unity between individual being and a plurality of beings. She remarks:

> We must therefore try to understand how the multiplicity and the unity of existents, i.e., the particular being of each individual existent and *the oneness* of being, can be found side by side. And in this attempt we may be guided by what we have said concerning the meaning of the good and the beautiful. If every existent has for other existents the meaning of "that which imparts perfection," and if each existent is formed according to a structural law that is integrally adapted to a universal, then all existents together form a coherently ordered *whole:* the *oneness* of *all that which is* [*das Seiende*]. And all self-enclosed (and in their self-enclosure comprehensible) meaningful units must then be regarded as parts of all that which is. The *oneness of being* is the being of the *whole*, a being of which all the parts "partake." (*FEB* 334)

Here, she articulates the being of God, the Trinity, the analogy of being, and the sense of being. She also introduces love as qualifying the bond between the members of the Trinitarian and human communities. Stein reworks the analogy of being, understood in a deep existential sense and not merely as logical (because the trace between the existent and the creator is real and relational), in order to explain how individual existents can "participate" in the sense of the whole (*FEB* 352–54).

In the end, though Stein continues to use concepts such as the person, phenomenology, and consciousness in her later works, they must not be understood as identical in meaning with their earlier use. As Stein grew and developed as a philosopher, her philosophy also grew and changed. We will see evidence of this change when we look at her political philosophy. This being said, however, it is not the case that Stein's earlier writings cannot accommodate what came later, but we must be careful not to elide the important distinction between her earlier and later work. Perhaps one way to characterize this distinction in relation to her social ontology is this: It would be fair to say that Stein was consistently concerned with developing a social ontology rooted in the lives of human persons, but in her earlier period her social concern falls under the rubric of the phenomenological synthesis that she produced between Husserl and Reinach. In this period, she developed her own unique understanding of the person and empathy. In her later thought the person remains central, but her understanding of the person is layered with additional theological and metaphysical possibilities that did not appear in her earlier phenomenology.

Other Roots of Stein's Social and Political Philosophy

As mentioned earlier, the sources upon which Stein drew in order to develop her own early social ontology are located in phenomenology. But other significant influences, including sociology and psychology, also helped to shape Stein's social ontology. Her *Beiträge* are deeply structured by the sociological categories of thinkers such as Scheler, Georg Simmel, and Ferdinand Tönnies.[39] From Tönnies she found useful the distinction between society (*Gesellschaft*) and community (*Gemeinschaft*), and from Simmel she took not only the distinction between society and community, but the notion of the masses as well. Stein uses these sociological distinctions to justify the claim that social objectivities are actual concrete entities with an ontic structure that contributes to our lived experience of said social objectivities, including society and community. Her phenomenological claim is that, in addition to an ontic social structure that is marked by some kind of personal, associative life as well as certain economic, geographical, political, historical, ethical, and religious structures, social objectivities, especially that of community, require a concomitant mental structure as well as conscious content that deeply inform how communities are lived and represented in experience. For Stein, a peculiar lived experience of community helps constitute the sense or being of a community—this is what she calls a *Gemeinschaftserlebnis,* or lived experience of community. (I will say more about this in chapter 3.) In drawing upon sociology, understood in the German sense of a science or *Wissenschaft*, and especially the founding fathers of sociology, Stein continues Husserl's project by pointing out that our understanding of what social reality is cannot proceed only by an objective description of the constitutive elements of our social and political world. We must also admit that our own experience and the structures that permit such experience are also constitutive and conditioning of what (read: phenomenological essence) our social and political world is. Stein's early phenomenology draws heavily from the social sciences (her later work does so less), and she saw herself as supplementing what is given in those sciences by uncovering phenomenological structures and content that condition our descriptions of what is thus given. In this way, Stein took very seriously Max Scheler's assertion that philosophy must engage the other sciences in order for it to be able to give a concrete analysis of the phenomena under investigation.

Stein began her university education by studying psychology, but she was deeply perturbed by psychology's failure to justify and ground many of its key concepts. This is why she found Husserl's attempt to give the sciences some logical ground so vital, which led to her decision to leave psychology and pursue the new philosophy of Husserlian phenomenology. This being said, however, Stein's break with psychology was never complete. In fact, if one examines her early, and even her later, works, one finds constant reference to the works of relevant psychologists. In her earlier works on empathy, for example, she examines the work of Theodor Lipps and commented upon his fusional view of empathy.[40] In her Münster lectures, she engaged with depth psychology.[41] One cannot deny that early psychology and phenomenology focused on similar questions and problems. Stein was critical of early psychology for two primary reasons, the first being psychologism. Following Husserl, Stein maintained that the reduction of mental phenomena to psychic causality fails to appreciate the complexity and transcendence of consciousness in general. The project of the *Logical Investigations* was to demonstrate how key logical operations, including the establishment of truth as logical adequation in the *Sixth Logical Investigation,* could not be traced simply to a body-psyche relation of psychic causality, which at the time was conceived in very mechanistic, physical terms.

In appendix 2 of *Philosophy of Psychology and the Humanities,* Stein devotes a substantial portion of text to tackling Münsterberg's approach to the sciences.[42] Münsterberg is generally known for two significant contributions to psychology and philosophy. An early psychologist, he claimed that psychology was indeed its own science, distinguished from philosophy by its emphasis on empirical evidence acquired through and confirmed in testing and analysis. Invited to Harvard from Germany, Münsterberg worked closely with William James to establish a psychology laboratory there. What the human sciences had failed to yield, especially in philosophy and phenomenology, was sound empirical and rigorously tested evidence for what they claimed as clear and distinct phenomena. The project of phenomenology was regarded as solipsistic, rooted in an understanding of consciousness as self-referential and hyperegoic. Münsterberg's second proposition concerned psychophysical parallelism, the idea that all physical processes are accompanied by parallel brain processes. Moreover, all mental states and neurological disorders were seen to be caused by cellular-metabolic functions. Applying his theories, Münsterberg made great headway in what is known as forensic psychology by demonstrating that brain processes can explain what witnesses in a court trial claim to perceive, and how they speak about it. Experimental psychology began to be applied to all kinds of fields, including labor, law, and other sciences in order to supplement them. Münsterberg writes:

> In this way all kinds of scientists who cared little for psychology had gathered the most various psychological results with experimental methods, and the psychologists saw that they could not afford to ignore such results of natural science. It would not do to go on claiming, for instance, that thought is quick as lightning when the experiments of the astronomers had proved that even the simplest mental act is a slow process, the time of which can be measured. Experimental psychology, therefore, started with an effort to repeat on its own account and from

its own point of view those researches which others had performed. But it seemed evident that this kind of work would never yield more than some little facts in the periphery of mental life—borderland facts between mind and body. No one dreamed of the possibility of carrying such experimental method to the higher problems of inner life which seemed the exclusive region of the philosophising psychologist. But as soon as experimental psychology began to work in its own workshops, it was most natural to carry the new method persistently to new groups of problems. The tools of experiment were now systematically used for the study of memory and the connection of ideas, then of attention and of imagination, of space perception and time sense; slowly they became directed to the problems of feeling and emotion, of impulse and volition, of imitation and reasoning. Groups of mental functions which yesterday seemed beyond the reach of experimental laboratory methods, today appear quite accessible. It may be said that there is now hardly a corner of mental life into which experimental psychology has not thrown its searchlight. It may seem strange that this whole wonderful development should have gone on in complete detachment from the problems of practical life. Considering that perception and memory, feeling and emotion, attention and volition, and so on, are the chief factors of our daily life, entering into every one of our enjoyments and duties, experiences and professions, it seems astonishing that no path led from the seclusion of the psychological workshop to the market-place of the world.[43]

For Stein, Münsterberg represented a serious challenge. Stein did not wish to deny the existence of a psychophysical parallel between various mental and physical states and brain processes and functions, but she regarded the experimental psychological approach as reducing that which is uniquely human and proper to the life of human spirit and history to mechanistic, natural causality; the spontaneity and creativity of spirit cannot be accounted for exclusively in natural, mechanistic terms. In her *Beiträge,* Stein argues instead for the distinction between psyche and spirit. Furthermore, she wondered how psychological experimentation and brain function, which focuses on an individual, can begin to explain and make sense of communal and social events, superindividual realities, especially as they unfold through time and space. Stein claims that the mechanistic view of psychology tended to see social phenomena (recall that this was a time prior to the development of social psychology) simply as the conglomeration of the results of various individual phenomena. For Stein, although such a conglomeration would typify the behavior of the masses and even society generally, it could not account for communities. She argues for a unique lived experience that typifies the mental life of communities, an experience that psychology could not explain in purely mechanistic terms. Contrary to Münsterberg, Stein, at the end of her *Einführung in die Philosophie,* argues that the reduction of psychology to natural theories of causality that focus on the individual fails to account for broader concepts of evidence and proof. In short, for Stein, the whole of human history, meaning, and human being, as well as being in general, is not reducible to a sum of parts. Philosophy and phenomenology proper, as well as the other human sciences, can give valid accounts of how the sense of the whole is to be understood and how it comes to be. Stein's insistence on the capability of the human or cultural sciences, the *Geisteswissenschaften,* to understand and advance the life of the human spirit was not merely psychological. Although psychology can certainly help in understanding what goes on in these cultural sciences, the human sciences create and study more than that which can be verified through experimental psychology. Moreover, experimental psychology must give an account of the language, logic, and mental structures that condition it and allow it to speak and assume authority in the way it does. Here, Stein follows the classic Husserlian critique of the sciences in general. Finally, she addresses the question of evidence. Is evidence constituted merely at the level of external observation and verification, or is there not clear, distinct, and forceful evidence that arises not only from external testing, but from inner experience and the inner verification of sense (*Sinn*) that is undeniably part of human experience—one's own as well as others'? Stein affirms that this is what phenomenology can yield. The phenomenological method shows how we can understand and be sure of what appears to us in consciousness as objectively meaningful or sense-laden. This is what eidetic variation can achieve but experimental observation can only verify by other means.

Stein's second general critique of psychology is its inability to account for the very conditions that make it possible as a science.

Psychology is a particular practice of a specialized science with certain determined goals and objects of inquiry, but, according to Stein, it cannot account for the conditions that make it possible as a science. Phenomenology, however, especially as laid out in Husserl's *Logical Investigations* and parts of his *Ideas I*, can do so. It would be a gross exaggeration to claim that all of psychology was practiced in the way of which Stein was so critical, particularly if one thinks of the development of Freud's own thought and methodology, which became highly self-reflexive as a practice. We can fairly say, however, that, while a student at Breslau, the psychology to which Stein was exposed through the work of William Stern, with its heavy emphasis on experimentation, certainly led her to question the purpose and methodology of experimental psychology.

Just as Stein was critical of certain psychological approaches to mental life, she was also deeply influenced by more phenomenological approaches to psychology, especially the work of Alexander Pfänder,[44] one of the founders of the Munich school of *Realphänomenologie*. Pfänder claims that the deep structures of willing and feeling play significant roles in how we view and understand the world. Husserlian consciousness and the logic of sense-giving constitution, though important, cannot on their own account for the foundations of all knowledge. For Pfänder, unlike Husserl, meaning is neither simply ideal nor transcendental; rather, it is real and deeply embedded in the world and the natural attitude that Husserl so forcefully tries to bracket through his (in)famous *Weltvernichtung* in the first edition of *Ideas I*. Pfänder's rich studies of willing, striving, and motivation color much of both Stein's and Husserl's treatment of the realm of spirit or *Geist*, especially in Stein's early phenomenology and in Husserl's *Ideas II and III*, texts transcribed, edited, and augmented by Stein.

Stein's political philosophy, as elaborated in her *Eine Untersuchung über den Staat (An Investigation concerning the State)*, is the last important element of her social ontology, and the sources that profoundly conditioned her analysis were drawn largely from the phenomenologies of von Hildebrand and Reinach, as well as from the political philosophy of Hegel, Aristotle and Kjellen. Her ethical and religious considerations of the state drew from the works of Hegel and von Hildebrand.[45] As mentioned earlier, she drew upon the work of sociology, which also extended into her political analyses. Stein found Reinach helpful for her discussion of the a priori foundation of the state as right (*Recht*), and she relied upon Aristotle's notions of autarchy, or sovereignty (*Souvranität*) in arguing that the essential foundation of the state depends upon it—it is the *conditio sine qua non* of the state. Stein's treatment of the state is a synthesis of the ideas of various thinkers and of various approaches to political philosophy, but it also constitutes her own attempt at a political intervention in discussions about the future of the German state in Weimar Germany. One of the challenges of Stein's treatise on the state is to determine just what is unique about the text and how it fits into her own phenomenology and social ontology in general. More will be said about this when we examine the role of the state in Stein's philosophy.

This chapter explains three background considerations key for an examination of Stein's early phenomenology and social ontology. First, we must resist the temptation to color her early phenomenology with her later Christian philosophy. Her early work, though meaningful for her later work, is nevertheless distinct. Second, Stein has her own phenomenological project in mind when she presents her social philosophy. She must not be regarded as derivative or as simply synthesizing the arguments of her colleagues. In dialogue with the social sciences and her fellow phenomenologists, Stein made her own peculiar philosophical intervention in social ontology and phenomenology. Finally, we must remain mindful of the sources for Stein's thought, which include phenomenology, psychology, sociology, and political theory, as well as history. Failure to consider this rich backdrop of problems and sources runs the risk of yielding a selective picture of Stein, thereby contributing to the plethora of problems that plagued her life and continue to shape her legacy, as outlined in the opening sections of this chapter.

CHAPTER 2

Empathy and the Beginnings of a Social and Political Philosophy

Scholars traditionally maintain that Edith Stein's social ontology begins with empathy, or *Einfühlung*.[1] *On the Problem of Empathy*—an extract from her doctoral dissertation, which was successfully defended in 1916 at Freiburg under the direction of her mentor, Edmund Husserl—constitutes her first major work in phenomenology.[2] I argue, contrary to more standard views, that though Stein's treatment of empathy yields knowledge of other minds, it also claims rich and certain self-knowledge, which serves as an important base for all knowing, including scientific knowledge. What empathy as an act of consciousness yields is an awareness of others that is analogously similar to an awareness, an inner experience, of oneself. The other, employed as a tool in eidetic variation, allows me to bring myself into "relief": when varied, the other can verify knowledge about myself and about the human person in general—the human person understood in its most general and constitutive sense as a phenomenological essence. The subjective knowledge of oneself as a human person is vital for understanding science, especially the sciences of the spirit or *Geisteswissenschaften*, sometimes called the cultural sciences. Knowledge of oneself is important for the self-appropriation so dear to phenomenology, as Husserl declares at the outset of his *Cartesian Meditations*, as well as for understanding the fundamentals, the practice and ultimate meaning, of any science.

Apart from its capacity to obtain empirical, objective knowledge about things, science aims at uncovering knowledge about ourselves and about how what we are conditions the practice and enterprise we call science. It is phenomenology, according to Stein, that can best account for that intimate subjective structure.[3] Our knowledge of others' minds, however, is never absolute, as complete identification of oneself with another is impossible. We can speak approximately of the other through empathy; what allows one to identify and share similar experiences with the other is another kind of experience, a communal experience, which, in her later texts, Stein called a lived experience of community or *Gemeinschaftserlebnis*. In this chapter, I argue: (a) empathy yields some knowledge of other minds, but it also allows us to acquire and verify deeper knowledge about ourselves and about what it is to be a human person *generaliter;* (b) like Descartes and Husserl, Stein maintains that self-knowledge and knowledge of what it is to be a human being—recall that the other shares in the general essence of human being—is essential for all knowing, including scientific knowledge; and (c) empathy is a low-level starting point for experiencing larger social and political objectivities, but social and political realities include larger and more complex structures of mind than empathy alone can provide.

Before proceeding to Stein's treatment of empathy, I will discuss some key scholarly interpretations of it. Sadly, two significant errors persist in the Anglo-American reception of Edith Stein's account of empathy. First, some scholars continue to read her notion of empathy through the philosophical interventions of the sentimentalists, especially their view of the close connection between morality and sympathy.[4] But Stein never claims that empathy is the same as sympathy. This error occurs, I think, because of the mistranslation of *Einfühlung*, a German concept for which there is no English equivalent. The closest neologism is "intropathy," which is not an English word. Second, though philosophers are largely correct to place Stein's work on empathy within the broader Husserlian concept of intersubjectivity, two mistakes generally occur with this reading—one in the analytic reading of Stein and the other in the Continental reading. In the analytic account, Stein is usually invoked within treatments of the philosophy of mind. Here, Stein's account is read as trying to justify the possibility of knowledge of other minds, always against the presupposition of a Cartesian mind-body dualism.[5] But if one pays close attention to Stein's project, it is clear that the knowledge of other minds that she elaborates is not as robust as analytic philosophers wish to make it. The most intimate knowledge Stein has is of herself as a corporeal-psychic-spiritual unity. Knowledge of other minds helps her achieve clearer self-knowledge, which allows her to understand herself and others in broader, more universal terms as a human person: we can grasp the essence of the human person—an essence that we all share. Analytic philosophers miss this logic. Continental philosophers, though admittedly cognizant of the intersubjective nature of her thought, tend to privilege the discussion of the foreign other, or alterity, in her treatment of empathy.[6] Empathy gives us access to otherness, which, in turn, shapes us. Stein is thus read as overcoming an early form of Husserlian solipsism, which Husserl himself claimed to overcome. Though this approach is probably more faithful to Stein's project than the analytic reading, what the Continentalist reading of Stein overlooks is her emphasis on self-knowledge as essential to achieving or grasping the full sense (*Sinn*) of the idea of the human person. Continentalists, inspired by the works of Levinas, Derrida, Lyotard, and other postmodern figures, ignore the role of the universal and communal essence of what Stein calls the human person. I do not wish to enter the debate between analytic and Continental interpretations of empathy; rather, I wish to address three prevalent interpretations of Stein's treatment of empathy: (a) empathy as knowledge of other minds and as the solution to the problem of solipsism; (b) empathy as intersubjectivity; and (c) empathy as a hermeneutical tool for interpersonal understanding.

The first and dominant interpretation of Stein's view of empathy centers on knowledge of other minds: empathy is the act of mind whereby one acquires knowledge of other minds. The topic of empathy had received much attention prior to Stein's investigation of it. The term "empathy" was first formally employed by the

German philosopher and art historian Robert Vischer (1847–1933) in his 1873 work *On the Optical Sense of Form: A Contribution to Aesthetics*. Drawing from the work of his father, Theodor, and other German Romantics such as John Gottfried von Herder and Novalis, who viewed empathy as a "feeling into," Vischer used the word *Einfühlung* to describe how it is that we see into and feel the form of a work of art through perception. The German term was first translated into English as "empathy" by the British psychologist Edward Titchener (1867–1927).

The psychologist and philosopher Theodor Lipps (1851–1914) was the first to treat empathy systematically, as both an aesthetic and a psychological phenomenon. Through his reading of Hume, Lipps came to incorporate empathy into his own theory of psychology. He read Hume's treatment of sympathy as allowing the content of one's mind to be mirrored in the other, and vice versa. Originally, Lipps thought that empathy could be used to explain optical illusions and, following Hermann von Helmholtz, he argued that deceptions or errors about the content of another's mind were caused not by errors in perception but by errors in judgment. Judgments are achieved through what John Stuart Mill and others called analogical inference. Defining empathy as a fusion between the observer and the observed, Lipps maintains that empathy can be used to understand inanimate objects as well as other minds. One understands the content of the other's mind either by some natural instinct or by some form of inner imitation. Using the classic example of watching an acrobat on a tightrope, Lipps claims that one understands and feels amazed by the acrobat's performance because one can imitate what the acrobat does, but one does so in the mind. There is a fusion between the acrobat and the observer. Lipps pays close attention to the fusion that arises in both understanding and feeling, and his work deeply influenced philosophers such as Edmund Husserl, Wilhelm Dilthey, Max Weber, Max Scheler, and Edith Stein.

Scholars have widely interpreted Stein's view of empathy as granting us access to other minds.[7] One has access to other minds through some kind of analogical comparison: one puts oneself in the place of the other or into relief vis-à-vis the other. The comparison allows us to see similarities and differences between ourselves and others, and this analogical key, to borrow Husserl's term,[8] gives us knowledge of others and self. While this is true, for Stein knowledge of other minds follows one's acquisition of a robust sense of oneself though inner and outer experience. More will be said about this later, but for now it is important to note that empathy works only when it is posited on this primal sense of self as an embodied psycho-physical unity. Most accounts forget this very important starting point, a point to which Stein returns at the end of her treatment of empathy, namely, the sense of self and how we uncover a sense of ourselves as human persons, and how the I and others all share this common essence.

The second common interpretation regards Stein's treatment of empathy as offering a truly intersubjective experience that allows us to transcend our own personal sphere of immanence and move into an intersubjective social world.[9] While it is true that empathy, for Stein, permits a genuine transcendence out of the self into the mind of the other, thereby granting us knowledge of self and other, this interpretation forgets the fundamental role of self-knowledge as well as the role of the knowledge that we share a common essence as persons. Stein is a genuinely modern thinker with a Greek twist: she wishes to preserve the force of something like an Aristotelian genus, namely, human being, which deeply informs who we are and what we are about, as well as our knowledge of ourselves and others, but she also wishes to retain a strong modern core of individuation—the I/ego, the self, the person, and the personality core. In fact, Stein's potent sense of personal individuation is maintained throughout her philosophical corpus: the I and a personality core are discussed in her early work; the I and the self feature in the Münster lectures; and the I and the principle of individuation figure prominently in her later work, *Finite and Eternal Being*. Furthermore, the accounts that focus on intersubjectivity and empathy usually, but not always, restrict themselves to empathy. But empathy constitutes only one sense of intersubjectivity: Stein's early work provides a richer or thicker account (a pregnant sense, as Husserl says) of intersubjectivity in terms of the social and political world, which she develops in her later works.

Finally, we come to an important interpretation of Stein's work on empathy: empathy as a hermeneutical key that both yields understanding of oneself, others, and the world, and serves as a foundation for the sciences. Marianne Sawicki is the foremost proponent of this view, which she lays out in her remarkable book, *Body, Text, and Science: The Literacy of Investigative Practices and the Phenomenology of Edith Stein*. I am sympathetic to this view of empathy; not only does Sawicki have a good grasp of Stein's larger project, but she also develops a hermeneutical practice deeply rooted in Stein's person and writings. Though empathy can give us a richer understanding of ourselves, others, the human person, the sciences, and hermeneutics, as well as facilitate interpersonal understanding, it alone cannot give us sufficient knowledge for a fuller understanding of these things. Rather, we require other mental acts and experiences, including a social psychology as well as lived experiences of community and unique social objectivities such as the masses, society, communities, and the state, to assist us. Sawicki, in the aforementioned work, does not fully account for how we acquire deeper meaning or a sense of larger, more complex superindividual realities beyond the rubric of empathy. I will show how this happens in subsequent chapters. Let us now turn to a discussion of Steinian empathy.

What Is Empathy?

Stein describes empathy, or *Einfühlung*, as an act of consciousness that is *sui generis*. She begins her analysis with an example of empathy: "Let us take an example to illustrate the nature of the act of empathy. A friend tells me he lost his brother and I become aware of his pain. What kind of awareness is this?...I would like to know, not how I arrive at this awareness, but what it itself is" (*E* 6). Stein admits that she can easily infer from her friend's pale and disturbed face, as well as his "toneless and strained" voice, that her friend is in pain. Following Husserl, she wishes to investigate not so much the inference of pain as the process that allows her to arrive at her awareness of the pain. Stein claims that there is something foundational in consciousness that structures her awareness of the other, allowing her to bring the mind of the other into greater relief in consciousness. Empathy is the act that accomplishes this.

In order to distinguish empathy as a unique act of consciousness, Stein has to distinguish it from other acts of consciousness that seem similar to empathy but are, in fact, different. She commences by asking if empathy is simply a perception of an outer state of affairs. In other words, is it just like any other act of perception, such as seeing, hearing, feeling, etc.? Stein argues the negative, claiming that when one perceives something, this thing "comes to me in embodied givenness" (*E* 6). When I hear a loud noise, the sound affects me and is perceived as my own and not another's perception. Though Stein perceives her friend as an embodied being, she argues that her awareness of her friend's state of mind is not perceived in the same way as she perceives her friend's physical presence. The pain of her friend is given in a way different from the perception of her friend's outer body:

> Needless to say, I have no outer perception of the pain. Outer perception is a term for acts in which spatio-temporal concrete being and occurring come to me in embodied givenness. This being has the quality of being there itself right now; it turns this or that side to me and the side turned to me is embodied in a specific sense. It is primordially there in comparison with sides co-perceived but averted. The pain is not a thing and is not given to me as a thing, even when I am aware of it "in" the pained countenance. I perceive the countenance outwardly and the pain "at one" with it. (*E* 6)

The person before her in consciousness, as well as his pain, is primordially present, but the two are not given in the same way; the pain is not seized in the same way as the perception of her embodied friend before her. Stein claims that acts of empathy admit both primordiality (*Originarität*) and nonprimordiality (*Nicht-Originarität*).

Stein defines our own experiences as primordial. Indeed, there is nothing more primordial; our experiences are primordial because they are our own (*E* 7). "But not all experiences are primordially given nor primordial in their content" (*E* 7). She states that acts such as memory, fantasy, and expectation are not primordial because the objects of these acts do not stand present before us in an original way as is the case with outer perception. In such acts, the objects or content of said acts are re-presented or presentified to the mind. The technical term for this kind of re-presentation is *Vergegenwärtigung*, literally, a making-present in consciousness. When I perceive the green house before me, the house is embodied before me as an object. When I remember the green house that I once saw, the house is not before me. I call it up and re-present it in my memory. "Memory, expectation, and fantasy do not have their object bodily present before them. They only represent it, and this character of representation is an immanent, essential moment of these acts, not signs from their objects" (*E* 7). There are, before the person, no embodied objects that signify meaning; rather, what is re-presented in consciousness is immanent to consciousness itself. Here, we encounter the reflexivity of consciousness upon itself. Stein's discussion of nonprimordiality will become important later when we delineate the exact nature of an act of empathy, but it is important now to elaborate further what happens in nonprimordial acts.

In memory, fantasy, and expectation, the content or objects of such acts are not primordial or directly present before us, but one can be aware that one is executing an act of memory, expectation, or fantasy in the present, here and now. When I remember the green house, the green house is not present, but I am aware that I am presently carrying out an act of re-presentation in memory. Furthermore, I can remember now what I have remembered in the past. "Thus the present 'I' and the past 'I' face each other as subject and object. They do not coincide, though there is a consciousness of sameness" (*E* 8). Stein even avers that I can project myself backward in the past and see myself in a different way. "However, the memory always remains a representation with a nonprimordial subject which is in contrast to the subject doing the remembering. The reproduction of the former experience is the clarification of what was vaguely intended at first" (*E* 9).

In empathy, Stein notes that

> we are dealing with an act that is primordial as present experience though non-primordial in content. And this content is an experience which, again, can be had in different ways, such as in memory, expectation, or in fantasy. When it arises before me all at once, it faces me as an object (such as the sadness I "read" in another's face). But when I inquire into its implied tendencies (try to bring another's mood to clear givenness to myself), the content, having pulled me into it, is no longer really an object. I am no longer turned to the content but to the object of it, am at the subject of the content in the original subject's place. And only after successfully executed clarification does the content again face me as an object. (*E* 10)

Stein's analysis here is important: what happens in acts of empathy is the discovery, first, of another subject and, second, the I stands in the other subject's place. But I stand in the other's place not as identical with that subject, but as myself. Stein describes empathy as an act that allows one to leave one's sphere of immanence (*Eigenheitssphäre*), one's own interior life, and move into the place of another subject as oneself. This is what grants one some kind of understanding of the other. In this case, the I understands the sadness of the other as sadness. Recall that in Stein's example of her friend's pain, she declares that she is not so much concerned with the awareness of pain as with the condition of obtaining such an awareness. Now, we can see that Stein is arguing that what allows me to be aware of the other's pain is not so much the pain itself but my capacity to enter into the other subject's place with my own mind. I literally enter into the feelings and lived experience of the other. Stein remarks:

> The subject of the empathized experience, however, is not the subject empathizing, but another. And this is what is fundamentally new in contrast with the memory, expectation, or fantasy of our own experiences. These two subjects are separate and not joined together, as previously, by a consciousness of sameness or a continuity of experience. And while I am living in the other's joy, I do not feel primordial joy. It

does not issue live from my "I." Neither does it have the character of once having lived, like remembered joy. But still much less is it merely fantasized without actual life. The other subject is primordial although I do not experience it as primordial. In my non-primordial experience I feel, as it were, led by a primordial one not experienced by me but still there, manifesting itself in my non-primordial experience. (E 10–11)

Insofar as it allows us to leave our own I-center and move into the place of another I-center, empathy is a transcending act. Furthermore, the I is led by another I's experience; this is why it can be said that empathy is led and not projected. Empathy is not a projection of the I into the other; rather, my I is led by the other, the act of empathy allowing me to stand in the other's place. I undergo another I's experience, but its sense and objectivity are constituted by my own ego.

Stein maintains that empathy is a special kind of experiencing (*eine Art erfahrender Akte*). "Empathy...is the experience of foreign consciousness in general, irrespective of the kind of experiencing subject or the subject whose consciousness is experienced. We only discussed the pure 'I,' the subject of experience, on the subject's as well as on the object's side.... The experience which an 'I' as such has of another 'I' as such looks like this. This is how human beings comprehend the psychic life of their fellows" (E 11). Empathy *in nuce* is an act of consciousness whereby the immanence of the ego is transcended and the I thereby enters into the place of the other. It is by being in the place of the other, then, that one can begin to bring the mind of the other and oneself into clearer relief. How one brings the mind of the other into relief and the results yielded by such processes will be discussed later.

Stein admits that her general description of empathy "does not accomplish much" (E 11). She maintains that her analysis must be brought into dialogue with other theories, both in order to critique them and to show points of convergence between them. Ultimately, too, she wishes to show why the phenomenological approach is both valid and unique in comparison with, say, the psychological approach. I do not wish to rehearse all of the detailed arguments here; instead, I will focus on four accounts that Stein deals with at length, including that of Lipps, Scheler, Mill, and Münsterberg.

Theodor Lipps's theory of empathy was probably, in Stein's day, the most prominent. Though Lipps's account, which covers various forms of empathy and sympathy, including positive, negative, and reiterated empathy, is quite rich, Stein challenged one particular claim he made when describing the fullness or full sense of an act of empathy. Stein agreed with Lipps that the ego and the alter ego enter into relation with one another through acts of empathy, that some kind of participation exists, but Lipps argued that the I can more or less fully enter or resist entering into the fullness of a particular experience of consciousness. In response, Stein offered the example of joy (*E* 13–14). According to Stein's reading of Lipps, one can experience the joy of the other by entering into what Lipps calls the other's primordial experience of joy. Stein was critical of Lipps because he failed to recognize the full extent of the nonprimordiality involved in acts of empathy. Lipps did admit, concedes Stein, that there may be something in the ego that holds it back from fully entering into the other's experience of joy (*E* 13–14, 17). But Stein argues that while the ego may enter into the minds of others, one need not experience the content of the other's mind as primordial; that is, one need not identify with the content in order to understand what it is or how it is being experienced by the other. Moreover, that one does not experience the joy of the other as primordial does not mean that the ego is holding itself back. Stein remarks:

> It seems to me that in neither case is it a question of a specific trait of in- or with-feeling (*empathy or sympathy*), but of one of the forms of transition from "cogito" to another in general. There are numerous such transitions: A cogito can be completely lived out so that I can then "entirely spontaneously" flow over into another one. Further, while I am living in one cogito, another can appear and pull me into it without causing conflict. Finally, the tendencies implied in the cogito and not yet entirely consummated can obstruct the transition to a new cogito. And all this is just as possible in perception, memory, in theoretical contemplation, etc., as in empathy. (*E* 16)

Stein also criticizes Lipps's insistence on some kind of feeling of oneness that typifies the essence of the act of empathy. "Lipps says that as long as empathy is complete (exactly what we no longer recognize as empathy), there is no distinction between our own and the foreign 'I,' they are one. For example, I am one with the acrobat and go through his motions inwardly. A distinction only arises when I step out of complete empathy and reflect on my 'real "I"'" (*E* 16). Two critiques arise here. First, the supposed feeling of oneness that Lipps describes is impossible because my body does not experience what the acrobat's body is doing; I can understand what the acrobat is doing, but I do not feel what the acrobat feels. For Stein, Lipps claims an impossible fusion because the body of the acrobat and that of the observer do not experience identical feelings. Second, Lipps's account also denies that one's own body and one's conscious awareness function differently from those of the acrobat; that is, the acrobat is not conscious of performing an act of empathy. How, then, can there be some kind of simultaneously experienced feeling of oneness between the feeling of the acrobat and the observer's empathic act? "What my body is doing to my body and what the foreign body is doing to the foreign body would then remain completely obscure, since I am living 'in' the one in the same way as in the other, since I experience the movements of the one in the same way as those of the other" (*E* 16).

Stein's treatment of Lipps brings to the fore several insights about the nature of empathy and its role in constructing social reality. First, empathy does not imply a fusion of or identity between minds. Stein is adamant about this point on two grounds. First, one's own embodied ego can never be identical with another's: the ego retains its own sphere of immanence, and this is primary for Stein. Second, the very nature of the act of empathy as both primordial and nonprimordial means that the act itself has to be undertaken by each individual ego: empathy as a particular form of re-presentation or presentification has to be executed by an individual ego. A kind of collective act of empathy in which a group of individuals performs the same act of empathy is not possible; being embodied in a certain time and space, and being physically separate from other individuals, renders this kind of collective act of empathy impossible. Another important aspect of Stein's critique is the role of the lived body in understanding another, about which more will be said later. But here one can see that being embodied is important not only for being able to distinguish oneself from another, but also for entering into the place of the other as oneself, not as another. The implication of this is clear: one can never become the alter ego, or other. The I obtains its own individuality as well as its distinct understanding of itself and others through empathy, which permits lived experiences to revolve around the pure ego that is the zero point of orientation of constituting consciousness.

I would now like to consider Max Scheler's treatment of sympathy, which Stein both admired and critiqued. Scheler's *The Nature of Sympathy* was probably one of the richest phenomenological accounts of both empathy and sympathy available to Stein at the time.[10] Scheler describes sympathy as a co-feeling; individuals can feel together certain emotions and experiences. One of Scheler's most famous examples is that of parents grieving the death of their son.[11] He argues that though each parent may feel profound sadness at his or her individual loss, both also feel a communal loss, the loss that properly belongs to both of them as parents, not just to one or the other parent.

For Scheler, unlike Edith Stein, community does not begin in empathy. In fact, in *The Nature of Sympathy,* Scheler argues that empathy cannot explain how we are able to know other minds or how we form human communities. He criticizes Lipps's account of empathy—as aesthetic mimesis—but he also criticizes Stein's view, noting that the account of empathy that is posited on analogical inference or analogical re-presentation presupposes that one can know oneself fully and absolutely.[12] Stein argues that the I knows and understands the other because it can re-present and compare self and other, bring the other into "relief" within the understanding of self, or, to borrow Stein's language, bring the other into relief with one's own knowledge of oneself. The other becomes a modification of oneself. Scheler remarks that self-knowledge is very difficult, and he notes that the projective accounts of empathy by thinkers such as Lipps and Stein, given their strong emphasis on ego structures, do not provide adequate grounds for assuming the existence of others, let alone individuals.[13] To be fair, Stein qualifies the projective account of empathy, commenting that though one experiences empathy as the mind's attempt to bring the other into relief within one's own ego consciousness, one does not, however, merely project onto the other one's own understanding of what is going on. The other, or alter ego, may modify, negate, or confirm one's knowledge of oneself. For Stein, empathy is bidirectional; egos modify one another.

Scheler's account of empathy and co-feeling neglects this mutual modification, which is vital for Stein. Scheler, according to Stein, collapses the distinction between inner perception (i.e., reflection upon acts of consciousness) and reflection in general. Scheler, according to Stein, maintains that "we perceive the foreign 'I' with its experience inwardly just as we perceive our own 'I'" (*E* 27). Stein reads Scheler as arguing that I perceive both my own ego and that of the other in the same way. This bold thesis asserts that we take a certain position in consciousness that allows us to observe both ourselves and the other; the judgments we make about our own I and that of the other, especially when it comes to the acts executed by both, are based on our own perceptions. Stein, however, rejects this inner perceptual stance as a description of empathy because it negates the primordiality and nonprimordiality structure discussed earlier. The I primordially experiences the other as other, but the I can only bring the consciousness of the other into relief by standing in the other's place. This standing in the other's place happens through a particular act of re-presentation, and this is what Stein identifies as empathy. For Stein, Scheler's account means that ego and alter ego give themselves in the same way to consciousness. Stein believes this to be patently false. She remarks:

> If I experience a feeling as that of another, I have it given twice: once primordially as my own and once non-primordially in empathy, as originally foreign. And precisely this non-primordiality of empathized experiences causes me to reject the general term "inner perception" for the comprehension of our own and foreign experience. Should one desire to stress what these two experiences have in common, it would be better to say "inner intuition" [*innere Anschauung*]. This would include, then, the non-primordial givenness of our own experiences in

memory, expectation, or fantasy. But there is still another reason why I object to including empathy under inner perception. There is really only a parallel on the level of empathy where I have the foreign experience facing me. The level where I am at the foreign "I," and where I explain its experience by living it after the other, seems to be much more parallel to the primordial experience itself than to its givenness in inner perception. (*E* 34)

Finally, I would like to turn briefly to Stein's critiques of Hugo Münsterberg and John Stuart Mill. The former's account of understanding the other as an act of will is important for Stein, whereas the latter focused on inference. Stein agrees with Münsterberg that the possibility of entering into "foreign" consciousness exists (*E* 35), but, according to Münsterberg, this is accomplished primarily as an act of will on the part of cognizing ego. Moreover, Stein asserts that he treats all attitudes and anticipations as acts of will. She remarks that all kinds of empathic acts, not only those rooted in the will, can yield insight into the nature of the act of empathy in addition to the specific content seized in the act. "He agrees with our analysis by characterizing this act of understanding as an act in which the 'foreign will enters into mine' and still remains that of the other. But we cannot see why this understanding should be confined to acts of will" (*E* 35). Significant here is Stein's insistence that empathy is a unique kind of mental act that can express itself in many forms, including the seizing of another's capacity to make decisions of will. Furthermore, she is faithful to the act of empathy itself. In many cases, we naturally drift into an awareness of the other with no cognition of the execution of an act of willing in order to do so.

John Stuart Mill's account of knowledge of foreign consciousness is predicated on analogical inference. At the time Stein was writing, Lipps's new account of empathy, based on aesthetic mimesis and the fusion of minds, was considered superior to Mill's because it moved beyond the strongly logical foundations of Mill's account. Stein explains the argument for inference by analogy: "There is evidence of outer and of inner perception, and we can only get at the facts that these perceptions furnish by means of inferences. This applies to the present case as follows: I know the foreign physical body and its modifications. Further, I know that the modifications of the latter are conditions and implications of my experiences, likewise given. Now, because in this case the succession of physical appearances can only take place when linked with experience, I assume such linkage where physical appearances are given alone" (*E* 26). Stein, albeit conceding that inferences by analogy do occur in knowledge of foreign consciousness, finds this theory problematic on numerous grounds; analogical inference, however, occurs only in some instances and is not itself the deep structure of knowledge of foreign consciousness (*E* 27). Stein maintains that according to Mill, one can perceive others as bodies and as possessing minds. I can claim to "know" the other's mind only insofar as I first compare it with mine and then infer from my own experience that what is given to me as the other's consciousness is similar to mine. The mind makes the judgment of an inferred similarity. Stein argues that this theory is restrictively logical and fails to appreciate the complexity of the rich layers of human being. "This theory maintains that we see nothing around us but physical, soulless and lifeless bodies, though I do not see how its advocates could actually hold such a belief" (*E* 26). The force of Stein's critique is that the theory lacks lived experience; it offers only logical comparison and inference, but the experience of the self is not lived in a unique way. Though Stein admits that Mill gives an account of the knowledge of the content of the experience, she insists that he does not explain how we can have awareness of the other as a general act of consciousness. More precisely, Mill ignores the value of such knowledge for the person and his or her life. "Further, this theory...intends to demonstrate the validity of our knowledge of foreign consciousness. It specifies the form in which knowledge of foreign consciousness is 'possible.' But the value of such an empty form, not oriented toward the nature of knowledge itself, is more than doubtful" (*E* 27).

Recall that phenomenology's unique claim is that it mines and delineates a specific field of knowledge, namely, lived experience, which is not reducible to merely empirical or logical facts. When Stein critiques Mill for his failure to situate his account of knowledge of foreign consciousness with regard to its value "for me" and "for us," as well as for his failure to connect his account to the larger purpose and value of knowledge itself, she is seeking to distinguish empathy from a mere form of perception or inference. Phenomenologically speaking, empathy is crucial in order for us to understand how it is that we bring to awareness the lived experiences of others, which are valuable and meaningful for us and for others. This being said, I wonder whether Stein's critique is too harsh, especially given that she, like Husserl, makes much use of analogical comparisons in her own work. Moreover, is it really fair to accuse Mill of failing to consider the value of his account of foreign consciousness? Mill's ethical and political commitments, as well his vast writing on various ethical, social, and political issues, in which he displayed a profound awareness of the value of knowledge, especially of others and of what is necessary for a society to thrive, are well known and highly regarded. His treatment of the nature of pleasure, for example, in his essay *Utilitarianism*, valiantly attempts to connect an awareness of the other's need and desire for pleasure with the common good.[14]

Thus far, I have done two things: First, I sketched a general picture of the nature of empathy as a particular act of consciousness; second, I contextualized Stein's analysis by comparing it with key elements of other leading theories of her day. It must be said that much work on empathy continues to be carried out, especially within the contemporary domain of the philosophy of mind. In particular and as previously mentioned, the works of Frédérique de Vignemont and Vittorio Gallese are important in this respect. Their work, which tries to link cognitive science and neuroscience with certain central phenomenological insights, draws heavily from the empirical sciences. For Stein, though these accounts may establish the validity of how empathy works from an external or observer-dependent perspective, they do not explain how it is that I live the experience. This is the intent of Stein's project. Cognitive and brain science may tell us what the brain and neurons are doing, but one does not *experience* the brain carrying out its commands, firing neurons, releasing chemicals, managing its own electric systems, etc. I experience myself engaging the other, and it is this experience that Stein, like phenomenology itself, focuses on, for it is pregnant with sense, or meaning (*Sinn*).

Empathy Debates Today

I would be remiss not to briefly discuss recent treatments of empathy, especially in analytical philosophical circles, which were inspired by the work of Karsten Steuber and others.[15] Philosophers of mind are divided over the issue. Though the literature on the topic has grown and cannot be taken up here at any great length, we can say that, at this point, two analytic approaches to the question of empathy dominate: simulation theory and stricter neurological accounts. The divisions between them are not fast and neat, as they draw upon one another, but their specific emphases can help us situate them as each offering a distinct view of empathy. In fact, one of the contributions of recent analytic philosophy and cognitive science is that they both provide neurological evidence for some of the possibilities described in the phenomenal account of empathy.

By far, the more prevalent school of thought is the simulation theory account, which generally maintains that it is possible to read or know another's mind because we can put or project ourselves into the mind of another, we can place ourselves in another's mental state. Some have even claimed there has to be an isomorphism between the empathizer and the empathee.[16] In any case, a relationship between the empathizer and the empathee is key. As we saw with Stein, we can trade places with the other in order to bring into profile or relief what the other mind may be experiencing. Thinkers like Alvin Goldman, Frédérique de Vignemont, and Pierre Jacob advance the simulationist point of view.

Goldman, whose contributions to the discussion are invaluable, argues that since simulation happens at all kinds of levels, especially at an emotional level, as psychology rightly explains, one could also argue that it happens in the case of empathy, which he understands to be a kind of mindreading. He differentiates between high-level and low-level mindreading. He notes, "'Low-level' mindreading... is comparatively simple, primitive, automatic, and largely below the level of consciousness."[17] He distinguishes high-level mindreading in the following manner: "'High-level' mindreading is mindreading with one or more of the following features: (a) it targets mental states of a relatively complex nature, such as propositional attitudes; (b) some components of the mindreading process are subject to voluntary control; and (c) the process has some degree of accessibility to consciousness.[18]

For Goldman, empathy is possible because we are able to simulate the other by projecting ourselves into the mind of the other. The distinction between higher- and lower-level empathy prevents the unilateral attribution of knowledge of other minds simply through a kind of projection of one's inner state into the mind of another. In lower-level empathy, there is a primitive recognition of emotive state that does not require this kind of mental trading places as described by Goldman. Zahavi, however, notes that Goldman's account suffers:

> Simply put, the general idea is that if I want to reach an understanding of other minded creatures, be it their emotions, their desires, their beliefs, etc., I must project what I know about my own mind into their minds. Why is this circuit through self deemed necessary? I need to project what I know about my own mind into the mind of others, because the only mind I have any direct and non-inferential knowledge of is my own, whereas the minds of others are closed territory. They remain concealed and hidden. All that I have experiential access to is their behavior. Without a commitment to a view like this, the constant appeal to internal imitations and projections would make little sense. This commitment is rarely spelled out explicitly.[19]

It would be fair to say, as we shall see, that Edith Stein also makes the distinction between direct perception of others' mental states and empathic acts, which require a presentification based on analogical comparison, very similar to the projecting oneself into the mental state of another advanced by simulationists like Goldman. Unlike Goldman and like Zahavi, Stein too recognizes that empathy is not a solipsistic process, for empathy allows us to understand that we share a common essence, namely, personhood. The common elements of that personhood act as the basis for our understanding of other minds: as persons we understand and share certain experiences in analogously similar ways. It is this shared personhood that grounds and helps us interpret other minds at bodily, emotional, or psychic, and even higher, spiritual levels.

De Vignemont and Jacob give a more textured reading of empathy. Not only do they use cognitive experimentation to justify their views but they also make similar distinctions that one finds in the phenomenological literature on empathy. In their famous article on empathy and pain, the philosophers distinguish different kinds of pain vis-à-vis the other: standard, contagious, and empathetic pain. De Vignemont and Jacob give a nice illustration of the differences:

> The following commonsense example will illustrate the threefold distinction among standard pain, contagious pain, and empathetic pain. Imagine a screaming infant who feels standard pain after being injected with a vaccine into his shoulder. Now consider the 6-year-old infant's sister watching the needle penetrate her little brother's shoulder. She tenses up and shrinks as if she were anticipating the pain caused by the needle in her own shoulder. Her vicarious experience of pain is an experience of contagious pain. Finally, consider the mother holding her son in her arms. Unlike her daughter, she is not imagining the painful vaccine injected in her own body. Her vicarious experience of pain is an experience of empathetic pain: she is painfully experiencing her son's standard pain. She believes that her son is in pain.[20]

What is interesting about de Vignemont and Jacob's distinctions, which we already find in Stein's philosophy, as we shall see, is that simulation theory needs to distinguish more precisely different kinds of mental acts and different levels of mindreading. One sees in this article an implicit attack against Goldman, whom de Vignemont criticizes for not giving an adequate account of the distinction between high-level and low-level mindreading. The distinctions that de Vignemont and Jacob arrive at, without ever recognizing the work of Edith Stein on this question, would allow Goldman to be more specific about what counts as high- and low-level mindreading. De Vignemont remarks,

In summary, Goldman offers a distinction between two levels of mindreading that should help to clarify the field. However, one remains frustrated by the elusiveness of this distinction. He lists a small set of conditions that appear to be sufficient, although not necessary. However, after examination, it turns out that they are neither necessary nor sufficient. More particularly, low-level mindreading cannot be reduced to a purely bottom-up automatic process of low fecundity, but reliable. We have seen that it can be contextualized, and thus that it can be rich in information, but at the cost of egocentric biases.[21]

The neurological accounts of empathy, as advanced by scientists like Vittorio Gallese and Christian Keysers, draw upon the centrality of the work of mirror neurons. When these neurons fire in animals one can see the same neuron firing in another animal, while it is observing the action of the other animal. Gallese contends:

> The point I want to make is that beside—and likely before—the explicit ascription of any intentional content to others, we entertain a series of "implicit certainties" about the individuals we are confronting with. These certainties deal with our implicit knowledge about other individuals, encompassing the way they look, the way they act and, ultimately, the way they feel and think. These implicit certainties are constitutive of the intersubjective relation, and contribute to the sense of oneness, the sense of identity with the other, which basically makes s-identity possible. It is this sense of identity that enables the possibility to ascribe *any* content to the individual we are interacting with. Our possibility to see or think that we are different from other living and nonliving objects is determined by our capacity to entertain i-identity. But i-identity depends in a constitutive way on the development of s-identity, which enables the possibility to entertain a meaningful dialogue with others.[22]

Empathy is predicated on a kind of mirroring, which is similar to the simulationist account, but with some significant differences, namely, the mirror account stresses the use of imagination. One must imagine what it is like to experience the other's experience in order to understand what the other is experiencing as one has no immediate direct experience of the other's experience as one's own. Philosophers like Patricia Churchland have expressed doubts about the reduction of intersubjectivity to mirror neurons as they feel the account neglects other significant aspects necessary for human intelligence. De Vignemont and Jacob criticize the mirror account for its incapacity to distinguish between contagious pain and empathetic pain, thereby ascribing to itself a greater justification of intersubjective cognition than what it actually is capable of doing. They remark,

> At the core of our account are the joint assumptions that empathetic pain is a vicarious experience of pain (caused by another's standard pain) and that vicarious experiences of pain are generated by a process of mental imagery, that is, a special kind of nonpropositional imagination involving the offline use of one's own pain system. There are two main current alternatives to an imagination-based account of empathetic pain: the direct-perception and the mirroring models. The direct-perception model erroneously construes empathetic pain as a perceptual experience of another's pain. Although a vicarious experience of pain can take as input the perception of cues of another's pain, it is not a perceptual experience. Perceiving cues of another's pain is neither necessary nor sufficient for empathetic pain: empathetic pain can be triggered by testimony, and it is not the default response to the perception of cues of another's pain. The mirroring model fails for a distinct reason. We took it as a condition of adequacy that a satisfactory account must be able to distinguish empathetic pain from four related, although distinct, phenomena: standard pain, contagious pain, sympathy for pain, and standard pain ascription. The mirroring account fails to offer a principled distinction between empathetic and contagious pain. Thus, we surmise that the imagination-based account currently offers the best prospect for meeting the above condition of adequacy on empathetic pain.[23]

Edith Stein would probably be leery of the mirroring account, simply because it proposes ideas similar to those of Lipps. The imagination that is crucial for their mirroring, Stein would prefer to ascribe to a specific kind of presentification that she calls empathy, though Stein would also be sympathetic to de Vignemont and Jacob's critique.

So far, I have briefly presented some current analytical views of empathy largely rooted in simulation theory. But contemporary phenomenologists like Shaun Gallagher and Dan Zahavi[24] have also presented a contemporary phenomenological account of empathy that draws form the transcendental phenomenological tradition. Both authors are very aware of Stein's work, but they see Stein as refining positions already taken by thinkers like Husserl, Scheler, and even Alfred Schütz. Though this is true to a certain extent, Stein has an interesting take on empathy that is unique, themes that will be developed in the rest of this chapter. Analytic philosophers have taken note of Zahavi and Gallagher's work, either dismissing it as classic Continental philosophical folk psychology, a characterization that is simply misguided, or as a direct-perception view of empathy. The latter description is inaccurate and has been rejected by Zahavi and Gallagher. Both thinkers view empathy as an act of consciousness *sui generis*, as does Stein. They defend the classical phenomenological view, with some revisions. Zahavi reads empathy as a means to understand other minds, though he is critical of any attempt to understand empathy purely in terms of analogical inference, as did Mill.

There are points of convergence and divergence between Zahavi and Stein, and it would be good to signal them here, before we advance with our reading of Steinian empathy. Both Zahavi and Stein admit that intersubjectivity cannot be restricted simply to empathy. The analytic and neurological approaches seek a basis for intersubjective understanding, and it would be an exaggeration to claim that cognition, though vital, is not the only basis for sociality and intersubjectivity. Zahavi poignantly and rightly remarks about empathy:

> To be more specific, empathy is typically taken to constitute a unique and irreducible form of intentionality, and one of the traditional tasks of this approach has consequently been to spell out the difference between empathy and other forms of intentionality, such as perception, imagination and recollection. This descriptive enterprise has often been associated with the phenomenological tradition, in fact the empathic approach has occasionally been taken to constitute *the* phenomenological approach to intersubjectivity. It is exactly this claim which I wish to contest in the following. In my view, some of the most interesting and far-reaching phenomenological analyses of intersubjectivity are all characterized by going *beyond empathy*. Not because they deny the

existence of empathy or the validity of the criticism of the argument from analogy, but because empathy understood as a *thematic encounter with a concrete other* is either taken to be a derived rather than a fundamental form of intersubjectivity—because it is taken to disclose rather than establish intersubjectivity—or because there are aspects of the problem of intersubjectivity which simply cannot be addressed as long as one remains narrowly focussed on empathy.[25]

Zahavi notes that there is something like prior intersubjectivity, which precedes consciousness, the transcendence of the other and world. Stein admits this too, but there are also specific mental states that accompany the being of specific social objectivities, including the mass, society, and community. She also admits that history, economics, religion, geography, and even gender[26] affect empathy and broader social relations in unique and interesting ways.

Key differences mark Stein's account of empathy as unique from other phenomenologists, and I will bring these out in the rest of the chapter. First, Stein argues, and Zahavi admits that this is important to understand the phenomenological approach to empathy, that the personal structure of empathy is vital as subjectivity is disclosed as one of the key results flowing from of an analysis of empathy. The first-person perspective reveals that the ego is shaped with a personal framework, which allows one to experience something like selfhood. Scheler makes this point often in his own work, though he does not see this as arising from empathy proper. Stein's analysis of the person, however, is not only a self-disclosure. It becomes an important ground for basic intersubjectivity and, more important, a ground for all human sciences. Furthermore, Steinian empathy is not only about access to other minds and our personal nature, it is also a means to greater self-knowledge. The egoic aspect of empathy is highlighted in Steinian analysis in a positive manner, giving greater context to the problem of solipsism as Husserl later presented it in his *Cartesian Meditations*. Given this discussion of contemporary empathy, let us proceed to unpack Stein's account of empathy where we will see similarities and vital differences between her account and more contemporary analyses.

EMPATHY AND THE CONSTITUTION OF SELVES AND INDIVIDUALS

Stein admits that her discussion of empathy thus far undertaken is limited—she has simply established what empathy is as a specific act of consciousness. She turns to the content of such an act. What kind of noema or phenomenological object of consciousness is constituted by empathy? "We must treat empathy as a problem of constitution and answer the question of how the objects in the usual theories, such as the psycho-physical individual, personality, etc., arise within consciousness" (*E* 37). Anticipating the response to the question of the noema of empathic acts, Stein posits both a psycho-physical individual and a spiritual person that possess a personality-core. For Stein, the human being is defined as a person—a unity of body, psyche, and spirit. According to her, empathy in its highest sense yields an awareness of the meaning of what it is to be a human being, namely, the personal unity described above. This knowledge of what it is to be human will be the real ground of the sciences, especially the human or cultural sciences (*Geisteswissenschaften*). I argue that, as we carry out various acts of empathy, the eidetic senses we obtain from our analyses not only yield knowledge about ourselves and others, but, more importantly, advance that knowledge to a concrete essence of what it is to be human. It is in our shared humanity that we can begin to discuss what it means to have and to build a social and political world. I believe my argument corrects the view that empathy yields only knowledge of other minds.

Another question immediately comes to mind: Cannot the person, understood as a transcendental (*E* 38) structure, be revealed through regular empirical and scientific inquiries? It cannot, first, because from an empirical point of view, the notion of the person assumes that all that constitutes a human being can be quantitatively and qualitatively measured, that the human being is completely accessible and present. Stein would deny this claim. There are profound limits to our knowledge of ourselves and not all we are is obtained through what is posited and obtained through the senses. Second, transcendental personhood is able to explain what fundamentally conditions all of our enterprises of knowing, firmly grounding science in the human subject rather than in some kind of objective investigation that disregards the role of subjectivity in conditioning knowing and the knowledge obtained. Moreover, and this is essential, the transcendental person that Stein uncovers offers the most intimate and proper sense of what it is to be human, for it is properly our most intimate selves through which we live our existence, others, and worlds. What the phenomenological account of transcendental personhood can do is yield the means and content that we can employ to make profound sense of what it is that "we" do and experience when we live our lives—it can provide an account that is not reducible to what the sciences tell us about what we do and how we do it.

So, how does empathy work and what does it reveal? It works at various levels, moving from a lower constitutive function to a higher, and, ultimately, the highest one. Low-level empathy begins firmly in the body: I understand the other and what she is experiencing by putting her body in "relief" alongside my own, thereby allowing me to comparatively understand certain bodily-psychic mental states. Husserl and Stein agree on this point (see Husserl's wonderful analyses of the body in his *Ideas II*). Higher, more complex forms of empathy allow us to grasp spiritual states of the other person, including the knowledge of the nature of the human person as a unity of body, psyche, and spirit (*Geist*). Before Stein can proceed to analyze the movement from more basic forms of empathy to higher forms of empathic understanding, she insists that we need to understand the basic, fundamental structural components of ourselves through what she calls inner and outer experience. Inner experience consists of immediate perceptions of internal states or facts about ourselves, for example, one's own perceptual experience of one's own body as it is experienced spatially within one's own consciousness. The classic way of experiencing this bodily space is through indexicals: here and there. I can experience what it is to be here, even though I am unable to perceive myself being here with my own senses. Another example of internal experience is emotion. I can experience what it is for me to experience something like joy or fear. Phenomenologically, this kind of inner experience is known as auto-affection. External experience is knowledge about oneself acquired by observing oneself from an external point of view. One can both see one's own hand resting on the table and perceive what the hand feels like resting on the table, and the table's resistance on the hand. Both inner and outer experience can provide us with knowledge about ourselves, and this knowledge can always be tested and verified. Contrary to Scheler's opinion of Stein's view of empathy, Stein never claimed that empathy can give one absolute knowledge of self. Believing that humans can make mistakes in their judgments about states of affairs, she never discussed absolute knowledge.

Pre-Empathic Givens Acquired through Inner Experience

Prior to discussing empathy, as well as notions of the self and the person, Stein pauses to remind her readers of certain fundamental phenomenological concepts acquired through inner perception or experience: the pure I, stream of consciousness, and the soul. Stein readily adopts Husserl's terms for the first two concepts. These terms serve two functions: First, they are the tools that will guide Stein's investigation—they are the specific means that will enable her to carry out her phenomenological study of the constitution of the human being. Second, they are key elements of what it means to be human. It should be said that, as we progress from lower to higher forms of empathy and toward the constitution of more complex human structures, it is tempting to regard all of these layers and parts as separate, but from the very beginning of her investigation of empathy, Stein posits a unified human being that is guaranteed by the pure I, stream of consciousness, and the soul. This unity is both necessary and real as it guarantees not only the whole individual as a human person, but as it is also the condition for the possibility of any kind of enduring, coherent, and consistent sense.

The pure I is described as the qualityless subject of experience (E 38). Stein sees the pure I as the fundamental experience of individuation that allows one to understand what is "mine" and not another's. This is the fundamental starting point of phenomenology and, as we have seen, it is central to understanding phenomenology's claim of delivering an analysis of a unique form of human experience. Stein describes the pure I that is given in the primordial experience of oneself in the following way:

> What does this individuality mean? First of all, it means only that it is "itself" and no other. This "selfness" is experienced and is the basis of all that is "mine." Naturally, it is first brought into relief in contrast when another is given. The other is at first not qualitatively distinguished from it, since both are qualityless, but it is distinguished simply as an "other." This otherness is apparent in the type of givenness; it is other than "I" because it is given to me in another way than "I." Therefore, it is "you." (*E* 38)

The ego is not projected or posited, as it is for Fichte.[27] Neither is the I a deduction, as it is for Kant.[28] The I simply appears, and its individuation as an I is not given by the other; rather, I and other, ego and alter ego, become individuated and develop a fundamental sense of mine-ness and otherness/you-ness when the two appear to one another. However, it is not their appearing alone that constitutes individuality; there has to be some kind of empathic act in which one ego brings into "relief" the other ego. "Thus the 'I' does not become individualized because another faces it, but its individuality, or as we would rather say (because we must reserve the term 'individuality'[29] for something else), its selfness is brought into relief in contrast with the otherness of the other" (*E* 38). The most basic kind of empathy allows one to enter into the mind of the other in order to be able to bring the other into relief, thereby establishing what is properly mine and what is properly other. My selfness belongs to me.

Stein also defines the I as a stream of consciousness (*E* 38). Though we have an experience of the I, when we reflect upon this experience, we realize that it is set up against a flow or stream of such experiences. The I moves in and out of experiences, one experience fading into another. This stream of consciousness also yields a sense of time — inner time-consciousness — whereby one notices that, as experiences pass, they are no longer in the present—they are past. It is precisely the experience of having past lived experiences, and their fundamental relation to present experiences, that, for Stein, means there is a unity that characterizes this stream of experiences, against which the I experiences itself and other experiences. "Precisely this affiliation of all the stream's experiences with the present, living, pure 'I' constitutes its inviolable unity" (*E* 39). As the I brings the other into relief and vice versa, both selves undergo a stream of conscious experience. But it becomes apparent that the I can vary its stream of experiences in different ways from the other.

"This does not mean that its affiliation with the same 'I' ceases; the stream only becomes another by belonging to another 'I.' Selfness and qualitative variation together—thus individuality in two senses—constitute a further step in the progress to the individual 'I' of common parlance, i.e., a characteristically structured psychophysical unity" (*E* 38). Individuation, then, is assured both by bringing the other into relief (i.e., empathy) and by variation in streams of consciousness, which can likewise only be brought into relief through empathy.

Stein now comes to a most curious point in her preliminary discussion of empathy, namely, her discussion of the soul (*Seele*). Here, soul is not meant as a religious structure in which immortality and the locus of encounter with God are posited. Stein understands soul in its more classic psychological sense, though not as the principle of motion in the Greek philosophical sense. Rather, she describes the soul both as unifying and as a kind of retainer or bearer (*Träger*). "Among our experiences there is one basic experience given to us which, together with its persistent attributes, becomes apparent in our experiences as the identical 'bearer' of them. This is the substantial soul.... This substantial unity is 'my' soul when the experiences in which it is apparent are 'my' experiences or acts in which my pure 'I' lives" (*E* 40). But how does Stein come to the conclusion that there is a soul, understood as both unifying and retaining? Her argument is as follows (*E* 40): First, when we examine our experience, we find that every experience not only has content—that is, it is an experience of something—but it also is characterized by a certain act, such as willing, perceiving, desiring, etc., but, as well, has a certain intensity or lack of intensity that accompanies my understanding or sense of both act (noesis) and content/object (noema). For example, we experience objects and acts more or less intensely, with greater or less fatigue, and so on. There are numerous attributes that accompany and deeply condition our experience. These attributes coincide, and in some cases are identical with, our experience, but they are not reducible to it. Mental fatigue, for example, does not come from the experience of something or from an act of consciousness; it is part of the whole structure of experience. The presence of such attributes and elements colors our experience in a deep way and bespeaks the presence of a soul that holds such attributes in place and allows them to coincide with both noetic and noematic aspects of experience. As Stein notes, "We have already become acquainted with such single psychic attributes.... The acuteness of our senses apparent in our outer perceptions is such an attribute. Another is the energy apparent in our conduct. The tension or laxity of our volitions manifests the vivacity and strength or the weakness of our will. Its persistence is found in its duration. The intensity of our feelings, the ease with which they appear, the excitability of our sentiments, etc. disclose our disposition" (*E* 40). The soul is the locus of the attributes mentioned as well as of other categories and elements, including causality and the life-force (*Lebenskraft*).[30] What Stein has given thus far are the rudiments of the human being: an ensouled ego that is aware of itself by experiencing self and other through empathy. It should be remarked that one of the distinguishing features of Stein's phenomenology is the attention she pays to the psychological dimension of human reality and its indispensable conditioning role in our understanding of the sense of things. Husserl was aware of this, too, but his officially published phenomenology did not dwell significantly on the force of the soul or psyche in phenomenology (although we find a good deal about it in his unpublished manuscripts, especially those that Stein edited for publication, such as *Ideas II*).

The Lived-Body Pre-Empathy

Having sketched the rudiments of what it is to be an "individual," understood in a general sense, based on inner and outer perception on the part of the conscious I, Stein begins to unpack the fuller constitutive sense of the human subject that precedes the experience of empathy. Again, self-knowledge comes first, in both importance and sense, and in a deep way, it makes possible the transition to the foreign other through empathy. She begins at the body. Stein asks, "How is my body [*Leib*] constituted within consciousness?" (*E* 41). She also asks, "What is the body? How and as what is it given to us?" (*E* 41). The first question is one that other sciences may ask, but phenomenology, at least in the Husserlian vein, begins with what it is for me to understand and experience myself as a body. How is my body given to me in lived experience? Stein commences with outer experience: I am embodied, I have a body. This is a given: I can perceive my body as I would perceive any object of perception. But if my body is given to me only as a physical body through outer perception, it becomes, Stein argues, a strange object; I can see only various points of my own physical body. I can never perceive it wholly as a body, but can see only aspects of it. I can feel and touch my body at various points, but I can never see it move as a whole. Again, I can see only parts of it move. The discussion of movement may seem odd at first glance, but Stein is trying to uncover a primordial sense of what it is to be embodied, a sense that outer perception cannot deliver because of its limited view. She defines her own lived experience of the body as an always-being-here, as opposed to a being-there. "But this one object (my physical body) is given to me in successive appearances only variable within very narrow limits. As long as I have my eyes open at all, it is continually there with a steadfast obtrusiveness, always having the same tangible nearness as no other object has. It is always 'here' while other objects are always 'there'" (*E* 42).

There is a duality in the way one lives one's body. First, although the body can be distinguished as an object distinct from psyche and spirit, it is not separate from them because they form a unity. Second, the body is always there; it accompanies us. Third, there is always a "tangible nearness," a proximity or intimacy that marks the body as our own. The body's quality of belonging to one is experienced as a distinction between what is my own, what is here—for the body is always here—and what is over there, what is not my own. Thus, at a very physical and bodily level, I experience individuation and separation.

How is the body given to the I? It is given through sensations; that is, we inwardly experience being affected by our own bodies (*E* 42–43). Sensation makes evident (it literally gives *Evidenz*, to borrow from Husserl) the living experience of the body. The certainty that comes from bodily sensation is not like the certainty that comes from other acts of the cogito. There is no reflection that can yield an I. Stein remarks that,

> in contrast with these acts, sensation is peculiarly characterized. It does not issue from the pure "I" as they do, and it never takes on the form of the "cogito" in which the "I" turns toward an object. Since sensation is always spatially localized "somewhere" at a distance from the "I" (perhaps very near to it but never in it), I can never find the "I" in it by reflection. And this "somewhere" is not an empty point in space, but something filling up space. All these entities from which my sensations arise are amalgamated into a unity, the unity of my living body, and they are themselves places in the living body. There are differences in the unified givenness in which the living body is always there for me as a whole. (*E* 42)

This passage is striking because Stein argues that sensations (*Empfindungen*, literally sense impressions), though certain and undeniable, are incapable of yielding the pure I or ego. Moreover, sensations themselves do not constitute an identity with the living body. In other words, that one has sensations is not proof of one's sense of a lived body. The sensations need to be synthesized and localized for there to be a sense of the lived body. Sensations themselves occupy a space within the lived body, but they do not give a whole sense of the lived body. What sensations do, for Stein, is bring into relief the fact that there is a certain feeling that is distinguishable from the larger reality against which they manifest themselves. I feel a tickle on my neck, but the tickle is not the body; localized in a certain part of my body, it makes manifest the larger reality of the body. Sensations localized in different parts of the body manifest that space is significant for understanding what a lived body is. "The various parts of the living body constituted for me in terms of sensation are at various distances from me. Thus my torso is nearer to me than my extremities, and it makes good sense to say that I bring my hands near or move them away. To speak of distance from 'me' is inexact because I cannot really establish an interval from the 'I,' for it is non-spatial and cannot be localized" (*E* 42–43).

It is the localization of sensation and the distancing it reveals that are crucial for making evident something like a lived body, for they show the living body, in its most basic aspect, as a zero point of orientation. All of the many and different localized sensations not only relate to one another, but revolve around some kind of center. Stein explains:

> But I relate the parts of my living body, together with everything spatial outside of it, to a "zero point of orientation" which my living body surrounds. This zero point is not to be geometrically localized at one point in my physical body; nor is it the same for all data. It is localized in the head for visual data and in mid-body for tactile data. Thus, whatever refers to the "I" has no distance from the zero point, and all that is given at a distance from the zero point is also given at a distance from the "I." ... The living body as a whole is at a zero point of orientation with all physical bodies outside of it. "Body space" (*Leibraum*) and "outer space" are completely different from each other. (*E* 42–43)

At this point, Stein notes that there are different senses of spatialization: "However, the distance of bodily parts from me is fundamentally different from the distance of other things from each other and from me. Two things in space are at a specific distance from each other" (*E* 43). A sense of the lived body as a zero point of orientation thus emerges through sensation.

So far, the discussion has focused on the body at rest. But the same spatialized sense of the living body as a zero point of orientation emerges when the body is in movement. In what way is the body in movement given to consciousness? Stein says that in movement, the world shifts along with the zero point of orientation. The zero point of orientation is also revealed as an understanding of the concept "if…then," which will be important for the subsequent discussion of the phenomenological view of causality. Stein notes:

> Now the experience that "I move" becomes entirely new. It becomes the apperception of our own movement, based on manifold sensations, and it is entirely different from the outwardly perceived movement of physical bodies. Now the comprehension of our movement and the alteration of the outer world are combined in the form of "if…then." "If I move, then the picture of my environment shifts." This is just as true for the perception of the single spatial thing as for the cohesive spatial world, and, similarly, for movements of parts of the living body as for its movement as a whole. (*E* 45)

Stein goes on to note that the living body, understood as a whole, can be represented in consciousness, especially in fantasy. The living body, particularly the senses we have of it, can be the subject of various cogitative acts. Stein remarks that, "I can fantasize my room empty of furniture and 'imagine' how it would look. I can also take an excursion through the world of fantasy. 'In thought' I can get up from my desk, go into a corner of the room, and regard it from there. Here I do not take my living body along" (*E* 47). In fantasy as well as in other cogitative acts, the lived body can become an object of representation; it can even be excised from an act of mind insofar as one does not experience the act of mind even though one undergoes the experience in question. But this does not mean that the body does not exist. As Stein observes, "An 'I' without a body is a possibility. But a body without an 'I' is utterly impossible" (*E* 47).

Why does Stein undertake this discussion of the lived body, and how does it relate to empathy? Thus far, Stein's discussion of the lived body does not require empathy. In fact, there has as yet been no mention of empathy and the lived body. The lived body is a given, and how one experiences this body in consciousness, in one's own lived experience, is unique. The lived body serves as the locus of consciousness—where consciousness is housed—and as the place from which we begin to spatialize ourselves and the world around us, including other minds, as we shall see later. The lived body permits one to distinguish oneself from another at a fundamental level. This happens through the synthesis or unification of different sensations and movements; oneself as here and not there, oneself as here and the other as there. This is a perceptual given. The first layer of the sense of "my own" is constituted at the level of the lived body, and as the grounding level, it is by no means the least important. So in answer to our question, Stein treats the lived body in such detail because it not only helps us to form a sense of individuation and otherness, but it also yields a phenomenological description of what we are, of our nature or essence, namely, embodied consciousness. Furthermore, the way in which we are embodied is peculiar because the lived body is not experienced as an empirical or physical body having extension, material parts, and organs. The lived body reveals, rather, that we are situated and differentiated as human beings; moreover, we are spatialized and spatializing, always capable of bearing sensations. Finally, and this is an important point, the image or sense of what it is to be a lived body can be freely manipulated by various acts of consciousness, including desire, will, and fantasy. This means that we can have very personalized senses of what it is for "me" to be a lived body; but it also means that the ways in which the various sciences image and re-present the body in their own fields of investigation are an expression of how we conceive and image the body. One sees here a parallel with Henri Bergson's notion of the body as image, as he developed it in *Matter and Memory*,[31] although Stein would not argue that the image is an in-between reality as well as selective, as Bergson does. She would insist, instead, on the lived body's concrete manifestation and givenness, which can be delineated and investigated phenomenologically.

Stein extends her treatment of sensations and impressions to include the sensation of feelings (*Gefühlsempfindungen*) and sensual feelings (*sinnlichen Gefühle*). Unlike the previous discussion of sensations, in which impressions did not require an accompanying I-consciousness, here Stein maintains that there are feelings that include, or are accompanied by, an I-consciousness.

> Sensations of feelings...or sensual feelings...are inseparable from their founding sensations. The pleasantness of a savory dish, the agony of a sensual pain, the comfort of a soft garment are noticed where the

> food is tasted, where the pain pierces, where the garment clings to the body's surface. However, sensual feelings not only are there, but, at the same time, they are also in me; they issue from my "I." General feelings have a hybrid position similar to sensual feelings. Not only the "I" feels vigorous or sluggish, but I "notice this in all my limbs." Every mental act, every joy, every pain, every activity of thought, together with every bodily action, every movement I make, is sluggish and colorless when "I" feel sluggish. My living body and all its parts are sluggish with me. (*E* 48–49)

In short, sensations of feelings, or sensual feelings, "fuse" with the I; they are one. Stein distinguishes said feelings from moods, as moods may not be localized in the body. So, I may feel cheerful or melancholy, but my body does not feel these feelings as it does vigor or sluggishness. "Moods are 'general feelings' of a non-somatic nature" (*E* 49).

Thus far, what is given to us, what makes itself manifest or makes sense for us, is that we are embodied, and capable of sensations or impressions as well as feelings. Feelings express themselves in the body and are distinguished from moods. Unlike impressions or sensations, feelings are accompanied by an "I"-awareness. Again, presumably, and by extension (for Stein does not discuss this), my own sensate, feeling lived body can be distinguished from that of another, as what I experience and what is given to me in experience is here and not there, my own and not the other's. The distinction or difference between self and other is not deduced or inferred; rather, it is given at the very fundamental level of sensate, feeling embodiment and is perceived both from within and from without.

In terms of originary givenness, not only is the lived body made manifest, but the psychic and spiritual (*geistlich*) aspects of an "I," as well. How is the psychic aspect made evident in consciousness? How is it given to the I? Stein argues that psychic causality is given phenomenologically in the understanding of causality in general. Recall her previous statement concerning the "if...then" relation in experience. One lives this "if...then" relation as an awareness that brings the psyche to the fore. "The psychic is in essence characterized by this dependence of experiences on somatic influences. Everything psychic is body-bound consciousness, and in this area essentially psychic experiences, body-bound sensations, etc., are distinguished from accidental physical experiences, the 'realizations' of spiritual life" (*E* 49). For example, I can draw my thumb across my fingers, producing a sensation. Or, for another example, I hear of the near-death experience of a friend's mother, and I am aware of my own feelings of sadness and shock. I am not only aware of the content of the actual experiences and the acts of consciousness that accompany them, but I am profoundly aware of a causal link between what I experience and how I experience it: the link is localized in the body but it bespeaks the presence of a psyche.

Psyche, or the psychic, for Stein, is a complicated term. She sometimes equates the psyche with the soul, but at other points she distinguishes the psyche from the soul, the former referring to affectivity and causality (*E* 51), and the latter connoting a unifying principle that unites corporeality and affectivity (*E* 49), but which is not reducible to mere affectivity or causality. We can generally assume this double meaning of psyche and soul, except where Stein emphasizes a particular sense. Specifically, in the case of the awareness of psychic causality, Stein notes that the awareness of sensation or feelings is only possible if we understand at a basic level the "if...then" aspect of causality. This awareness of the "if...then" is not strictly localized in the living body, but, according to Stein, it is evidence of what she understands as the psychic realm, which allows one to unify or synthesize the sense of what is experienced and how it is experienced (i.e., feelings or sensations and their accompanying acts of awareness) with the lived experience of causality itself. Angela Ales Bello neatly explains the phenomenological sense of what Stein intends by psychic causality, which differs from physical causality as understood in the natural sciences.

> In actual fact, however, the type of causality that is thus identified is different from the one that underlies scientific research; Bergson's antipositivist attitude is thus maintained, for the causality that Edith Stein has in mind is not the "exact" causality that forms the basis of the physical sciences, but a "prescientific" causality of the kind that

sometimes presents itself in [our] experience of the physical world. The following are examples of causal connections in psychic life and the experience of nature: "I am so tired that I cannot read a book that makes intellectual demands on me," and, again, "today the air is so limpid as to assure good visibility"; these connections can certainly not be determined in a rigid manner; rather, they are somewhat vague, though this does not mean that they do not express some kind of "necessity."[32]

Causality, understood in its exact sense and as practiced in the natural and social sciences, especially psychology, is established through external means and observation. One gathers data based on experimentation and clinical practice in order to establish possible relations, which are always subject to margins of error and falsifiability. But the emphasis in phenomenology is the lived sense of the "if…then" relation and how it appears in consciousness to the "I." One lives the certainty, or undeniability, of a sensation or feeling and its causes. One naturally assumes that x→y. For Stein, this inner sense of causality is distinct and necessary to understand ourselves as human beings. This "if…then" synthesis is key to understanding ourselves and the connections between the various constitutive aspects, or profiles, of what it is to be a human being. Furthermore, the problem of induction, as raised by David Hume,[33] both applies and does not apply here. Hume is critical of those scientists and philosophers, including Descartes, who claim to establish the a priori nature of causality practiced in the pure sciences. This, of course, is not the kind of causality that Stein is proposing. Hume, however, designates a kind of inner causality, which he calls custom and habit. For Stein, habit may be evidence of a certain notion of causality (E 51), but it is only one aspect of the larger, more general "if…then" structure.

Bodily expression is one of the most fundamental ways in which the I can approximate and grasp what it comes to understand about itself. The body articulates not only what it senses and undergoes, but what the psyche and spirit experience and live through as well. "Since phenomena of expression appear as the outpouring of feelings, they are simultaneously the expression of the psychic characteristics they announce. For example, the furious glance reveals a vehement state of mind" (*E* 54). The first level of expression Stein describes is connected to feelings. She begins her treatment of expression by reminding her readers that feelings can be experienced as either an accompaniment or expression (*E* 51). In the case of the former, feelings are accompanied by some kind of sign that indicates to oneself (and, as we shall see, to others) a range of possible feelings. For example, one may blush with shame or embarrassment; the redness of the face accompanies the experience of shame. But the manifestation of psychic states of mind through the body alone does not guarantee a reliable understanding of what one is experiencing. In fact, Stein argues that observing the reddened face of another may indicate various things, including anger, shame, discomfort, etc. In order to bring the experience to a fuller sense of fulfillment, feeling must be made more precise through reflective understanding, and it is through this connection of feeling with reflective consciousness that one obtains a more exact picture of what is being expressed by the body.

> I blush in anger, shame, or from exertion. In all these cases, I have the same perception of my "blood rising in my face." But in one instance, I experience this as an expression of shame, and, in another, not as an expression at all but as a causal result of exertion. We have said that it requires an observant glance to make the bodily perceived expression into an intentional object in the pregnant sense. Yet the felt expression, even though experienced in the mode of actuality, also requires a particular turning of the glance to become a comprehended object. The turning of the glance is not the transition from non-actuality to actuality that is characteristic of all non-theoretical acts and their correlates. (*E* 53–54)

In order to understand the fullness of the meaning of the bodily expression of feelings, one must consider the context and situation. Stein is aware of this necessity. Circumstances certainly provide indicative signs as to what one might be experiencing in a given context. Stein recognizes that when dealing with feelings and expression, one must not be too quick to read the connection between them in a purely causal fashion. That is to say, a certain bodily manifestation of a psychic state of mind—for example, shame—must not be thought to appear only because certain circumstances caused it. Though this can certainly happen, Stein is seeking to expand the typically behaviorist, positivist account by arguing that the bodily expression of feeling is also connected to a broader spiritual conception of meaning, itself connected to deeper structures of will and motivation as well as to reflection (*E* 53). Through reflection, one can easily alter the meaning of bodily expression. For example, one can choose to smile, an act accomplished through reflection, even though the psychic state usually indicated by a smile is not what one is feeling. The body can indicate a feeling or state of mind that is the opposite of the actual psychic state. Here, the I has the freedom to alter what it wishes to signify bodily, to dissemble. For example, one may be very upset by the actions of another, but if cultural convention and circumstances prohibit the display of public irritation, one might smile instead, despite one's feelings of discomfiture or disapproval.

The final constitutive component of what it is to experience oneself as a psycho-physical unity, or subject, is the will, and Stein includes here a discussion of striving and motivation. In fact, when we enter into the realm of the will and motivation, we are properly in the spiritual realm, the domain of *Geist*. How does one experience will and how does it manifest itself in the lived body? Stein reports:

> Other phenomena of bodily expression do not appear to be the expression of volition itself, but the feeling components of complex volitional experiences. I may sit here quietly weighing two practical possibilities. When I have chosen, have made a decision, I plant my feet on the floor and spring up vivaciously. These movements do not express a volitional decision, but the resulting feeling of decisiveness, of activity, of unrest that fills me. Will itself is not expressed in this sense, but, like feeling, neither is it isolated in itself, having to work itself out. Just as feeling releases or motivates volition from itself (or another possible "expression" in a wider sense), so will externalizes itself in action. (*E* 54)

For Stein, there is a direct relation of the "*fieri*," or the "to make" or "to become" of what is willed, to the decision to bring about the willed thing and to the "*facere*," or carrying out, of the decision

(*E* 54–55). In short, the object to be willed, the decision, and the action that brings about the willed object conform. Describing what the I lives through when it wills, Stein presents a very strong definition of the will: (1) the delineation of something to be willed; (2) the review of possibilities and a decision about what exactly is to be willed; (3) and, finally, the execution of the will in an action that makes actual the willed object. The body itself may not display any direct signs of the will, but it must cooperate if the will is to fulfill its function.

Stein amplifies the I's experience of the will by attributing to it other phenomenological descriptions. Noting that the will can ultimately help to bring about a certain action, she observes that, "to act is always to produce what is not present" (*E* 55) and "action is always the creation of what is not" (*E* 56). I take this to mean that actions in and of themselves do not necessarily make manifest the activity of willing that helps to bring them about. The production of a new state of affairs may not make the agent's will or motivations evident. Furthermore, the will is associated with creativity, for it can bring about new states of affairs; it is capable of creating new things, things that are not but can be. This creative aspect of willing is traditionally identified as one of the greatest aspects of spirit: it can create new, spontaneous realities through its capacity for willing and the thinking and decision-making that willing requires. Moreover, Stein describes the will as the "master of the soul as of the living body" (*E* 55). But she is not an absolute voluntarist; objective reality imposes a limit on the will.

> The world of objects disclosed in experience sets a limit to the will. The will can turn toward an object that is perceived, felt, or otherwise given as being present, but it cannot comprehend an object not present. This does not mean that the world of objects itself is beyond the range of my will. I can bring about a change in the world of objects but I cannot deliberately bring about its perception if it itself is not present. The will is further limited by counter-effective tendencies which are themselves in part body-bound (when they are caused by sensory feelings) and in part not. (*E* 55)

Finally, Stein describes willing in terms of resistance and conflict. The will can be divided by conflicted strivings; St. Paul discusses this phenomenon as the "divided will." According to Stein,

> The will employs a psycho-physical mechanism to fulfill itself, to realize what is willed, just as feeling uses a mechanism to realize its expression. At the same time, the control of the mechanism, or at least the "switching on of the machine," is experienced. It may be experienced step by step if it means overcoming a resistance at the same time. If I become tired halfway up a hill, this causes a resistance to the movement to lift my feet, and they stop serving my will. Willing and striving oppose each other and fight for control of the organism. Should the will become master, then every step may be willed singly and the effective movement experienced by overcoming the counter-effect. (*E* 55)

Transition to the Foreign Individual

Up to this point, Stein has been describing the subject, but the subject experienced from within himself or herself. Phenomenological reflection, based on inner and outer experience, yields a subject that experiences itself as a lived body, a psyche, and a spirit, all of which are experienced in a unified fashion.

> We have at least outlined an account of what is meant by an individual "I," or by individuals. It is a unified object inseparably joining together the conscious unity of an "I" and a physical body in such a way that each of them takes on a new character. The physical body occurs as a living body; consciousness occurs as the soul of the unified individual. The unity is documented by the fact that specific events are given as belonging to the living body and to the soul at the same time: sensations, general feelings. The causal tie between physical and psychic events and the resulting mediated causal relationship between the soul and the outer world further document this reality.... The living body... is characterized by having fields of sensation, being located at the zero point of orientation of the spatial world, moving voluntarily and being constructed of moving organisms, being the field of expression of the experiences of its "I" and the instrument of the "I's" will. (*E* 56–57)

In her treatment of the essence of the self experienced as a subject, empathy has not been the focus of the discussion. When Stein transitions to the other, empathy becomes important, but, as Scheler rightly notes, Stein's account of empathy is conditioned by a deep self-awareness. The question, then, is: What evidence do we have that Stein's account of subjectivity—that is, her own subjectivity as she experiences it—is correct? Scheler also wonders whether such self-awareness is generally possible, as Stein maintains. In order for empathy to work as Stein proposes, a reflexive self-knowledge and an active awareness of the structure of experience—both the content of experience as it relates to the self and how one lives the experience—are required. Following Husserl, Stein develops a strong sense of egology that will serve as a vital condition for knowledge of other minds.

Essential for Stein is the experience of unity. This unity of the various aspects of what it is to experience oneself as human—namely, lived body, psyche, will—is justified phenomenologically in two ways. First, Stein maintains that this experience of unity is evidently given and, therefore, undeniable. For example, feelings and sensation properly belong to the fundamental experience of a body, and psyche makes manifest some kind of body-soul unity. Second, the experience of causality confirms the reality of a unified field of experience that is the I. When an event in the outer world occurs, both the body and the soul bear the effect of, or react to, this event. For example, a sad event will cause both the psyche and the body to display sadness as a reaction to the external event. As was pointed out earlier, a natural sense of cause and effect registers here in Stein's description. The discussion of causality and unity will play important roles in Stein's later text, the *Beiträge*.[34]

Once Stein has established the structure of the individual, always understood as an object of consciousness, that is, as self-consciousness, she begins to unpack the structure of empathy. Stein's description moves from the most basic level of empathy to its higher, more complex elements. What is primordially given to I-consciousness is the foreign other; the other is not a projection of the I's mind.

Facing the other, the I recognizes the other as another I. The ego and the alter ego are co-given (*E* 57). What allows the I to distinguish itself from the alter ego is the lived body of the other, which is given and seen as not my own; however, at the same time, both the I and the other share similar fields of sensation. "As we saw, we have a primordial givenness in 'bodily perception' of our own fields of sensation. Moreover, they are 'co-given' in the outer perception of our physical body in that very peculiar way in which what is not perceived can be there itself together with what is perceived. The other's field of sensation is there for me in the same way. Thus the foreign living body is 'seen' as a living body. This kind of givenness, which we want to call 'co-primordiality,' confronts us in the perception of the thing" (*E* 57).

It is the living bodies of the ego and alter ego, especially as they are spatialized and, therefore, capable of being seen and grasped from different aspects and angles (*E* 57), that are co-given and co-primordial. They both manifest fields of sensation, and this field of sensation, which is common to both, permits the very first form of empathy, what Stein calls "sensual empathy" (*E* 58). Stein offers the classic phenomenological example of a hand resting on a table, an example used by Husserl and reworked by Merleau-Ponty (*E* 58): My hand does not rest on the book in the same way that the book rests on the table. My hand feels various pressure points. I understand the sensation of the other's hand resting on the same book because I can bring the other's experience "into relief" with my own; I can also "take the place of the other," trade places with the other "as if" I were the other. The act of empathy, in Steinian terms, is described as trading places, as an "as-if" act, or as bringing the other's experience into relief with my own.

> The hand resting on the table does not lie there like the book beside it. It "presses" against the table more or less strongly; it lies there limpid or stretched; and I "see" these sensations of pressure and tension in a co-primordial way. If I follow out the tendencies to fulfillment in this "co-comprehension," my hand is moved (not in reality, but "as if") to the place of the foreign one. It is moved into it and occupies its

> position and attitude, now feeling its sensations, though not primordially and not as being its own. Rather, my own hand feels the foreign hand's sensation "with," precisely through the empathy whose nature we earlier differentiated from our own experience and every kind of representation. During this projection, the foreign hand is continually perceived as belonging to the foreign physical body so that the empathized sensations are continuously brought into relief as foreign, in contrast with our own sensations. This is so even when I am not turned toward this contrast in the manner of awareness. (*E* 58)

In sensual empathy, we are "sensing-in" to the experience of the other. My own experience is always primordial, and I can only become aware of the other's sensation, and understand it precisely as sensation, when I perform an act of empathy through the lived body and a shared field of sensation. But empathy is not confined to understanding specific acts; one may also experience more general acts of empathic understanding, such as empathically understanding what it would be like in general for a hand to rest on a table. Here, one must perform an eidetic act, that is, one must understand what it is in general for a hand to lie upon a table. Through free variation, one seizes an understanding of what it means for a hand, or any living limb, to have contact with a table in general. One moves, here, to the level of universal eidetic description. One preserves a type of experience and brings various instantiations into relation with the general type: "My physical body and its members are not given as a fixed type but as an accidental realization of a type that is variable within definite limits. On the other hand, I must retain this type. I can only empathize with physical bodies of this type: only these can I interpret as living bodies" (*E* 59). Stein remarks that there are various levels of generality to which various possible levels of empathy correspond (*E* 59). For example, I can speak of what it is like for a "human physical body" to experience contact with the table. Likewise, I can even project my empathy onto animals; for example, I can extend my experience of touch to the dog's paw and claim that I understand, albeit not in a fully adequate or fulfilled way, what it feels like for the dog to touch the table. Stein admits that these general types of empathy are very general and fall under a broader understanding of types; they clearly do not have the same fullness of sense as would the experience of one ego undergoing an analogous experience of the other.

Stein acknowledges that her view of empathy is analogical in nature; we analogize the experience of the other in relation to our own. Yet this analogizing is not identical with the analogical inference of other theories of empathy. In those theories, as, for example, in Johannes Volkelt's theory of empathy (E 59), one never analogizes one's experience directly with the other's. Rather, one must refer to an analogical type that is rooted in a logical or transcendental form that allows the comparison of the experience of the ego and that of the alter ego. Stein dismisses this logical formalism. She insists that one compares one's experience directly with that of the other (E 59). In analogical inference, one presupposes a myriad of logical forms that condition, and against which we measure our own experience of, reality.

From the beginning of her discussion of empathy, Stein tackles a problem that lies within the very structure of empathy: Why does one need to take the place of, or analogize oneself with, the other in order to obtain a presentification of the other's experience? Could we not, simply by performing Husserlian eidetic variation, understand the experience of the other as a more general instantiation of reality, as in the case mentioned earlier of the general possibility of the "human being" touching the table? Stein concedes that this would give us a general type of understanding, but this general understanding would not necessarily provide a full or "pregnant" sense of the act. Without the specificity of the experience of my own hand, rather than a hand in general, I would not be able to understand what it is like for different hands to have diverse experiences—my experience and understanding would be too general and insufficiently comprehensive. Empathy yields not only general understanding but also specific, varied and personalized experiences. It gives us a greater range of experiences rather than a series of general types of experience.

> Were the size of my hand, such as its length, width, span, etc., given to me as inalterably fixed, the attempt at empathy with any hand having

> different properties would have to fail because of the contrast between them. But empathy is quite successful with men's and children's hands as well, which are very different from mine, for my physical body and its members are not given as fixed types but as an accidental realization of a type that is variable within definite limits. On the other hand, I must retain this type. I can only empathize with physical bodies of this type; only these can I interpret as living bodies. (*E* 59)

In the end, empathy can not only analogize and thereby help us to obtain an understanding of what another may be experiencing, but it also enables us to better appreciate the varied, specific, and individual experiences of other minds. This is essential, especially in terms of understanding particular personalities and the specific body-psyche-spirit unity of other persons.

The lived body not only permits me to understand both my sensations and those of the other, but it also constitutes a zero point of orientation (*E* 61). The zero point of orientation simply refers to the lived body's experience of always having a reference point or ground. Phenomenologically, the pure I of consciousness, like the lived body, has a zero point of orientation. This zero point of orientation, or *Nullpunkt*, is vital for Stein as it not only localizes ego consciousness in the body, but because it permits one to see that others have a zero point of orientation as well. Stein maintains that this is immediately given in consciousness because one sees that one navigates space and spatialization by means of this zero point of orientation.

> We come to the second constituent of the living body: its position at the zero point of orientation. The living body cannot be separated from the givenness of the spatial outer world. The other's physical body as a mere physical body is, like other things, spatial and given at a certain location, at a certain distance from me as the center of spatial orientation, and in certain spatial relationships to the rest of the spatial world. When I now interpret it as a sensing living body and empathically project myself into it, I obtain a new image of the spatial world and a new zero point of orientation. (*E* 61)

Stein clarifies this by adding that the I does not literally shift its zero point to another place, for it always retains its primordial zero point of orientation. Moreover, the I does not experience some fantasized image of the spatial world. Rather, the I can presentify the other's zero point of orientation through empathy, even though, unlike the I's own zero point of orientation, the other's is not primordial.

The discussion of the zero point of orientation is important for phenomenology because it is the traditional way in which one discusses one's position in the world, both in relation to oneself and vis-à-vis others. We call this indexicality. For Hegel and Husserl, indexicality is expressed through spatialization in terms of being here and there.[35] This spatialization not only indicates a separation between ego and alter ego, but also establishes the centrality of the I-subject. Stein does not adopt the categories of here and there; rather, in her discussion of space and the zero point of orientation, she treats the spatial relations between subjects as both affirming the connection to the outer world, and outer perception to inner perception and intuition, as well as helping to bring us to a richer, fuller awareness of what the other is experiencing. Stein declares that, "this orientation [i.e., co-primordial zero point of orientation] takes us a long way in constituting the foreign individual, for by means of it, the 'I' of the sensing, living body empathizes the whole fullness of outer perception in which the spatial world is essentially constituted. A sensing object has become one that carries out acts. And so all designations resulting from the immanent essential examination of perceptual consciousness apply to it" (*E* 62). It is space and our orientation in space, both in relation to ourselves and vis-à-vis others, that allow us to see ourselves as part of the same whole.

Presumably, the fact that we all share the same space while being differentiated within it allows Stein to maintain that we also have an inner representation of that shared spatial world—what she calls a world image. She neither describes the content of that world image nor justifies its possibility, but she is clear that one has a world image and that others have one, too (*E* 62). "The world image I empathize in the other is not only a modification of my own image on the basis of the other's orientation; it also varies with the way I interpret his living body. A person without eyes fails to have the entire optical givenness of the world" (*E* 62). Stein claims that to have an orientation in the world means that one also has an accompanying world image. Again, this claim is not justified; it is simply asserted. One way to read this treatment of the world image is to look back at her treatment of spatialization. One can assume that space is not empty: it has content and is replete with all kinds of things. One stands in some kind of relation to this content, as her treatment of space indicates. Given that space is also the shared space of the outer world, which is common to all, one can argue that we share the common experience of sharing one reality, diverse as it may be. Also critical, and here I hark back to the opening thesis of this chapter, empathy is not only about the other; it also involves a deep building and awareness of self. Stein confirms this claim when she discusses the possibility of a world image and the modification of my own world image in relation to the other's.

The Importance of Reiterated Empathy

Consciousness and awareness of the other's mind occurs through an analogical projection or trading of place with the other. But before one can do this, one needs to have a sense, an awareness, of oneself. Earlier, we saw that through self-reflection one could recognize oneself as an ego-consciousness that experiences itself as a body-psyche unity. As I pointed out, such self-knowledge is possible, but how do we know whether it is true or accurate? It is empathy that allows one to confirm, indeed deepen, the sense of oneself as a human being, as a body-psyche unity, by understanding it analogically in another: there is wider confirmation of a shared understanding of self and other. But Stein, for the first time, also applies empathy to the self, and this special form of empathy is what she and Husserl called "reiterated empathy." In reiterated empathy, my empathic acts return to me and I can think them again; they are reflexive. The claim is that I can presentify myself to myself, presumably as an other (E 18), and this presentification (*Vergegenwärtigung*) allows me to see myself in a fuller sense. "In 'reiterated empathy,' I again interpret this physical body as a living body, and so it is that I am first given to myself as a psycho-physical individual in the full sense. The fact of being founded on a physical body is now constitutive for this psycho-physical individual. This reiterated empathy is at the same time the condition making possible that mirror-image-like givenness of myself in memory and fantasy.... It probably also accounts for the interpretation of the mirror image itself, into which we shall not go more deeply" (*E* 63). If we follow the structure of Stein's analysis, what constitutes the condition for an understanding of the experience of the other—and this is primary—is a self-reflexive awareness obtained through reiterated empathy. This makes sense, for in order to carry out the work of analogization, in order to trade places or act "as if," one needs to have a sense of self, itself constituted by an ego, body-psyche unity, and acts of will, etc. In order to project oneself into the other, what is projected cannot be empty. It must itself have content and a world in order to be able to understand the content and world of others. It is "seeing myself as another or as another sees me" (*E* 63) that enables Stein to extend her mind into the mind of the other. This split in self-consciousness that is achieved through reiterated empathy allows one to bring the image of the other into relation with one's own self-image, and then to modify it and vary it in fantasy, in order to obtain an understanding of the other's mind. If the self were not capable of reiterated empathy, one could not form a self-image or an image of oneself in the world at different points with different possibilities, nor could one separate oneself from the other. The otherness of the other is dependent upon the otherness that is already in me, an otherness guaranteed by reiterated empathy. Reiterated empathy also gives Stein the tools with which to challenge Scheler's critique of the premise of complete self-awareness. Self-awareness is possible only insofar as one is able to presentify self-images and vary them in consciousness, especially as they relate to others. One can have an awareness of oneself only if one can view oneself as an other; this is a necessary condition for Stein.

Given that reiterated empathy highlights the possibility of a non-identitarian consciousness, Stein believes that she can move to a description of the real outer world in intersubjective experience. If we concede that empathy works in the way elaborated by Stein, then our understanding of one another, and the modifications of both self and other that occur through empathy, give to us a comprehension not only of self and other but also of the world in which we dwell intersubjectively. Stein claims that, "the world I glimpse empathically is an existing world, posited as having being like the world primordially perceived. The perceived world and the world given empathically are the same world differently seen" (*E* 63–64). But given that the world is always described in relation to one's own consciousness, how do we know that the world really is the way we perceive or experience it to be? Stein will argue that empathy ensures that the world is not merely a projection of intersubjective consciousness and that it demonstrates the existence of a separate world, a world that is not purely dependent on consciousness.

Stein gives two arguments for the external reality of the world. First, in my own experience of what I perceive to be an outside reality, if I am faithful to what is given to me in my own experience, I note that, though there is a flow of the experience of something we call the world, this flow of experience appears to me as not being given by me; that is, the constitutive moments of the flow of the experience of the world are not motivated by me. Rather, the different perceptions of the constitutive moments of the experience of the world are motivated by the world itself. Hence, there is an external world that is not reducible to my own individual experience of it. Stein notes:

> The perceived world and the world given empathically are the same world, differently seen. But it is not only the same world seen from different sides, as when I perceive primordially and, traversing continuous varieties of appearances, go from one standpoint to another. Here, each earlier standpoint motivates the later one, and each following one severs the preceding one. Of course, I also accomplish the transition from my standpoint to the other's in the same manner, but the new standpoint does not step into the old one's place. I retain them both at the same time. The same world is not merely presented now in one way and then in another, but in both ways at the same time. (*E* 64)

My conscious experience of the world is dependent on the world continuing to present itself from a future standpoint that is not dependent upon my own projections. Second, external reality outside my own experience and perception is guaranteed by the perception of another, which I understand through empathy. I receive different images of the world that, because we share the same reality, are related to my own but are marked by another's consciousness.

> Were I imprisoned within the boundaries of my own individuality, I could not go beyond the "world as it appears to me." At least it would be conceivable that the possibility of its independent existence, which still could be given as a possibility, would always be indemonstrable. But this possibility is demonstrated as soon as I cross these boundaries by the help of empathy and obtain the same world's second and third appearance, which are independent of my perception. Thus, empathy as the basis of intersubjective experience becomes the condition of possible knowledge of the existing outer world, as Husserl as well as Royce present it. (*E* 64)

For Stein, empathy does more than allow us to "transfer" into the mind of the other; it also guarantees the nonreducibility of the world to my own experience.

Stein's logic progresses thus far as follows: Consciousness, when it reflects upon itself, knows that it is an I that constitutes a psychophysical unity capable of acts of will. This is what can be intuitively grasped as given to consciousness. Consciousness is also aware that others are co-primordial. Empathy allows one to know other minds (as sensate and as a zero point of orientation localized in a shared space), and reiterated empathy allows one to confirm, verify, and deepen the sense of the structure that is intuitively grasped in immediate self-consciousness. Finally, given is a shared world, albeit a world uniquely experienced by all subjects; this world is also independent of conscious experience, that is, it has its own independent status that does not depend upon human consciousness. Stein's analysis of empathy goes on to claim that empathy allows us to understand that all individuals are capable of experiencing, for themselves as well as in others, various aspects of individuality, including voluntary movement, phenomena of life (such as aging, health, sickness, vigor, and sluggishness, etc.), causality, and expression. Not only does empathy make us conscious of these phenomena about individual human beings, but it is the key that allows us to grasp that our structure as human being is constituted by the aforementioned subjects. At this point, I would like to discuss briefly what Stein means by each of these constituents, how it is that empathy reveals them, and how they operate intersubjectively.

First, let us examine voluntary movement. Stein identifies the lived body as the bearer (*Träger*) of voluntary movement (*E* 66). We saw earlier that it is also the bearer of sensation as well as a spatializing and spatialized zero point of orientation. Stein declares that a body can experience five kinds of movement, especially by observing these kinds of movement in others. These include mechanical, alive, spontaneous, imparted, and associated movements. Stein describes one hand moving another hand as an example of a mechanical movement. Here, movement appears in a very isolated form. Alive movement is accompanied by consciousness of the experience of moving—"I move." Mechanical and alive movement simply align with the distinction between the physical body (*Körper*) and the lived body (*Leib*). The consciousness of the living-through of the experience of moving—the "I move"—renders the movement alive for Stein. Movements may also be spontaneous, that is, they may arise out of nowhere and seem to have no direct cause other than the will. For example, I may choose to lift my arm and nothing other than my own will seems to cause my arm to move. In the case of imparted movement, the emphasis is on the passive elements of movement. When my left hand moves my right, I observe the movement and recognize that it was imparted by my left hand; the movement of my right hand was passively undergone, not simply enacted. Finally, associated movements are indirect movements caused by another movement—they are corollary movements. "For example, suppose a rolling ball strikes another and 'takes it along' in its movement. Here we have mechanical spontaneous and associated movement" (*E* 66).

All of these kinds of bodily movements of one's own lived body are analogously found in the other's. Again, Stein's logic insists that the primacy of my own movement is required in order for me to understand that of the foreign I.

> Movements analogous to our own are found in foreign movements. If I see someone ride past in a car, in principle, his movement appears no differently to me than that of the "static" parts of the car. It is mechanical associated movement and is not empathized, but is outwardly perceived.... The case is entirely different if, for example, he raises himself up in the car. I "see" a movement of the type of my own spontaneous movement. I interpret it as his spontaneous movement. As I participate in the movement empathically in the way already sufficiently familiar, I follow out the "co-perceived" spontaneous movement's tendency to fulfillment. Finally, I objectify it so that the movement faces me as the other's individual movement. (*E* 67)

Stein makes a crucial distinction here between movement that can merely be perceived and movement that can be empathized. She claims that voluntary or spontaneous movement is the kind of movement that empathy can properly understand. This is so because the importance of the "I will," or *Ich kann*, is constituent of such movements, and in order to grasp a full sense of this movement, one requires insight into the subjective structure and source of such acts as rooted in the will and the body. Moreover, an objectification or objectified sense of the voluntary movement is important. I understand not only what it is for the lived body to sense, to move in diverse spaces, but also what it is for the lived body to carry out voluntary movements. "This is how the foreign lived body with its organs is given to me as able to move. And voluntary mobility is closely linked with the other constituents of the individual. In order to empathize alive movement in this physical body, we must already have interpreted it as a living body" (*E* 67).

Another constituent element of our individual human being is what Stein calls the "phenomena of life," which include such specific phenomena as growth, development and aging, health and sickness, vigor and sluggishness (*E* 68). Stein criticizes Scheler, who regarded such phenomena as mere outward perceptions. For him, one simply perceives that another is tired, ill, etc. According to Stein, this view is too limited because we do more than simply observe these states. We empathically grasp them, we understand how the other feels as he or she undergoes these particular experiences. "In considering general feelings as our own experience, we have seen how they 'fill' the living body and the soul, how they definitely color every spiritual act and every bodily event, how they are then 'co-seen' in the living body, just as fields of sensation are. Thus, by his walk, his posture and his every movement, we also 'see' 'how he feels,' his vigor, sluggishness, etc. We bring this co-intended foreign experience to fulfillment by carrying it out with him empathically" (*E* 68–69). We interpret these phenomena much in the same way as we do feelings; we can give fuller meaning to these distinguishing aspects of our individuality by projecting and transferring ourselves into the place of the other. Again, an objective understanding of what the other feels—for example, vigor or health—requires that we first understand what these states would feel like for us. Of course, we constantly modify what we understand by such phenomena through the experience of it.

Stein's treatment of the phenomena of life helps us elucidate the position of empathy vis-à-vis knowledge obtained by outer perception. She offers the example of a doctor in order to illustrate what careful perception and knowledge can provide (*E* 70). The doctor, using his training and knowledge, can diagnose a case of carcinoma or tuberculosis simply by observing and studying the patient. But in order to understand the "cause" of illness and how it affects the life of the patient, empathy is required. Perception provides a certain kind of knowledge, but empathy gives us insight into how this knowledge is lived by others. The claim, then, is that this understanding of how others live a specific illness—an understanding acquired through empathy—may help the doctor to better locate the cause of the illness or even to alleviate the suffering caused by the illness. Empathy produces a fuller sense of the illness and how it affects the patient: projecting herself into the mind of the patient, the doctor more fully understands what the patient is experiencing, thereby learning more about the disease. I do not wish to say that empathy gives a deeper understanding of the disease itself, but it certainly adds to the cognitive richness of phenomena as they present themselves to consciousness. Stein remarks: "[The physician] sees [his patients] full of fresh strength or ailing, recovering or dying. He elucidates their condition for himself empathically.... He looks for the cause of the condition and finds ways to influence it" (*E* 70–71).

We come now to another constitutive element of the human individual and, in particular, of the psychic dimension, namely, causality. Like sensation, the zero point of orientation, voluntary movement, and the phenomena of life, causality can also be experienced in the lived body and can be empathized. Stein argues that because causality is lived and experienced bodily, one can both perceive and empathize the experience of it. Stein is not much interested in the problem of induction as laid out by Hume, because it becomes a matter of correcting the pretensions of a metaphysics that claims it can serve as an a priori science. The causality with which Stein is concerned is experienced bodily; it is a causality that both psychology and medicine draw upon in order to carry out diagnoses and cures. Stein observes that both Scheler and Bergson (*E* 72) argue that, given advances in psychological research, one must distinguish causality in the mental or psychic realm as well as the physical realm. Stein argues that, although this distinction is correct, the difference between mental and natural/physical causality is not so great as Bergson and Scheler maintain. She argues that, in terms of efficacy—that is, how natural and psychic causality play themselves out—they operate in similar ways. I cannot review the differences between Stein, Scheler, and Bergson in detail here, as doing so would lead us far from the task at hand. For our purposes, suffice it to say that causality, both natural and psychic, proves to be an efficacious way to validate empathy, and it can help us to build not only an understanding of ourselves, but an understanding of others and the world we share as well. Stein's account of empathy depends, in a significant way, on causality and an understanding of how it works.

What is the essential structure of causality? Stein argues that it takes the form of a cause-effect relationship: something causes *a* to affect *b*, or vice versa. What is important is the relation between the objects that stand in a cause-effect relationship. The doctor observes or perceives that a physical blow results in a certain kind of trauma to the body. As we have seen, the doctor can also empathize with the injured patient in order to better treat and understand the patient's suffering. In psychic phenomena, too, we can understand how one event may affect another.

> And of what finally concerns the efficacy of the whole life in every moment of existence [*Daseins*], we must say: Everything living in the present can have an effect, irrespective of how far the initiation of the affecting experience is from "now." Experiences of early childhood, even though pushed into the background by the profusion of later events, can also endure into my present. This can be clearly seen in dispositions toward other persons. I do not forget my friends when I am not thinking of them. They then belong to the unnoticed present horizon of my world. My love for them is living even when I am not living in it. It influences my actual feeling and conduct. (*E* 74)

The psyche undergoes the effects of past lived experiences—both those relatively closer to the present and those lodged in the remote past. A psychiatrist can perceive the effects of psychic trauma in the present life of her patient, but she can also empathize with her patient's trauma in order to acquire a deeper understanding of what the patient is going through. Causality, and understanding how cause and effect work, Stein argues, is part of our psychic constitution and can clearly be seen in and through the lived body. Recalling what was said above about the nature of space and voluntary movement, it is clear that causality can help us to understand how one movement leads to another, or how a particular spatialization produces certain given effects, etc. In terms of empathy, an understanding of the shared human structure of causality allows us to enrich our understanding of the nature of a given phenomenon and why it has come to be. But an understanding of causality also helps us to understand how it is that others, as well as ourselves, experience such phenomena and why we experience them the way we do. Causality is one of the key structures of embodied psychic life that permits us to penetrate more deeply into the sense and nature of reality. According to earlier understandings of causality, such as in Kant or Hegel, causality is a logical structure of (transcendental) consciousness; common to all human beings as part of their logical capacities, causality conditions all with which the mind comes into contact. Stein, however, does not root causality in logic; rather, she uncovers its structure as manifested in both physical and psychic life. Part of our psychic constitution, causality is lived at a very fundamental bodily level, as demonstrated by her example of the doctor and psychic trauma. In moving away from the metaphysical, epistemological, and logical roots of causality, Stein offers her readers a more robust and lived sense of causality that is fundamental to acquiring a deeper understanding of oneself, others, and the world in which all dwell together.

A further aspect of psychic life is revealed in Stein's treatment of expression. She notes that an understanding of self and others also requires some capacity for understanding expressive signs (E 76). The lived body of the other expresses or gives signs of (signifies) mental states that an I can understand through empathy. Stein offers the following example:

> Now there is still a group of phenomena that disclose to us a further domain of the psyche in a peculiarly characterized way. When I "see" shame "in" blushing cheeks, irritation in the furrowed brow, anger in the clenched fist, this is still a different phenomenon than when I look at the foreign living body's level of sensation or when I perceive the other individual's sensations and feelings of life with him. In the latter case, I comprehend the one with the other. In the former case, I see the one through the other. In the new phenomenon, what is psychic is not only co-perceived with what is bodily, but with what is expressed through it. (E 75–76)

When the "if...then" form of causality (E 84) begins to actualize itself within the embodied psychic life of the individual, it can yield an understanding of the how and why of a certain state of affairs, as we have seen. This was certainly the case with Stein's example of the doctor. In her treatment of expression, Stein claims that, as expressions manifest themselves to us in consciousness, the sense of our lived experience becomes richer because these expressions reveal a broader context in addition to providing the possibility of correcting empathic acts. How is this so? Stein notes that, in empathizing the expression of the other's lived body, "understanding of a bodily expression is based on comprehending the foreign living body already interpreted as the living body of an 'I.' I project myself into the foreign living body, carry out the experience already co-given to me as empty with its countenance, and experience the experience ending in this expression" (*E* 82). Linguistic meaning, which Husserl treats in the first *Logical Investigation,* is not the same thing as bodily expression. Although Stein accepted Husserl's understanding of spoken expressions, she was more interested in how such expressions are experienced bodily and how bodily expression is constitutive of understanding of the individual I and others. "As we saw earlier, we can neglect the speaking individual in the world. I myself primordially comprehend the meaning of this ideal object in the transition of understanding from word to meaning. And as long as I remain in this sphere, I do not need the foreign individual and do not have to empathically carry out his experiences with him. An intuitive fulfillment of what is intended is also possible through primordial experience" (*E* 82). Like Husserl, Stein believed that speech, especially the speech of the thinking I, can be meaningful when there is a fulfilled adequation between what is spoken and what is meant. Empathy is not required for this meaning fulfillment to occur.[36] If we agree with Stein that bodily expressions of inner states can be empathized in the way she describes, what is achieved? When I see the blushing cheeks or clenched fist of the other, I see, respectively, shame or anger in the other. When I empathize by projecting myself into the anger or shame of the other, I begin to ask why or how this state has come about. I thus obtain a deeper understanding of what I experience as an other's lived experience. But when we carry out further phenomenological reductions, expression points to another layer of sense. In order for us to understand how bodily expressions work, Stein argues that we need to have an understanding of meaning in general. Understanding the meaning of expression, in general, means that we have to understand the broader meaning-context that gives unity to the whole phenomenon. That which we experience in the other does not come to us as an isolated series of events and instants. Rather, it comes to us "progressively" in a unified, meaningful way; it is given sense by consciousness. And this act of *Sinngeben,* or what Husserl calls constitution, requires an understanding of the unity of word, meaning, and object.

> In order to comprehend the object intended right now, we always need a givenness of the intuitive basis of meaning experiences. There is no intermediate level between the expressed experience and the expressing bodily change. But meaning and symbol have something in common that causes them both to repeatedly be called "expression".... They constitute the unity of an object, that the expression released from the connection with what is expressed is no longer the same object (In contrast with the signaling [i.e., perceptual or perceived] physical body), that the expression proceeds out of the experience and adapts itself to the expressed material. (*E* 81)

Expression in the lived body, when empathized, points to something else; it reveals another layer of understanding that is both shared with and empathized in another, namely, the layer of expressive meaning. Husserl ultimately situates this layer in a transcendental logic or structure, but Stein uncovers it in an intersubjective and bodily way. "These relationships are present in simple form in bodily expression; they are doubled in a certain sense in verbal expression: word, meaning and object; and correlatively, having of the object, logical intention or meaning, and linguistic designation. The function of expressing, through which I comprehend the expressed experience as the expression, is always fulfilled in the experience in which expression proceeds from what is expressed" (*E* 81). When we empathize the lived experience of the other—when we project ourselves into it, especially in terms of bodily expression—we may not only understand certain moods or psychic states, but we also see a larger structure of meaning-making at work. We try to make sense of or give meaning to the expression and what lies behind it as manifested in the body-psyche unity of the other. We try to grasp the whole meaning in a unified way, and insofar as we do this, we render the experience of ourselves, others, and the world intelligible, richer, and pregnant with sense. "An action is a unity of intelligibility or meaning because its component experiences have an experienceable connection. And experience and expression form an intelligible whole in the same sense. I understand an expression, while I can merely bring a sensation to givenness. This leads me through the phenomenon of expression into the meaning-contexts of what is psychic, and at the same time, gives me an important means of correcting empathic acts" (*E* 84).

Stein concludes her treatment of the lived body and the psyche with an important consideration of deception and error. All human beings, even the phenomenologist, can make mistakes or be deceived about what they empathize, both with respect to themselves and to the minds of others. But Stein's treatment of deception and error must not be read only within the framework of eidetic variation. In other words, the correction of mistakes and deceptions of the objectivated presentification of both the I and other does not have as its only aim a more accurate picture of the essence of what has been empathized. Deception and correction have two functions, and should be read as part of the empathic act itself rather than as being rooted in the demands of the broader phenomenological method. How can this claim be justified? First, Stein claims that deception and the correction of empathic acts help one to negotiate the meaning-context, discussed above. "Experience and expression form an intelligible whole.... I understand an expression, while I can merely bring a sensation to givenness. This leads me through the phenomenon of expression into the meaning-contexts of what is psychic, and at the same time, gives me an important means of correcting empathic acts" (*E* 84). Second, deception and correction help us access another layer of the human person, namely, character. Concerning the first claim, Stein remarks:

> The basis for what would suspend the unity of a particular meaning must be a deception. When I empathize the pain of the injured in looking at a wound, I tend to look at his face in order to have my experience confirmed in his expression of suffering. Should I instead perceive a cheerful or peaceful countenance, I would say to myself that he must not really be feeling any pain, for pain in its meaning motivates

> unhappy feelings visible in an expression. Further testing that consists of new acts of empathy and possible inferences based on them can lead me to another correction: the sensual feeling is indeed present but its expression is voluntarily repressed.... The harmony of empathy in the unity of meaning also makes possible the comprehension of expressive appearances unfamiliar to me from my own experience and therefore possibly not experienceable by me at all. (*E* 84–85)

The unity of the whole of meaning is interrupted by an inconsistency, and this undermines the consistency of what is being empathized. Part of the empathic act is the ability to understand unified wholes of meaning and meaning-contexts. The disjunction that occurs when the unified whole of the meaning-context of injury and the meaning of pain is unsettled or contradicted by an untroubled countenance causes me to carry out further empathic acts and inferences. Deceptions and corrections help us to negotiate such meaning-contexts; they can confirm (or not disconfirm) what is being experienced, enriching our understanding of what is being lived in consciousness and in the world.

Turning now to Stein's claim about character, the analysis of deception and correction helps us to judge a large unified whole, namely, the character of a person. "But the possibility of correction goes further. I not only interpret single experiences and single-meaning contexts, but I take them as announcements of individual attributes and their bearers, just as I take my own experiences in inner perception. I not only comprehend an actual feeling in the friendly glance, but friendliness as an habitual attribute" (*E* 86). Stein posits that a leap can be made from single experiences to broader judgments about character. Empathy allows one to do this. When it comes to deception and character, a larger sense of a person helps us to make sense of their individual acts, especially if those acts do not fit the character that we have derived through empathy. "But having thus gotten a picture of the foreign 'character' as a unity of these attributes, this itself serves me as a point of departure for the verification of further empathic acts. If someone tells me about a dishonest act, I will not believe him. And, as in single experiences, there are also meaning-contexts for personal attributes" (*E* 86). Stein maintains that we understand the unity of character in relation to each specific attribute as we would the unity of any given thing with all of its constitutive attributes. Character, acquired through a broader application of empathy, can guide our understanding of what it is to be a self and what others may be experiencing. As an example, Stein identifies herself as a lover of music, especially Beethoven's. If she believes that an unmusical person may also enjoy Beethoven, her deception or error will be corrected when she observes the bodily expression of the other's utter boredom as he or she listens to the Beethoven symphony (*E* 87).

With the treatment of empathy as a psycho-physical phenomena, we discover that the human being, especially the I, is constituted as the bearer of sensation in a lived body that experiences itself as a spatialized and spatializing zero point of orientation, is capable of movement (voluntary and otherwise), and understands expression and meaning-contexts as well as character. It should also be remarked that empathy is always guided by outer perception (*E* 87). Perception yields all kinds of aspects of reality, but empathy allows us additional insight into deeper senses of ourselves, others, and the world we share (*E* 87). Prior to moving on to higher functions of empathy in relation to the spiritual, or *geistlich,* aspect of the human person, Stein emphatically reminds readers that her treatment of empathy, though it yields awareness of other minds, primarily reveals one to oneself; it is also about subjective self-constitution. Indeed, empathic awareness and understanding of the other is the condition for self-understanding. "Now, as we saw on a lower level in considering the living body as the center of orientation, the constitution of the foreign individual was the condition for the full constitution of our own individual self. Something similar is also found on higher levels" (*E* 88). But the self that is constituted in empathy vis-à-vis the other may still suffer from deception. The other may see one better than one sees oneself. That the I can acquire self-knowledge—following the ancient oracular wisdom, *gnothi seauton,* through empathy—is no guarantee that such knowledge is absolute. In fact, this was the error of the Moderns, especially Descartes and Hegel, who posited an I that was identical with itself. Let us not forget the force of Fichte's claim regarding the self-positing I. For Stein, the I is undeniably proper to the self, but it acquires deeper knowledge about itself not only through reflection about itself, but through the other, who, in empathy, becomes the condition for self-knowledge. For Stein, the other may know me better than I do myself.

> Empathy proves to have yet another side as an aid to comprehending ourselves. As Scheler has shown us, inner perception contains within it the possibility of deception. Empathy now offers itself to us as a corrective for such deceptions, along with further corroboratory or contradictory perceptual acts. It is possible for another to judge me "more accurately" than I judge myself and to give me clarity about myself. For example, he notices that I look around me for approval as I show kindness, while I myself think I am acting out of generosity. This is how empathy and inner perception work hand in hand to give myself to myself. (*E* 89)

Ultimately, we must recall that, for Stein, the I is given to itself, but a greater awareness of self is also achieved through the other.

EMPATHY AND THE UNDERSTANDING OF THE SPIRITUAL PERSON

In the consideration of spirit, or *Geist*, we must comprehend the peculiar Steinian understanding of the word. Spirit, in Stein's early works, does not have a religious meaning; rather, it is firmly rooted in the German tradition of nineteenth century philosophy, in which spirit, often badly translated in English as "mind," was broadly taken up. There are two senses in which Stein uses the term. The domain of spirit is marked by the classic Husserlian distinction between spirit as the domain of will and motivation and psyche as the domain of nature. In other words, the realm of spirit is intimately linked with all that stems from and is concretized by human spontaneity and freedom, whereas the psyche and sensation are rooted in our nature and subject to natural and psychic causality. Working from this view of spirit, Stein investigates the nature of acts of will and motivation, and of strivings. This constitutes the subjective side of spirit. But as it acts and lives, spirit produces objects; objectivated spirit is concretized in works of art, culture, history, religion, etc. The production that ensues from the life of spirit, that is, the life of human freedom and spontaneity, leads to the second, more peculiarly Steinian intervention into the domain of spirit: the products and objects of spirit and their lives—their unfolding and decline—can be studied as well. It is the study of the sciences of spirit and the understanding they yield which are important for Stein, both in her treatment of empathy as well as in her later work, the *Beiträge*. She calls the specific studies of the life of spirit *Geisteswissenschaften,* sometimes loosely translated as the "human" or "cultural" sciences, but this translation is inadequate. However, English has no equivalent that captures the sense of the study of human freedom and its products and movements.

> The *Geisteswissenschaften* [cultural sciences] describe the production of the spirit, though this alone does not satisfy them. They also pursue, mostly unseparated from this, what they call "history" in the broadest sense—history of language, art history, etc. They pursue the formation of spiritual products or their birth in the spirit. They do not go about this by causal explanation, but by a comprehension that relives history. Were cultural scientists to proceed by causal explanation, they would be making use of the method of natural science. This is only permissible for elucidating the genetic process of cultural products insofar as it is a natural occurrence. (*E* 93)

Stein's description of the cultural or spiritual sciences is very precise: these sciences help us "relive" what-is through what-has-been. They also contribute to the creation of further possibilities that may arise from reliving what has been historically. Though steeped in a German idealist approach to history, which marks her own phenomenological method in a unique way, Stein's notion of "reliving" is not marked by a dialectical unfolding or teleology, as was Hegel's approach to history and the science of spirit. Stein saw "reliving" as vital and central for these sciences, and empathy, as presentification, is the most intense form of reliving for her because, as it helps to uncover deeper layers of sense, the complexity of reality begins to unfold. This unfolding becomes clear through the application of her own phenomenological method. Stein observes that, "as it pursues the formative process of spiritual products, we find the spirit itself to be at work. More exactly, a spiritual subject empathically seizes another and brings its operation to givenness itself" (E 93). Essential to understanding Stein's notion of spirit are the spiritual sciences, which, in order to function, in order to achieve their aim, namely, to relive what they uncover rather than simply chronologically report the causes of what has been uncovered, require empathy.

Why do these sciences need to relive rather than merely provide an aetiological account of what they discover? Aetiological accounts, at least in Stein's day, were imbued with the spirit of positivism that reduced reality to what can be seen and quantified. This methodology, if applied to the traditional domains of the cultural sciences, including history and art, renders the products and expression of these sciences as a series of lifeless facts, which stand outside ourselves as banal objects. Contrariwise, a vivifying view of the cultural sciences seeks to uncover and make meaningful richer possibilities of sense that speak to the core of the projects of philosophy and of human being: to know oneself so that one may live fully.

Thus far, I have focused on the psycho-physical development of the individual, only alluding to various spiritual aspects of the human person such as volitional movements, the spiritual sciences, and some aspects of meaning-context. Stein concludes her treatment of empathy with a discussion of the spiritual layers that constitute the human person, both as a self and other, as well as how this spiritual domain helps to constitute a world that we share in common, a world that can be grasped and understood through the spiritual sciences. In her treatment of the person, the person begins to emerge as a supporting (*Träger*) structure for all that is human. In the psycho-physical account, "consciousness appeared not only as a causally conditioned occurrence, but also as object-constituting at the same time. Thus it stepped out of the order of nature and faced it. Consciousness as a correlate of the object world is not nature, but spirit" (E 91). Stein defines spirit not only as the domain of the lawfulness of will and motivation, but also as the world in which consciousness turns back on itself and begins to reflect freely on that which nature has given it. This is a classic definition of the spiritual, or *geistlich,* realm that one finds in German Idealism and phenomenology. Stein identifies, *ab initio,* one of the proper relations of empathy to the spiritual. The personality (*Persönlichkeit*), and the understanding of it, in others as well as in ourselves, is one of the elements of the person that empathy can help us to understand.

Stein is staunchly committed to the value of the *Geisteswissenschaften.* She lauds the work and unique insights of Jacob Burckhardt (*E* 93) and Wilhelm Dilthey (*E* 94) as defending the rightful place of the cultural sciences within study. In her discussion of these sciences, she focuses on the work of Dilthey, who was influential for both Husserl's later work and Stein's own thinking. Dilthey believed that the cultural sciences could draw upon the work of the natural sciences, especially psychology, but could also develop their own account of things that come to be reflected upon, especially human beings. Like Simmel, Dilthey drew upon a rich understanding of perception and reflection, albeit not in an a priori way as did Simmel, to form ideal types of human beings. Stein notes: "From Dilthey's mistaken expositions, we learn that there must be an objective basis for the cultural sciences besides the clarification of method, an ontology of the spirit corresponding to the ontology of nature. As natural things have an essential underlying structure—for example, the fact that empirical spatial forms are realizations of ideal geometric forms—so there is also an essential structure of the spirit and of ideal types. Historical personalities are empirical realizations of these types" (*E* 95). Dilthey is convinced that the same tools employed by the natural sciences could be employed to glean insight into the structure of other minds, namely, perception and intuition. Distinguishing herself from Dilthey, Stein argues that the establishment of types is not acquired through outer perception alone; one also requires empathy in order to obtain the deeper structure of the person: "If empathy is the perceptual consciousness in which foreign persons come to givenness for us, then it is also the exemplary basis for obtaining this ideal type, just as natural perception is the basis for the eidetic knowledge of nature. We must also find access to these problems from the point of view of our considerations" (*E* 95–96). Admittedly, Stein's treatment of Dilthey is perfunctory; she justifies neither her own critique of Dilthey nor her own position. I think this is why Stein needed to write the *Beiträge*—in order to flesh out the claims she makes about other approaches, particularly those that claim a privileged understanding of how we know ourselves and the minds of others, as well as the world in which we dwell, namely, psychology and Dilthey's *Weltanschauungsphilosophie*. I shall take this point up more amply in the next chapter, which focuses on Stein's *Beiträge*.

What Dilthey and Stein share, however, is the conviction that in order to understand the cultural sciences, one must understand what the self, the human person, is. It is self-understanding, according to Stein, that acts as the base upon which we can understand persons not only as individuals but also as types, as following certain typical traits and characteristics; both the I and others may be typical types of persons (*E* 115). Personalities may also have an experiential structure of atypical character (*E* 114). Understanding the material of the cultural sciences can be truly understood only in relation to a self; empathy is the act that allows us to develop our understanding of ourselves, others, and human nature by leading us constantly to modify ourselves and our understanding according to what others claim to be experiencing. Empathy allows me to enter into the very claims, actions, events, and personalities described by the cultural sciences. Self-understanding, then, is pivotal. Stein remarks: "Now we see what justification Dilthey has for saying, 'The interpretative faculty operating in the cultural sciences is the whole person.' Only he who experiences himself as a person, as a meaningful whole, can understand other persons. And we also see why Ranke would have liked to 'erase' his self in order to see things 'as they were.' The 'self' is the individual experiential structure" (*E* 116).

The spiritual subject, for Stein, is not separate from the psycho-bodily unity described in her earlier treatment of empathy. Again, the human subject is revealed as a unity of body, psyche, and spirit. In her preceding descriptions, the subject was seen to be capable of spiritual acts of will, evident in the experience of spontaneous movements of will. As Stein charts the spiritual domains constitutive of our own and others' subjectivity, she maintains that the revelation of the structure called "person" does not emerge with the lower spiritual functions such as motivation, striving, and willing; rather, these basic components of the spiritual subject reveal a stronger sense of the I, personality, and the role of value in our lives. The human being begins to emerge with these later elements and is located within this very structure Stein calls person. In sum, Stein's phenomenological account of spiritual subjectivity moves from an account of motivation, striving (*Streben*) and will to more precise, personal layers: a richer sense of the I with a personality and the ability to value. Stein identifies two sources as pivotal for her analysis, namely, Pfänder and Scheler.

Let us turn to an exposition of Stein's treatment of the spiritual layers of the human person. Reflecting upon herself—again, the self is always the starting point of any act of empathy—Stein claims that the psycho-physical I is capable of movements or acts of will. How does she prove this? Examining the flow of consciousness, one notices that one moment of experience flows into another. When conscious of my own acts of will and the movement of the will, I observe various things. First, the moments constitutive of the flow of lived experience, called "willed acts," flow one into the other; they unfold in time. (Stein reiterates this at the beginning of her *Beiträge*.) One's acts of will are not experienced as a whole duration, but consist of moments that once were (past), are now (present), and anticipate another (future). There is definitely an I in such acts, but no experience of a substratum that one can call a person (*E* 96). This substratum will emerge later. But what connects one moment to another in a coherent fashion? How does a meaning-unity emerge from this flow of the conscious moments of a willed act? "Spiritual acts do not stand beside one another without relationship, like a cone of rays with the pure 'I' as the point of intersection, but one act experientially proceeds from the other. The 'I' passes over from one act to the other in the form of what we earlier called 'motivation.' This experiential 'meaning context,' so strangely experienced in the midst of psychic and psycho-physical causal relationships and without parallel in physical nature, is completely attributable to spirit. Motivation is the lawfulness of spiritual life" (*E* 96). As we move to the domain of meaning and unified meaning-contexts, we break away from causality and move into a spiritual domain, because what is here presupposed is not only the production of a given effect, but a reflective consciousness of the effect that produces meaning; this meaning orients and elicits us in different ways from those of a purely passive effect. Stein admits that psychology and the other natural sciences can study the meanings that emerge from her understanding of the motivations that lie behind the flow of consciousness of lived experience. Here, presumably, the flow of lived experience acquires a richer sense as we begin to reflect upon its meaning, rather than merely describing how one effect produces another, as we do in cases in nature. A spiritual understanding of meaning, motivated by a unified meaning-context, leads us to an understanding of expression, both our own and that of others, as we saw earlier.

> The experiential context of spiritual subjects is an experienced (primordially or empathically) totality of meaning and is intelligible as such. Precisely this meaningful proceeding distinguishes motivation from psychic causality, as well as empathic understanding of spiritual contexts from empathic comprehension of psychic contexts. A feeling by its meaning motivates an expression, and this meaning defines the limits of possible expressions, just as the meaning of a part of a sentence prescribes its possible formal and material complements. This asserts nothing more than that spiritual acts are subject to a general rational lawfulness. Thus, there are also rational laws for feeling, willing, and conduct expressed in a priori sciences as well as laws for thinking. Axiology, ethics, and practice take their place beside logic. (*E* 96–97)

The unity of a meaning-context bespeaks a certain coherence and rational lawfulness; without such a unity, there would be no sense or only contradictions. We do not usually, however, experience reality in a nonsensical fashion. That there is a rational lawfulness of unified meanings of feelings, willings, and practice or doing means that we can study such rational acts in sciences such as axiology and ethics.

But Stein gets ahead of herself here, for she has thus far established only that some kind of rational lawfulness marks the flow of constitutive moments of lived experience, that these moments are motivated. But this discussion of motivation in experience does not yield a spiritual person (*E* 98). Stein goes on to discuss feeling and emotion as revealing something about our spiritual nature that is not purely affective. In reflecting upon her own experience of emotion, she observes that one is not merely affected in a certain way, producing joy or sadness or a certain mood; more is given than a purely psychic experience of emotion. Emotions and feeling not only give us an object, that is, a certain feeling such as joy or sadness, but they reveal something about the structure of the I itself.

> Feeling is an experience when it gives us an object or something about an object. The feeling is the same act when it appears to be originating out of the "I" or when it appears to unveil a level of the "I." Yet, we still need a particular turning of the glance to make the feelings, as they burst out of the "I," and this "I" itself in a pregnant sense, into an object. We need a turning specifically different from reflection because reflection does not show me something not previously there for me at all. On the other hand, this turning is specifically different from the transition from a "background experience," the act in which an object faces me but is not the object toward which I prefer to turn as the specific cogito, the act in which I am directed toward the object in the true sense. (*E* 99)

Stein observes that when one experiences oneself undergoing a certain emotion or feeling, the I, too, is objectivated. Furthermore, one's subjectivity is not only objectified (i.e., "I" am sad), but one is given to oneself in a certain way. "For turning to the feeling, etc., is not a transition from one objective givenness to another, but the objectifying of something subjective. Further, in feelings, we experience ourselves not only as present, but also as constituted in such and such a way. They announce personal attributes to us.... We gave examples of such persistent attributes, among others, memory, announced in our recollections, and passion, revealed in our emotions" (*E* 99). Through feelings and emotions, I experience myself as given to myself in a certain way, with certain personal attributes. So the experience of emotion "motivates" in consciousness another aspect of my own subjectivity, not merely the specific feeling or meaning-context of the feeling I am undergoing presently. Stein's account, which draws from Husserl, is fascinating because the objects of consciousness always transcend themselves, always point to other layers and senses that make possible our very experience. This excess, which comes from intentional consciousness and always points to more than what is given, encourages us to bring other aspects of our experience to further consciousness, ultimately giving us further sense—sense understood in its "pregnant" or thick phenomenological use.

I contend that self-knowledge is primary in empathy, and Stein affirms this claim by considering how one comes to be given to oneself in emotion or feeling, how one undergoes this "self-experiencing" (*E* 100). When I experience a certain feeling, such as pain, the pain alone is not the only thing revealed. I, too, am in pain. Likewise, when I experience joy or sadness, my mood—something about myself—may be given to myself. Moreover, emotions and feelings, as well as moods, may color the way one experiences certain acts in consciousness. Moods, which are not experienced as specific feelings resulting from specific triggers, occupy a special place in consciousness. Moods occupy no specific locality in the I; rather, they suffuse, completely inundate, and fill the I. "For example, cheerfulness of character is not an experienced attribute that is localized in the 'I' in any way, but is poured over it entirely like a bright luster. And every actual experience has in it something of this 'total illumination,' every experience is bathed in it" (*E* 100).

The discussion of emotions, feelings, and moods produces in Stein a certain self-affectivity or autoaffection that reveals something about the very structure of the I, that it is given to itself in a certain way. This self-giving points beyond itself to make evident another aspect of spiritual subjectivity, namely, value. The same feelings, moods, or emotions are not all given with the same intensity, nor do they correspond to the same object all the time. The pain of a broken fingernail is not the same as the pain of the loss of a piece of jewelry, or the pain of the death of a loved one. There are grades and hierarchies to the same emotion. It is this very hierarchy within emotion that points to the phenomenon of value: we care about or find valuable certain things. "Anger over the loss of a piece of jewelry comes from a more superficial level or does not penetrate as deeply as the loss of the same object when it is also the souvenir of a loved one. Furthermore, pain over the loss of a loved one himself would be even deeper" (*E* 101). From her analysis of pain, Stein derives a hierarchy of "felt values" (*E* 101).

Values are also located in the domain of the will. The lived experience of one's will always comes in the form of the Husserlian "*Ich kann*" or "I will or I shall...." One can will certain values, especially higher ones that are more immediately connected to one's freedom. Freedom, for Stein, though posited metaphysically, is never justified philosophically. She follows Husserl's assumptions here. What is fundamentally made manifest in the experience of willing is the reflexive I's power or capacity to choose. In striving, *a contrario*, the object of striving is primary. Of course, there are values that are received and transmitted by larger social and political realities, so one may inherit certain values, based, for example, on one's family structure and commitments. Furthermore, living in a particular country may color one's perception of the values of other countries. But despite these received and passive values, which form our unique backgrounds and ethos, Stein maintains that we nevertheless have the capacity to choose freely or will our values.

If the I has the capacity to choose or reject certain values, and thus to form a hierarchy of values, how does this capacity point to the possibility of a person? Stein's argument is threefold. Acts of willed value are reflexive, as the I reflects upon its own acts and choices. "The acts of reflection in which knowledge comes to givenness can thus always become a basis for valuing; and knowledge, like every felt value, therefore becomes relevant for [the] personality's structure" (*E* 107). Stein claims that, in choosing certain values, we become aware that these values affect and structure who we are; they shape certain of our attributes and help to structure and unfold what Stein calls the personality. For example, if I choose a certain value—say, the belief in equal marriage for all—I begin to see myself as liberal. I begin to attribute to myself liberal values, which can color my personality. "Accordingly, every time we advance in the value realm, we also make acquisitions in the realm of our own personality. This correlation makes feelings and their firm establishment in the 'I' rationally lawful, as well as making possible decisions about 'right' and 'wrong' in this domain. If someone is 'overcome' by the loss of his wealth (i.e., if it gets him at the kernel of his 'I'), he feels 'irrational.' He inverts the value hierarchy or loses sensitive insight into higher values altogether, causing him to lack the correlative personal levels" (*E* 101).

Stein admits that certain sentiments can also form a personality. "Sentiments of love and hate, thankfulness, vengeance, animosity, etc.—feelings that have others as their object—are also sensitive acts that expose personal levels. These feelings, too, are firmly established in various levels of the 'I'" (*E* 101). Interestingly, with sentiments that have other people as their object, one crosses into the other's hierarchy of values. "For example, love is deeper than inclination. On the other hand, their correlate is other people's values. If these values are not derived values, such as other realized or comprehended values, but his own values, if they come to givenness in acts rooted in a depth other than the feeling of nonpersonal values, if, accordingly, they unveil levels not to be experienced in any way, then the comprehension of foreign persons is constitutive of our own person" (*E* 101–02). Stein claims that when we experience love or hate or animosity toward another person and their values, we stand in a certain relation to that person, who, as a bearer of value, becomes constitutive of our own values; we see ourselves in relation to that particular other's values. Again, we see here the primacy of self-awareness when we stand in relation to the other, whereby we presumably bring the other's values into our own consciousness through empathy. Stein never explicitly mentions empathy in this context. Outer perception allows us to see those values that inherently belong to the other, but empathy allows us to compare and modify our own values in relation to those of the other as we stand in the other's place. We understand what it is for the other to experience a certain value that we seize through empathy.

Stein identifies love as the most important value, for it allows us to recognize the person purely as a person and nothing else. In love, the other is valued for herself and for no other derived value. The other is given fully as a person in love. "Now, in the act of love we have a comprehending or an intending of the value of a person. This is not a valuing for any other sake. We do not love a person because he does good. His value is not that he does good, even if he perhaps comes to light for this reason. Rather, he himself is valuable and we love him 'for his own sake.' And the ability to love, evident in our loving, is rooted in another depth, from the ability to value morally, experienced in the value of deeds" (*E* 102). When we love the other simply for being that very other, and not according to her deeds or accomplishments or possessions, we come to experience the full value of the person as a person. Here is the full recognition of what constitutes the person: to be loved unconditionally as a person and for nothing else. It is the I that recognizes this value in the other. The value of the person is made evident to my consciousness, and I thus value this person simply as a person. While other acts of valuing help us understand the self and others as persons, the fullest sense of personhood manifests itself in love, which Stein suggests is not given by acts of empathy.

Most curiously, the traditional structure of empathy, which Stein has maintained until this point, breaks down in this claim. In love, I cannot take the place of the other because the other is loved for who they are as a person. We have uncovered here a limit of empathy. Again, personhood, in its fullest sense, is revealed not through empathy, but through love. In the highest expression of spirit, empathy has no role; rather, recognition of the personhood of the person is revealed in love. So, if love makes manifest the value of the other as a person in the fullest sense of the word, and if empathy as a project of self-constitution thereby breaks down, how is the I to recognize itself as a "full" person? Does the I need to be loved in the same way?

The recognition of myself as a person, in the fullest sense of the word, is not acquired through an act of empathy, nor is it dependent upon the recognition of the other as beloved. The I's personhood is recognized in its own awareness of its independent ability to create value. This ability is fundamentally the I's capacity brought to fullness through its own acts of self-reflection and personality-building.

> The value of our own person seems to be only reflexive and not constituted in the immediate directedness of experience; we need yet another investigation to decide this. Not only comprehending, but also realizing, a value is a value. We want to consider this realizing in more detail—its emotional components rather than as willing and acting. In realizing a value, this value to be realized is before me, and this feeling of value plays the role in constituting personality that we have attributed to it. But, simultaneously, with this feeling of value, there is an entirely naïve and unreflected joy in "creation." In this joy, the creation is felt to be a value. At the same time, I experience my creative strength in this creation and myself as the person who is provided with this strength. I experience creativity as valuable in itself. The strength I experience in creation, and its simultaneous power, or the very power of being able to create itself, are autonomous personal values and, above all, entirely independent of the value to be realized. (*E* 103)

This capacity for self-creation and creation in general is not reducible to an act of empathy; it is fundamental. Stein claims that there is an independent value in which the I comes to be revealed as a person—the value of creating value. Self-recognition as a creator of value, and the joy that ensues from such a creation, allow us to see ourselves as persons, always within the register of value. Empathy, then, is an adjunct, a way to continue this project of self-value and value-creation, especially at various levels of feeling, movement, and certain valuing acts that show forth a personality. But the primary act that makes all of this possible is dependent not on empathy, but on one's own sheer capacity for creating value and recognizing such a capacity.[37]

Undoubtedly, the influence of Scheler (and Nietzsche, through Scheler) runs deep here. To situate the person within the domain of values, in addition to limiting the reach of empathy within the fundamental manifestation of the other in love and positing the self as value-creating, are very Schelerian moves. Also important here is the fact that, though consciousness plays a role, what is revealed in consciousness is fundamental, namely, the persons of the I and other, which are not reducible to sense-bestowing consciousness in any way. With her discussion of the person, we reach Stein's highest conception of the human being from the standpoints of the I and other. At this point, we must ask: Are Stein's claims tenable? More precisely, why is it that love alone can reveal the person of the other? It would seem that hate, too, or jealousy, might reveal the same structure. The alterity of the other can be manifested in my inability to relate to him or her, and, furthermore, I might hate the other simply for being the person they are. I might even hate the other person to such an extent that I can attribute no value to his existence and alterity.

My second objection to Stein's argument is that it creates two unrelated poles. The self is self-creating through values, its own and those it attributes to others, both good and bad. The other is revealed as a person through my love for him. The person that is revealed, however, is not dependent upon my love, even though my love is what makes him manifest as a person. How, then, do I and the other actually relate? Even if both are co-given in consciousness, the descriptions Stein gives of them seem to isolate the personhood of the person and that of the I. They are in no way shared, unless, of course, we claim that all "I"s are value-creating and aware of their capacity to create value, and all others are recognized as such. Without trading places with the other in empathy, or bringing the other into relief, or projecting oneself into the other's consciousness, one wonders how both I and other relate at a fundamental level.

Finally, Stein's claim that the other is revealed in love as a person, and that the other's personhood is somehow independent of my love for him, seems odd. It seems that the personhood of others is dependent on my love for them, and my loving them for who they are. Noble as this may be, it is highly improbable, even rare. Can there be other ways, outside of love—especially a love that is solely dependent on my feeling of it—by which the other person is revealed to me?

If I read Stein correctly, we have to take her account of empathy in both an objective sense and as a self-understanding. Empathy can also yield an understanding of other minds as well as of other disciplines, such as the cultural sciences. Objectively speaking, we also uncover, through empathy, outer perception, and inner reflection, a layered account of the human being: a body-psyche-spirit unity. Furthermore, if empathy is to work, a deep sense of self and self-understanding is required. By projecting ourselves into the minds of others, empathy helps us to modify our own self-understanding. Stein's notion of the person as unfolding in value—the highest manifestation of that which is properly personal—must not be read in Platonic terms. Though she highlights structures that are constitutive of the person, they need not be fully present all the time. For example, Stein argues that there are incomplete persons.

> On the other hand, a stronger organism continues to support life when its meaning is already fulfilled and the person has completely developed himself. The incompleteness is here similar to the fragmentary character of a work of art of which a part is finished and only the raw material for the rest is preserved. A defective unfolding is also possible in a sound organism. He who never meets a person worthy of love or hate can never experience the depths in which love and hate are rooted. To him who has never seen a work of art nor gone beyond the walls of the city may perhaps forever be closed the enjoyment of nature and art together with his susceptibility for this enjoyment. Such an "incomplete" person is similar to an unfinished sketch. Finally, it is also conceivable for the personality not to unfold at all. He who does not feel values himself, but acquires all feelings only through contagion from others, cannot experience "himself." He can become, not a personality, but at most a phantom personality. Only in the last case can we say that there is no spiritual person present. In all other cases, we must not put the person's non-unfolding on a par with his non-existence. Rather, the spiritual person also exists even if he is not unfolded. (*E* 111–12)

Individuals who do not experience, or are incapable of experiencing, certain things are, for Stein, lacking the fullness of sense that exists within the broad range of possibilities. To speak of a person as an incomplete spiritual person because they lack or are incapable of certain experiences is highly problematic and can be read as a case of chauvinism. If there are individuals who are, as she claims, incomplete spiritual persons, then their values or capacity to value are not fully developed. This notion of fullness is worrisome, perhaps even repugnant, because it suggests that some cultures and individuals are spiritually fuller than others: some are more fully persons than others because they possess a full spirituality. Moreover, there seems to be some ideal standard against which one can measure development and fullness. If values are essentially hierarchical, as Stein claims, then it would seem that the values that connote personhood are also hierarchical. Here, we encounter a remarkable blind spot in Stein's philosophy. This early philosophy is markedly different from her later philosophy, which extended personhood to all human beings by virtue of their being stamped in creation by a tri-personal God. In her first work, although all persons are spiritual, if they live only at an unreflective level of sentient contagion, much like Nietzsche's herd, the spiritual dimension, if it fails to unfold, remains undeveloped. The question then becomes, What would a full spiritual person look like?

By way of concluding this chapter, I would like to point out, again, that empathy, for Stein, has an important end: it presupposes and aims at self-knowledge. This self-knowledge serves as the basis for the cultural sciences. The other is co-given in experience and comes to be recognized as a full person, understood in and through the experience of "the value of the person." But the presentification of the other that I obtain in empathy allows me to understand and develop myself. It allows me to see myself as a certain type, with a certain personality, and to become aware of my own volitional, valuing acts.

> We also see the significance of knowledge of foreign personality for "knowledge of self" in what has been said. We not only learn to make ourselves into objects, as seen earlier, but through empathy with "related natures," i.e., persons of our type, what is "sleeping" in us is developed. By empathy with differently composed personal structures, we become clear about what we are not, in what respects we are more or less than others. Thus, together with self-knowledge, we also have

> an important aid to self-evaluation. Since the experience of value is basic to our own value, at the same time as new values are acquired by empathy, our own familiar values become visible. When we empathically encounter ranges of value closed to us, we become conscious of our own deficiency or disvalue. Every comprehension of different persons can become the basis of an understanding of value. Since, in the act of preference or disregard, values that remain unnoticed in themselves often come to givenness, we learn to assess ourselves correctly now and then. We learn to see that we experience ourselves as having more or less value in comparison with others. (*E* 116)

Empathy, however, is a limited mental act. It is not the only way by which we get to know other minds. In fact, it works to help us understand very specific phenomena, including sensation, feelings, moods, spatialization, meaning, and certain values and personalities. The person of the other is revealed in love as the "valued person" and the I is manifested as value-creating. Stein admits that empathy needs to work with other mental acts, including acts of outer perception and self-reflection, in order to arrive at the proposed structure she calls "person." Recall that empathy is led by outer perception. The knowledge that is obtained through empathy always stands in relation to the self, and in this way, Stein remains faithful to one of philosophy's most ancient tasks: *gnothi seauton*. We know ourselves, more or less, by measuring ourselves with and against the other. This is how one comes to some kind of clarity about who one is, what type one may be, what personality traits one may have and share, etc. Empathy, then, is not only about acquiring self-knowledge; it is also a constant measuring—a comparing and contrasting—of the self with others in order to have some kind of picture of the self, always in relation to others. The self, for Stein, only comes to be as measured with and against other selves, as well as by participating in the essence "human person." Empathy also serves as a limit: the contrast achieved through bringing the other into relief and trading places with the other makes clearer the limits of what we are and are not. For example, Stein never claims that any kind of fusion of individuals is possible; absolute identification is impossible. Furthermore, empathy as analogizing shows us how we are both similar to and different from others. This difference can serve as a limit, indicating what we are not and even what human persons are not. If empathy allows us to understand what we are—and we are human persons—it is not necessarily the case that larger social and political communities are reducible to empathy—empathy alone cannot account for how we experience superindividual bonds between persons. In order to understand such bonds, we need to invoke other structures and ontic realities, including states and communities. This will be the focus of the next chapter.

Chapter 3

The Move from Individuals to Superindividual Social Realities

The broader sense of Steinian subjectivity and intersubjectivity are not reducible to empathy. In fact, as an act of consciousness, empathy is largely I-centered; it is heavily dependent upon what Stein calls internal and external experience, which allows the I to acquire a denser sense of itself—necessary before it can even begin to compare itself with another I, or alter ego. Though the I and the alter ego are co-given, their respective senses can only be deepened through I-consciousness, be it of oneself or another. Empathy gives us a low-level intersubjectivity that grants us awareness of ourselves and others, and leads to the conclusion that we all share in something larger and more complex than the I, namely, the essence or idea of the human person. If scholars persist in reading Steinian intersubjectivity within the empathic framework, the result can only be a very stunted notion of intersubjectivity. If we turn, however, to Stein's *Beiträge*,[1] we will acquire a larger sense of Steinian sociality.

In this chapter I will argue that a fuller sense of intersubjectivity, according to Stein, requires us to move beyond empathy to another kind of consciousness: we-consciousness, or what Stein calls "superindividual consciousness." Stein identifies three kinds of social relationships that bespeak three kinds of social bonds that typify most of our human social relations. Phenomenologically speaking, these bonds are essentially constituted by a certain form of consciousness.

Whether in relation to family, friends, coworkers, or anonymous people on the street, all social relationships can be described by one or more of the phenomenological modes of consciousness identified by Stein. But Stein is aware that consciousness alone cannot account for the broader sense of sociality or intersubjectivity she advocates. She also notes that there are material, geographical, cultural, historical, and economic requirements. But she does not devote much time to these requirements, believing that they can be better discussed by sociology and political science as well as the other humanistic and social sciences. There is, however, another unique Steinian contribution for which I would like to argue, especially as it relates to her phenomenological descriptions of superindividual acts of consciousness. Like the I that requires a full sense of itself, acquired through inner and outer experience, in order to engage in fruitful acts of empathy, Steinian social consciousness requires a complex psychological apparatus that makes possible the phenomenological experiences she describes. Unlike Husserl, who emphasized the transcendental conditions of intersubjectivity in his published works, Stein posits a psychological foundation, a foundation deeply rooted in an understanding of the lived body and psychic causality. Just as the lived body and psychic causality are important for Stein's account of empathy, they are likewise important for Stein's understanding of a phenomenology of intersubjectivity.

The Phenomenological Experience of the Social World

Empathy certainly gives us knowledge of other minds, but this knowledge and understanding of others gained through one's own analogizing, though it involves the body-psyche unity and parts of the spiritual aspects of subjectivity, constitutes one basic form of intersubjectivity. One of the critiques of this comparative or analogizing view of empathy, which one finds in simulation theorists, is that it requires robust self-knowledge. We saw this critique in Scheler's views as well. Stein resolves this problem, I think, by positing a more general essence that derives from her analyses of empathy, namely, the essence of the human being understood as person, a universal essence that we all share in: we are all corporeal-psycho-spiritual unities also capable of higher social and intersubjective interactions. Higher levels of sociality, according to Stein, have their own proper meaning, form, or lived experience, which allows us to recognize them as uniquely intersubjective and as experienceable at various grades of intensity. These forms include the mass, society, and community. Stein takes these categories straight out of the sociology of her day, especially that of Tönnies and Simmel, but to these accounts she adds the perspective of phenomenological consciousness.[2]

Stein develops these higher forms of subjectivity in the major phenomenological work that followed her treatment of empathy, *Beiträge zur philosophischen Begründung der Psychologie und der Gesiteswissenschaften* (*Philosophy of Psychology and the Humanities*). This work is divided into two major parts: "Psychic Causality" (*Psychische Kausalität*) and "Individual and Community" (*Individuum und Gemeinschaft*). The earlier work on empathy and this work can certainly be read together, for we can see a movement outward from an ego-centered to a more superindividual account from the first to the second. The *Beiträge* engages the work of then-contemporary experimental psychology and various social sciences in order to develop its own unique thesis. One question that needs to be asked is, How do these two works stand together?

There is no extended discussion of empathy in the first part of the *Beiträge*. Rather, Stein presents a straight phenomenology of the structure of psyche. But we can read backward insofar as the first part of the text discusses how one constitutive moment of the flow of consciousness flows into the next by virtue of the processes of causality, association, and motivation. Again, it is largely motivation that is connected to the spiritual life and that helps to unfold meaning-structures and meaning-contexts, which form the complex layers of the flow of consciousness—what Stein calls a *Komplexbildung*. As we saw in our discussion of empathy, motivation helps us to understand the unity of sets of meaning acquired through the flow of consciousness. We not only understand how motivation works and how it works analogously in others, but we also understand that what is being seized by the other is a unified meaning of a given flow of consciousness.

The extension of Stein's treatment of intersubjectivity occurs in the second part of the *Beiträge*, "Individual and Community." The text opens with an acknowledgment that many of her ideas can also be found in the work of Theodor Litt,[3] which she read only after completing her own text (*PP* 129). Furthermore, she readily admits that she was deeply influenced by Husserl's unpublished manuscripts, which she edited and organized to form various of his works, including *Ideas II, Ideas III,* and *On the Phenomenology of the Consciousness of Internal Time*,[4] as well as by the works of Scheler, Tönnies, and Simmel. Before I present Stein's account of the higher forms of intersubjectivity, I would like to sketch out the logical form of her argument so that we may follow her claims. There are three significant stages of development in her analysis: (1) the presentation of what she feels is the essence of various forms of higher social, or intersubjective, relations—what she calls *Zusammenlebens* (various forms of togetherness); (2) a description of how it is that these phenomena, from the standpoint of consciousness, are possible; and (3) an ontic description of how these social relations are lived and experienced in the world. Points two and three, respectively, present the subjective and objective sides of the higher forms of intersubjectivity.

The Essence of the Lived Experience of Intersubjective Life

Following Simmel, Tönnies, and Scheler, Stein identifies three specific forms of social or intersubjective life: the mass, society, and community. From a phenomenological perspective, what makes these experiences distinct is that each of them is interiorly experienced or lived in diverse ways in consciousness. Precisely what, then, is experienced that helps us to distinguish one form of sociality from another? Stein claims that it is the unity of the bond that exists between members of a given social relation that essentially distinguishes one form of sociality from another. She hierarchizes the forms of sociality, from lowest to highest, though it should be remarked that all three forms of sociality can coexist. Community, however, can exist without society, though society ultimately cannot exist without community. In the lived experience of the mass, members of this relation exist and live next to one another. Generally, no reflective ego life is present here; one does not recognize the other either as a subject, as in the case of community, or as an object, as in the case of a societal bond (*PP* 240). One simply acts according to what others do and say. Stein describes the unity of the bond between members of a mass as "psychic contagion."

The psychic contagion (an unfortunate word choice) that typifies the lived experience of the mass is generally understood to be structured by a general typology of involuntary or instinctual imitation (*PP* 180). Members of the mass, according to Stein, imitate one another in three general ways: (1) by participating in foreign movements that do not have any form of expressive value; (2) by participating in expressive foreign forms; and (3) by imitating the expressive forms in which foreign psychic states announce themselves (*PP* 182). The first form, Stein says, can be seen in the example of a flock of sheep that simply follows the shepherd. One sheep follows the movement of another and, analogously, in the case of humans, one merely follows the movements of another. For example, when walking among a crowd, one follows the movement of the crowd without reflecting on where and why the crowd is moving; one simply imitates the movements of the crowd. The second form of imitative psychic contagion occurs when some form of expression is imitated by others. Stein gives the classic example of infants crying or laughing (*PP* 185). A crying baby may cause other babies nearby to cry, even though there may be no physical cause for the others' crying; babies imitate the expressive cries of the other. In the third case delineated above, not only does one have expression, but a low-level recognition of the source of the general state of affairs as well. Here Stein gives the example of a depressed person (*PP* 187–88). In the company of a depressed person, I may begin to feel depressed. Although my depression is not willed, I take on the depression of the other; I can even become aware of this, though I may not. Stein considers this, too, a form of imitation.

Following Scheler (*PP* 241), Stein asserts that the mass cannot carry out any act of consciousness that could deliver a unified sense of understanding. The members of a mass share space and comport themselves in a uniform way, but there is no "true, interior unity" that binds them (*PP* 241–42). In a mass, members are excitable and subject to suggestion (*PP* 252), but this does not mean that they are always aware of what they are experiencing, for there is no ground upon which such recognition could be based. Stein describes the movement of the mass psyche largely in terms of causality, according to which one member is psychically affected by another without recognizing why or how. One simply moves along with the others. Stein remarks that, though this behavior is prevalent in human nature, it is not always or necessarily bad. Like a community, masses of people can be moved by ideas, but they lack a communal interiority. Stein observes that "it is possible that within a social union with more of an associational character than a communal character, mistrust was the *motive* for the transition into the associational orientation, that one closed oneself off from the personal environment out of mistrust, instead of making oneself available to its influences.... Here the association appears as a deficient mode of community, which in principle it doesn't need to be" (*PP* 261). Communal conduct in a mass that is oriented toward some ideal or value can exist, but such communal conduct does not imply a lived experience of community. Stein's language here is very powerful, because community is characterized as "interior." Recall that the self, as Stein described it in her treatment of empathy, was a project of interiority. The discussion of interiority continues here. Community is lived within one's interiority. More about this communal interiority will be said later, when we treat community proper.

Society is another form of sociality Stein describes. As mentioned earlier, society is conceived in objective terms. Unlike the mass, whose unifying relationship between its members is located in the psyche and largely animated by a natural form of causality, society, according to Stein, who follows Scheler here, is both spiritual and personal (*PP* 259). These concepts automatically set society within subjective and reflective terms, and are always infused with acts of will, motivation, and willing. Largely conceived in objective terms, however, society, though consisting of persons who are aware or conscious of their nature as persons through reflection, is unified by the consciousness of its members' common goal, which is external to their very being as persons. As an example, Stein offers the program or agenda of a political party, which guides its life and work. Societies are founded—they require a founding act; they do not naturally grow out of human relationships (*PP* 259–60). The members of a society, however, are not limited to its founding members. More members can join a society, usually according to the rules and conventions of the society in question (*PP* 260). Stein says that one can speak of a society as developing and having a life, but only in a very restricted sense. A society has life insofar as it is organized around its conscious end and moves toward the achievement of that end. Its development is also marked by mechanisms and stages of growth, which are also conditioned by this external goal. For example, if a banking society forms to earn money for its shareholders, the society has a life and organization that revolve around and aim at fulfilling this end (*PP* 260–61).

The life of individuals who belong to a given society is determined by that society; they take on certain roles and functions in light of the society's end. The society also admits certain types of individuals; for example, a society has workers, guardians, executives, etc. There is an infinite variety of types that belong to various societies (*PP* 258–61). Though societies are determined by their ends, and though functional types populate any given society, its members are not purely functionaries. A personal foundation is required to enable the society. In other words, societies require spiritual persons as their basis (*PP* 256). But the fullness, or full expression, of the individual members' personalities is subject to the ends of any given society. A society can have a multiplicity of types of employees, or even persons, specific to itself (*PP* 256–57). For example, a marketing firm requires outgoing, creative individuals to promote the work of the agency. As members of the society work together to achieve their end, their typological traits as well as their personal traits help to form the specific character of a particular society (*PP* 256). This character bespeaks certain attitudes toward various states of affairs, as well as some "inner life" (*PP* 256). Stein is quick to point out that societies have an interior life that is delineable, especially if one considers not only societal typologies but also the personalities of those who belong to a society. Societies acquire a certain character (i.e., noble, vulgar, etc.) according to their ends. This character affects the life of a society's members (*PP* 257), who treat one another mostly as objects aiming at the same end. They have functions to carry out and jobs to be done. The way in which they function depends on the character of the society.

Stein notes that societies may be formed in two general ways (*PP* 257–58). First, membership may be explicit and direct—one asks or is asked to become a member of a society. One may even sign a contract. Second, societies can come about simply by assigning certain functions to people; if those tasks are carried out, a collectivity with an implicit understanding of a given aim is formed. What is striking about Stein's analysis is the force of the objective aim of a given society. Though she gives some scope to character and personality, she does not admit the possibility that a strong or charismatic personality can gather around himself or herself people that will work toward a certain aim. But it is possible for the personality of a manager to completely alter the work environment, and even the aims, of a society. However, this case of a unique personality inspiring and shaping a society is not discussed in Stein's work. Although she admits that there is room for spontaneity in societies (*PP* 258–59), she reserves discussion of the strength of personality and the uniqueness of the person for her description of community.

Although Stein draws heavily from Scheler in her account of society, she distinguishes herself from him on two counts, namely, on the questions of the temporality of the society and the role of distrust. Scheler argues that a lived experience of time accompanies any experience or relation of society. Societies, according to Stein's reading of Scheler, experience no duration beyond their own specific time (*PP* 259). This is because, presumably, all members of a society work together at a given moment to carry out a task that is meant to be accomplished in the present or near present. This means that the goal of a society is always directed to the present moment and cannot exist outside the particular present moment. A society can thus leave behind no legacy and, hence, unlike other historical structures, has no epochal or historical significance. Stein argues, however, that societies are nevertheless temporal objects in the broad sense and that they thus have a history. Therefore, they can leave behind some kind of temporal legacy. It may not be as lofty as other legacies, but one simply cannot deny the historical significance of given societies, especially for their own, as well as future, epochs (*PP* 260). A society's members are completely replaceable, which contributes to the now-time of the society. A society need not die when a leader or employee dies; these can simply be replaced. In fact, this constitutes one of the key differences between society and community; whereas a society's members are replaceable, a community's are not. A community's members are highly unique and personalized individuals, and their loss is irremediable because they are defined not by their function or objective end, but as free persons with a unique personality and history.

Stein is also critical of Scheler's notions of distrust and competition, and perhaps even of the *ressentiment* that animates his social phenomenology (*PP* 259). Stein does not view societal relations as necessarily based on distrust. While there may be societies that live and function in a distrustful way, Stein points out that numerous societies do not (*PP* 259). Stein argues that if societies were always based on distrust, there would be no examples of truly excellent societies, yet the historical development of nineteenth century Europe presents many such examples. It was precisely the strong sense of Prussian liberalism set amid the Austro-Hungarian Empire and Germany that helped to create the vibrant Germany of the late nineteenth century—a theme developed in Stein's political work on the state. Furthermore, a unified German state created various societies charged with improving the welfare of citizens, including societies that would look after pensions and health care needs. There is no direct mention of empathy in Stein's analysis of the mass and society. Nevertheless, one can assume that empathy comes into play as societies are constituted by individuals, who still need to understand what others are thinking in order to carry out their specific purpose. The same is largely true for her treatment of community as well. Perhaps this can be read as verification of my original thesis about empathy as primarily geared toward self-understanding rather than an exclusive intersubjective understanding, which, in the case of community, requires not empathy but a certain kind of lived experience of solidarity, for the mass a certain unconscious imitation, and for society a kind of objective awareness of a particular end.

We come now to the highest form of Steinian intersubjectivity, namely, community. Whereas society is a relation between subjects and objects, community is generally conceived to be a relation of "subject to subject" in which the other is regarded and treated as a subject (*PP* 130). But here the subjects do not stand in relation to one another in a vis-à-vis relation; rather, one consciously "lives" (*PP* 130) with the other and is determined by the other's vital movements. Together, these subjects form a community, but Stein is clear that community never implies a fusion. She insists that in a society individuals are isolated; quoting Husserl's reworking of Leibniz, she maintains that the individuals in a society are monads with no windows. In community, however, solidarity is the essential nature of the relation between subjects. This lived experience of solidarity is conscious and is lived through consciousness.

There is a long tradition of social theorists, including Durkheim and Weber, that pinpoints solidarity as key to understanding the nature of social relations. Durkheim, for example, distinguishes two types of solidarity: one derived from the division of labor and the other stemming from one's own personal sphere of action.[5] All of the various notions of solidarity, of course, are situated within and deeply influenced by the larger context of law. Stein, in both her texts on community and her work on the state, defines solidarity very minimally: she views it as a kind of intentional state of mind whereby one lives in and with the other, a living experienced intensely in consciousness. Evidently, her understanding of solidarity is phenomenological, as she sets it within the framework of awareness and consciousness.

Stein uses the word *Gemeinschaftserlebnis,* or lived experience of community, to describe the specific, conscious lived experience that typifies the essence of community. She starts her analysis of community by emphasizing that it is always lived through the pure I. It is the pure I that experiences solidarity with others. She declares that it is wondrous how the individual pure I can enter into a community of life with other subjects (*PP* 133). The individual, according to Stein, can experience life within what she calls a "superindividual subject" (*PP* 133). Using the famous example of the troop (*PP* 134), she describes what she means by the convergence of the individual and the superindividual within the lived experience of community. Recall that this text was written after the experience of World War I, which Stein saw first-hand as a nurse at the front and as a result of which she lost many friends and colleagues. So she asks the reader to imagine a troop whose much-loved leader perishes. She observes that an individual certainly feels the sadness of the loss. This is one's own personal grief. But she goes on to say that individuals can also feel the collective grief of the community. One feels a communal sadness, and insofar as one does this, he or she lives with the others an experience of solidarity that consists of the communal sadness of the group.

> Certainly I, the individual ego, am filled up with grief. But I feel myself to be not alone with it. Rather, I feel it as *our* grief. The experience is essentially colored by the fact that others are taking part in it, or even more, by the fact that I take part in it only as a member of a community. *We* are affected by the loss, and *we* grieve over it. And this "we" embraces not only all those who feel the grief as I do, but all those who are included in the unity of the group: even the ones who perhaps do not know of the event, and even the members of the group who lived earlier or will live later. We, the we who feel the grief, do it in the name of the total group and of all who belong to it. We feel this subject affected within ourselves when we have an experience of community. I grieve as a member of the unit, and the unit grieves within me. (*PP* 134)

I am simultaneously conscious of my own grief and that of the group of my fellow troop members. In this way, Stein says, the I has an individual as well as a superindividual experience. Notice that the I is never absorbed into the superindividual experience, but experiences both simultaneously. Stein also differs from her colleagues, such as Gerda Walther, who argues for a total fusion of subjects, a feeling of oneness.[6] Scheler's example is of parents grieving their dead child. He argues that the grief experienced here is not only lived individually, but felt collectively—both parents feel each other's sadness; insofar as they experience the same sadness together, they share a communal sadness—there is an *Auseinanderfühlen*.[7] Scheler emphasizes the feelings of love and hate, as well as certain values. Values play a role in Stein's account, too, but she will take the Husserlian route and stress the conscious lived experience of solidarity as primary.

Absent from Stein's description of the lived experience of community is a sustained discussion of empathy. Why is this significant? And what prohibits this lived experience of community from being understood simply as a case of shared feeling instilled in us by means of "psychic contagion?" First, the absence of empathy at the level of the higher forms of intersubjectivity, including society and community, is significant because it reveals Stein's awareness of the limited function of empathy, which is useful for self-understanding and for helping us to understand analogously what others may be thinking, but, in the end, cannot fully account for other forms of social consciousness. Community has its own proper essence, which is superindividual solidarity. This being said, we still require empathy in order to have communal experiences, as it is an important act that grants us access to other minds. Concerning the second, important question, Stein makes clear that the solidarity one experiences in community is not simply a feeling, although it requires sensibility in order to manifest. More will be said about this later. One must understand the "sense" of an experience as lived communally. The lived experience of community can be shared reflectively as properly superindividual, as well as individual (*PP* 135). Insofar as individuals make sense or meaning as well as understand it, we are here dealing with a rationality that is communicable and shared. In empathy or even co-empathy (*PP* 136), the individual subject is able to experience what it would be like for the other to suffer grief, even to understand what it is for the other to suffer the loss of, say, a beloved troop leader, but this remains an individual experience. The collective experience of community is its own unique experience. Stein notes: "Not every sense need be available to a plurality of subjects. If I lose a friend, this loss affects me like no other human being. And accordingly, the sense-content of the grief that's appropriate to this loss belongs to my experience and only to mine. The sense is available for appreciative empathizing and sympathizing.... However, in comparison with the originally experienced sense-content, the empathized grief as such, even though the sense is fully received into it, still exhibits a modification of sense that permits you to designate the sense itself, disregarding its existential coloring as a private experience" (*PP* 136).

Stein remarks that as a lived experience of community is lived (*erlebt*), it can acquire greater color and depth and even grow in significance, especially if it endures; it grows in the continuity of its living (*PP* 136–37). There can be many variations within the living of the lived experience of community, but these always take place within the unity of its "fulfilled" sense (*PP* 137) and its meaning-context.

> But only in the experience of the one who feels the "appropriate" grief is the intention which runs throughout the collective experience of community fulfilled and satisfied. It must be stressed that besides the purely objective intention, an intention toward the communal experience is inherent within the experiences that are directed toward a superindividual object—inasmuch as that object stands before us as superindividual—and that our experience is constitutive for that object. We feel the grief as something belonging to the unit, and through this grief we are calling for the grief of the unit to be realized. (*PP* 137)

And if there is no continuity or duration of sense within the unified experience of solidarity, then the lived experience can fade away. Likewise, if the troop members do not feel a communal sadness at the loss of their leader, then there is no communal lived experience.

Furthermore, it should be remarked that though the lived experience of community is typified by one living in the experience of the other in solidarity, the sense of solidarity can arise and grow with a myriad of experiences that may have many forms and many intentional objects (*PP* 138). Stein uses the example of the troop's sadness, but many other experiences, including love, joy, boredom, etc., can serve as a communal sense around which one can live the experience of community. Finally, the lived experience of community can be felt with varying intensities. In a lived experience of community, all members experiencing solidarity in relation to a specific intentional object are not required to experience it identically, with the same level of intensity. Stein notes that the lived experience of community is filtered and lived through individual personalities; it can be felt passionately, superficially, persistently, or even fleetingly. What is seized is the sense of solidarity that typifies the lived experience of community and, therefore, one lives within the other in an experience of community.

Stein concludes her analysis of the lived experience of community by reaffirming that superindividual experience occurs within the consciousness of individuals. There is no superconsciousness or flow of lived consciousness outside individuals. One lives the experience of the other in solidarity with the other, but one never loses one's individuality; there is no communal pure I. There are only individual pure I's that direct consciousness toward the superindividual experience of community.

Stein goes on to ponder the question of temporality and communal lived experience. Admittedly, she describes only present experiences, which allow some kind of living here and now. But might there be communal experiences of the past, historical communal experiences? And can there be future lived experiences of community? With regard to the latter question, Stein says nothing, and it would be hard to say what future lived experiences of community might look like. The closest approximation of such an experience might be the unification of people around utopian writings toward whose ideals they work, but in such a case, the lived experience of the community would nevertheless occur in the present, even though the living is directed toward the future. More precisely, the lived experience of a community based on a future utopia, though futurity is built into its sense, can only be lived by its subjects in the now of the present, despite the fact that their experience of lived solidarity is focused on achieving said utopia.

In response to the question of past communal experiences, Stein explicitly considers the possibility through a reflection on Simmel and historical lived experiences of community (*PP* 141). Historically, we can identify lived experiences of peoples that can fairly be described as communal. Stein cites the example of oppressed groups and peoples. Through empathy, we can understand the nature of their suffering, and by observing historical evidence, we can identify the experience as communal. But can we now experience as a community the lived experience of a community of the past? Stein thinks not. She remarks: "The specifics of the historical are not concerned with the relationship of individual and community; the exposition of this relationship is presupposed, and Simmel's constructions imply something about it" (*PP* 142). Here, one might assume that empathic understanding would be more effective as one could presentify a comprehension of what others experienced, even across time. But the uniqueness of community is that it is a living-now experience. It is firmly marked by a present here and now; it may endure and grow in sense as it is experienced, but it cannot extend into the future or into the past. Gerda Walther, however, argued that habit and the structure of habit, as well as memory, can help us to experience a past communal experience as our own communal lived experience. I take this up elsewhere,[8] but one should be aware that, in Stein's account, the question of the temporality of communal lived experience remains a significant problem.

Stein's account of the lived experience of community raises questions not only about temporality and the structure of inner time-consciousness of community, but about intentionality and objectivity as well. First, one wonders whether Stein, in restricting the analysis of community to a structure of solidarity in which one lives with and seizes the experience of the other, defines community too narrowly.

Given the complexity of human social relations, lived experiences of community need not be experienced only as solidarity. Moreover, one might have experiences that entail solidarity without community—for example, the solidarity of anonymous strangers who engage in an intimate sexual encounter. They may feel exactly as Stein describes, but they could rightfully say that there was no experience of community. Second, given the variety of experiences that emerge within lived experiences of community, one wonders where, precisely, solidarity falls within the structures of subjectivity and intentionality. If what we experience in the lived experience of community is solidarity, does solidarity always become the intentional object? Can it also be understood as the objective correlate of communally experienced consciousness? Stein never delimits the actual phenomenological structure, especially *qua* intentionality, noesis and noema, of the lived experience of community. Her insistence on sense places her squarely within the phenomenology of Husserl's *Logical Investigations* rather than the transcendental logic of the *Ideas*. I must confess that I believe something like a communal lived experience, as Stein describes it, exists. I can certainly comprehend it in an objectivated sense, understood phenomenologically. Stein describes the experience very well and very convincingly. But when it comes to the details of the structure of consciousness that permits this communal experience, outside the problem of sense, her description raises these sorts of questions. Notwithstanding such questions, however, Stein realizes that she had to provide an account of what in the structure of consciousness allows us to experience what she calls a lived experience of community. To this end, she argues that it is the human being, understood as a body-psyche-spirit unity, and the inherent structures of consciousness that allow us to have such experiences, as discovered in the previous chapter. Lest we limit Stein's understanding of community to consciousness, again, it must be noted that community is more than a state of mind: it has material, historical, economic, ethical, cultural, and religious components to it as well. We will discuss these when we address Stein's ontology of community.

Insofar as Stein argues for the possibility of social objectivities like society and community, and insofar as she maintains the viability of an experience of collective consciousness or group mindedness, that is, her notion of a *Gemeinschaftserlebnis*, we have to go back to the question of collective personhood, which arises from her analysis of the essence of human beings as persons. Is there such a thing, for Stein, as group personhood? Is there a collective person that is distinct from individual persons? Stein's answer is negative, but in her analysis of the state, she claims that the state does possess a life of its own and we can understand it as if it is a person, but not in any objective way. Higher social objectivities are analogous to persons as we speak as if they have personal traits, but they are not objectively persons. The bearers of all collective experiences are individual persons, and Stein's strong sense of individuation, especially in her analysis of the body and its spatio-temporal configurations as well as the personality core, negate the possibility of collective personhood.

Finally, I would like to address the question of gender and community. Though Stein never discusses this question in her early phenomenology, one does find the themes of empathy, the nature of the state, and community reappearing in her later writings on woman from the late 1920s and 1930s.[9] These texts are largely set within the discussion of Catholic education, and discuss matters both theological and practical. I do not wish to discuss ideas of faith and education, but I do wish to highlight that Stein believes women, precisely because of their sex, exhibit a maternal essence. This, of course, does not mean that all women are by nature called to be mothers. The maternal aspect of women is important for the education of all children and, in particular, for young women. The argument is rooted in role modeling: older women serve as concrete guides and models for younger women, and this role modeling affects not only how women live and experience their bodies but also their psyches and spirits. In many ways, Stein is an essentialist: she maintains that women have a nature and a vocation, albeit she also believes there are many types of women and, thus, her essentialism is not to be read as rigidly determinative.

This being said, we also find in these texts a very strong advocate for women's education: women should be educated in all things just as men are, although Stein also calls for women to be educated separately from men in order to develop their unique female strengths outside the judgment of men; women should be able to participate in professions traditionally reserved for men; she believes women's education should be comprehensive and must address the needs of body, psyche, and spirit.

When it comes to the question of empathy, Stein maintains that women are generally more capable of it. I have explored how this might translate into empathy being a particular form of female consciousness in my other book on Stein's philosophy, as mentioned in the previous chapter.[10] But when it comes to the question of community and the state, Stein clearly sees particular communities—namely, family, the Roman Catholic Church, and the state—as being responsible for the complete education of women. Each of them plays specific roles. She states that each of the members of these communities does so in solidarity with one another: mothers and fathers are responsible for the physical well-being of their individual children but they are role models of how to behave in society and the state as well as in the home. Children have the right to be educated and parents have the responsibility and obligation to ensure that they are educated; the state has the obligation to educate both men and women, and it can decide what this education will consists of, as this is its sovereign right—this notion of sovereignty of the state to organize and determine itself will be discussed in the next chapter; the Church is responsible for the spiritual well-being of the young and it dispenses sacraments and theological education as its right. In the end, when we read Stein's later interventions on women, the community, and the state, especially as they relate to her early phenomenology, we must take note that she is faithful to her own analyses of how the forms of sociality she describes function: they are particular meaningful relationships between persons, who are aware of both solidarity and state sovereignty.[11]

STEIN AND CONTEMPORARY SOCIAL ONTOLOGY

Over the last 20 years or so, analytic philosophy has poignantly turned to questions of collective mind and social realities. Eminent thinkers like John Searle and Raimo Tuomela, along with philosophers like Margaret Gilbert, Philip Pettit, Michael Bratman, have made significant contributions on this score.[12] The accounts offered by such thinkers are notable because they add layers not present in Stein's account, aspects to which she would not have access, given her time and the state of science of her day. In particular, recent discoveries in neurology and cognitive science as well as evolutionary and social biology all amplify our understanding of social reality. Though Stein cannot add to these more recent scientific approaches, she does bring psychology to the table or, more precisely, phenomenological psychology, which most current philosophers do not do. Also, she brings the force of history and the study of the cultural sciences, as we shall see, to bear on the nature of sociality, which present-day philosophers largely ignore.

This being said, there are two aspects of contemporary social ontology that I would like to address here, especially as they have a direct relation to Stein's own philosophy, namely, the pragmatic and performative nature of language, as discussed by Searle and John Austin, and the ethico-commitment approach discussed by thinkers like Tuomela and Gilbert. Concerning the former, Stein conceives of language as expressive. Language is not only symbolic, that is, words and sounds do not only point to or represent another reality, for example, a stop sign ordering us to halt before an intersection. Following Husserl, Stein maintains that language can communicate senses (*Sinn*) of things and reality without any necessary mental picture or representative image. Indeed, this is what Husserl's *First Logical Investigation* reveals. While Husserl certainly mentions the practical or pragmatic nature of language, Stein does not take this aspect up in any significant way. Neither does she maintain that language can perform or bring about the reality that it describes simply through its articulation and collective consent to that which it articulates. Searle, however, maintains this possibility and gives the example of a marriage license. Those that sign the license and pronounce the promises of marriage enact or perform the marriage. The marriage does not legally exist except through the promise and signing of the license. Stein was certainly aware of speech acts as promises through the work of her teacher Adolf Reinach, but she sees promises as expressions of sense, understood in the Husserlian sense: a promise expresses a certain expectation. It is the practical or pragmatic force of such speech acts that Searle, through Austin, highlights. Furthermore, Searle argues that many of the key ingredients that are vital for society to flourish are precisely these kinds of performative speech acts, including laws, contracts, economic forecasts, money, etc. Stein's expressive understanding of language grants us understanding, but it misses the practical aspect discussed above.

Raimo Tuomela's monumental works on social ontology and group action represent in an eminent way the view that groups or collectivities are precisely groups because of an epistemic affirmation of members' intentions to belong to a group as well as the holding of certain ethical stances. He maintains,

> Let me accordingly reformulate the above account of a we-mode group (g) in a way making the artifact nature of we-mode groups clearer: A collective g consisting of some persons (or in the normatively structured case position-holders) is a (core) *we-mode social group* if and only if
> (1) g has accepted a certain ethos, E, for itself and is committed to it. On the level of its members this entails that a substantial number of the members of g, including its specially authorized operative members (if any), when functioning as group members have accepted E as g's (viz., their group's, "our") ethos and are collectively committed to it, with the understanding that the ethos is to function as giving authoritative reasons for thinking and acting for the group members.
> (2) Every member of g ought to accept E (and accordingly to be committed to it as a group member) at least in part because the group has accepted E as its ethos.

(3) Necessarily, the members collectively accept (with collective commitment) E as g's ethos if and only if (it is correctly assertable for them that) E is g's ethos.
(4) It is a mutual belief in the group that (1), (2). Clause (1) entails that a we-mode group (in contrast to an I-mode group; see below) is a collective artifact and indeed an institutional entity, as will be argued in Chapter 8. Acceptance as a group member will be analyzed in Chapter 6, and I will not here clarify it. A we-mode group is capable of action in virtue of the collective commitment to the group ethos (this contrasts with an I-mode group).... Let me note that the present account of course assumes that the group members have some mastery of the concepts involved, e.g. they must know what it is for a group to have an ethos and what it is for them to be collectively committed to the ethos.[13]

Tuomela stresses commitment based on a kind of epistemic assent to belong and be a member of a group. A strong emphasis on rationality and epistemic awareness color Tuomela's account. Stein admits that the ethical commitment as well as the epistemic assent that Tuomela describes can factor into the lived experience of the community. We could place many of Tuomela's criteria within Stein's discussion of motivation in the *Beiträge* and in the ethical considerations of her ontology of community, which I will discuss later. The solidarity that Stein says marks the life of the community has its deep roots in her phenomenology of the body and sensation, as well as in the life of psyche and spirit, for she sees human beings as unities of body, psyche, and spirit. Privileged in Tuomela's and other accounts—for example, Gilbert's work—is the rational will, as informed by recent analytical understandings steeped in the Liberal tradition of politics. Stein does not negate the force of rationality and will, but she is also aware that one can belong to a community and experience solidarity but also not be aware of the epistemic and ethical conditions of commitment that Tuomela so carefully lays out. In families and in belonging to a certain people (*Volk*), for example, being a Jew, members need not have to fulfill Tuomela's requirements. Both Stein and Tuomela agree that some kind of consciousness is constitutive of group experience as is commitment, but for Stein the rigorous demands of Tuomela need not be met in order to experience something like a group: one may feel part of a group and never have consciously assented or committed. These may happen at a later point, perhaps in times of crisis.

The Psychic and Logical Foundations of the *Überindividuelle* World

Mass, society, and community—all of these social relations, understood phenomenologically, require certain psychic and logical foundations, despite the apparent fact that the mass seems incapable of an awareness of such logical structures. The mass is understood as lacking awareness or consciousness of others and as being affected by emotions without understanding them; the mass is simply reactive. But the basic capacity for sensation and affectivity are required even for the mass. Furthermore, society and community, though distinct, share basic logical and psychic foundations: society needs them in order to function and to strive toward their desired ends, and community needs them in order to live an intense social bond in solidarity. When it comes to community, one cannot speak of an I-independent communal consciousness. There can be no such thing as an original, absolutely individual-independent stream of lived experiences for either a community or a society. In other words, there is no communal consciousness apart from the ego (*PP* 135). There is, however, an experience that includes more than one's own subjectivity—an experience in which one is present and that lives within one as a "we." It is only in this sense that we may speak of a conscious experiencing of a "stream of lived experiences of the community"; it is lived experience of a communal nature, but it is not experienced in the way the individual I experiences the stream of lived experiences as an original consciousness. In other words, *communal* experience does not exist as communal per se, and is not, therefore, then somehow transmitted to each individual member. Rather, each member "lives" the experience, thereby rendering the experience communal (*PP* 141). An example of this communal lived experience is history, for we can speak of communal histories that account for the common experiences of certain communities of people. History can only be embodied in the individual members of a community; in and of itself, it does not exist outside of the individual (*PP* 141–43).

The first part of the *Beiträge* lays out the psychic and logical conditions for experiences of higher sociality, namely, society and community. Lived experiences of society and community, understood in the densest, richest sense, cannot come to be without these psychic and logical underpinnings. Before discussing these underpinnings, however, I would like to draw the reader's attention to the fact that Stein blurs the distinction between society and community vis-à-vis these substrata. I do not think this is an error on Stein's part; rather, I think she does this in order to show that we all share a basic psychic and logical structure. When we move to a higher awareness of the kind of relation we are in, it is up to us to make the distinction between the goal- or end-oriented relations of society's and community's more intimate relations of solidarity that are marked by an *ineinandergreifen*.

Again, Stein believes that communal lived experiences (*Gemeinschaftserlebnisse*), as well as societal and mass forms of togetherness, are grounded in both psychic reality and logical structures. Here, Stein blends Husserl's early logical work, which she had found so inspiring, with psychology. One of the basic psycho-bodily elements shared by all human beings is *Sinnlichkeit*, the capacity for sensation. We are affected by things that impress upon our senses and our psyche; we perceive these effects. The individual ego experiences sensations as affecting itself very easily. For example, I can feel the heat from a burning candle when I wave my hand over the flame. Does sensation work similarly in communal lived experiences? In other words, can a community have a collective experience of sensation wherein each member of the community experiences a given sensation in an identical fashion? According to Stein, the answer is no (*PP* 144). Although we can share a common understanding of one another's sensation of pain through *Einfühlung*, this understanding does not in itself qualify as a communal lived experience of the sensation of pain. Though we cannot experience sensation identically in community as directly as the ego can experience sensation in its own immediateness, the community can nonetheless have a lived sense-experience of a communal sort.

Sensation, or, more precisely, the capacity for sensation, is a human experience structured in such a way that human beings know its nature. There is a unity of meaning that marks experience in general, which makes it intelligible from person to person (*PP* 146–48). We learned in the earlier discussions of the empathy of which human beings are capable. Stein's discussion of the body made this evident. Sensation, as an experience, then, is something that all human beings are capable of understanding, expressing, and experiencing individually, but also communally to the extent that we share in a common human nature and traditions that allow us to experience things in common. Hence, a communal "we" lived experience of a given sensation is experienced not as an I experiences it, for that would require a group of individual Is to experience the same sensation in the same circumstances, but in its generality, accessible through the commonality of sense-experience that comes to be shared in what Stein calls the flow of the lived experience of community. For example, to turn to Stein's example of the death of a beloved troop leader: the capacity to feel sad and the sadness are experienced at the level of the individual. Individuals can experience at the same time the communal sense of loss. Stein illustrates how individual perception is shared and even, in large part, determined by the life of the community. When a subject begins to order the multiplicity of sensations received, giving to them some kind of sense, when these meaningful sensations are ordered and can thus be typologically or regularly understood, when they are repeatable and have the same sense of others, then we have the beginning of shared sensibility. Stein remarks that,

> where such a regularity and arrangement makes possible an object-constitution, that's where the possibility of commonality begins. The "arrangement" makes the "tumult of sensations," which is utterly irrational in itself and utterly individual in its concretion, a carrier of a sense and a possible base for the apprehension of an object. The arrangement can impinge upon other subjects, and, within the sensory

processes that each one has for himself or herself, can bring about an object's constitution as common to them all. With this is established the possibility of an object's apprehension as a communal experience. Just as within any stream of individual experiences, a unitary comprehension can encompass a plurality of sensory processes, each of which is continuous in itself but separated from the others by processes not governed by the same arrangement and therefore not constitutive of the same object—so the sensory processes of different streams of experience can contribute to the coalescence of a communal experience if they are comprehended in the same sense. (*PP* 147)

In this way, then, we can speak of a *Sinnlichkeit* that pertains not only to individual ego experiences but to the *überindividuelle* reality as well. One is reminded here of Husserl's description of *hylé*, the primordial strata of material sensibility that somehow guarantees a kind of universal intelligibility concerning sensibility of affectivity. We have to ask: What does a communal capacity for sensation mean for collectivities? I believe Stein would argue that an account of how individuals can experience the feelings of a group or that they are capable of doing so is necessary in order to account for super individual realities like the grief and sadness of a community or its collective joy. In these descriptions, it is always the individual who feels what the collective feels. Another example, in this instance, would be the sadness and mourning a nation can feel at the loss of a beloved leader or cultural figure. Undoubtedly, Stein's claim that phenomena of the collective capacity for sensation bespeak deeper, passive structures is certainly taken up by her own colleagues like Gerda Walther[14] and Husserl but also more contemporary thinkers like Michel Henry in his *Essence of Manifestation*.[15]

From previous investigations we learned that an individual consciousness can turn its attention to an object through intentionality. Are there, then, intentional acts within the life of a community? Yes. Intentional acts by the community can only be experienced through the individual, within individual consciousness, that is, through one's own consciousness of the community. At the same time, however, the community lives within the individual and is thus real. A situation wherein everyone in a community experiences the same intentional act to the same degree is ideal and virtually impossible. But the fact that the communal experience of an intentional act is lived through the individuals of the community in no way negates the reality or force of such communal intentional acts. Like the universality of *Sinnlichkeit* in the essence of human being, what makes the lived experience of an intentional act communally experienceable is the very *Allgemeinheit* or capacity for generalization of intentional consciousness: it renders a communal lived experience possible for the individual who finds herself or himself in an *überindividuelle* world—a person can experience the unity of a multiplicity of subjects through the general nature of the content across the individual experiences. To the extent that all human beings have an intentional consciousness, such a reality forms the basis for a communal experience of what consciousness can mean for everyone in the community, even though such an intentional consciousness is lived primordially in one's own egological life. Hence, when I intend an object, I can also have a communal experience of intentionality itself—a "we" intention. Intentional consciousness is not only experienced as one's own; there is also a communal experience of intentional consciousness that is shared with others. Because intentionality defines the essential structure of human consciousness, all individuals are capable of understanding intentionality. The significance of a communal understanding of intentionality is therefore possible.

Here, we find a rich phenomenological claim about intentionality that derives from Husserl's work on the topic. He claims that intentionality is a deep structure of consciousness: it directs our conscious gaze on specific objects, helping to reveal different aspects or *Abschattungen* of the object of consciousness. Intentionality works with higher logical capacities to grasp the sense of the object, and it can do so both in terms of the specific particularity of the object and its universal sense (*Sinn*). It is this very understanding of intentionality collaborating with logic that informs Stein's understanding of collective experience. A community can intend certain objects, always through individuals, in a meaningful way. For example, a religious community can intend and, therefore, focus upon an attempt to better comprehend specific revelations of dogmas, albeit it does that through individual agents.

Thus far, Stein has attributed intentionality and *Sinnlichkeit* to *Gemeinschaftserlebnisse* and, by implication, to lived experiences of society, despite the latter's being more object-oriented and the former's being more intimately constituted by solidarity. She attributes to communal lived experiences two other elements, which are ascertained by an investigation of two particular kinds of acts: *Kategoriale Akte* (categorial acts) and *Gemütsakte* (dispositional acts). The former, which are linked to the pre-given fundamental structures of logical understanding, are clearly drawn from Husserl's understanding of categorial acts as laid out in the *Logical Investigations;* the latter are concerned with the pre-given primordial structures of feelings and human dispositions that are rooted in the psyche. In categorial acts, the ego performs certain think-acts (judgments based on predication, drawing conclusions based on comparisons and contrasts, linking one thing to another, computation, etc.), and in so doing it reveals that there is a certain pre-given capacity for the ego to understand certain logical concepts and/or relations. For example, in mathematics, one may indeed understand that 2 + 2 = 4 by means of proofs, but insofar as human beings are endowed with certain capacities for rational and logical thought, the capacity to understand mathematical structures and concepts in general is not something we create. Our foundational capacity to think mathematically permits us to engage very specific mathematical problems. Stein calls such acts categorial acts. She goes on to give other examples of foundational or categorial ego acts, including acts of predication, judgment, comparison and contrasting, etc. (*PP* 151–52). When I predicate something about an object—"the tree is green," for example—I am making a judgment or saying something about an object. However, my capacity to execute such an ego act is not founded on or derived from anything else. It is an innate capacity, inherent to human minds in general. Given that all human beings are capable of categorial acts, it follows that there can be a communal lived experience of such foundational acts. Again, these acts do not occur outside the individual ego, but because of the universality of their structure (i.e., they belong to human nature and have a common meaning-structure [*Allgemeinheit*]), "we" can experience what it means to make a judgment, to make a predication, to see a similarity or difference on a more communal level. We can also communally intend the same object—for example, a mathematical problem. We understand that 2 + 2 = 4. This is an example of a shared or communal categorial act. We understand what it means to draw conclusions, to make comparisons, etc.; we also, according to Stein, understand what it is for objects to have a general meaning. In the *Logical Investigations*, Husserl aptly remarks that foundational categorial acts are acts of pure understanding,[16] and, to the degree that we cannot found foundational acts, that such acts impose limits on our freedom: "But we cannot really carry out 'foundings' on every foundation: we cannot see sensuous stuff in any categorial form we like, let alone perceive it thus, and above all not perceive it adequately."[17] Husserl helps us to understand what Stein means when she speaks of the foundational nature of categorial acts as nonreducible, that is, they are fundamental.

Dispositional or affective acts, sometimes called acts of sentiment, function in a similar way. Dispositional acts include such things as having the capacity to feel certain emotions or to make value judgments. One has a certain disposition toward particular objects, individuals, or states of affairs, but the very capacity (*Vermögen*) to be disposed in a given way is a universal human experience. The universal capacity as a human being to experience such dispositional acts serves as a bridge between the individual incarnation of such a capacity in the ego and dispositional acts as communal lived experiences. Using the example of an artwork, Stein observes that one experiences a certain feeling or emotion elicited by the artwork—a feeling of greater or lesser intensity. This feeling is characterized as one's own feeling. However, the "wonder" one feels before an artwork points to a more communal experience, an experience shared by those who appreciate or understand art (*PP* 165). One feels oneself united with those who have a general disposition toward art appreciation.

Others share a general sense of what it means to speak of something as "cold," "beautiful," "ugly," etc., as well. Such aesthetic judgments, which concern feeling and sentiment, can be expressed communally through the shared capacity to understand and carry out dispositional acts. In other words, out of one's own feeling there also can emerge a *Gemeinschaftserlebnis* between those capable of understanding art. For Stein, certain values, dispositions, and sentiments can be experienced communally as well as experienced individually. We have the capacity to experience this communal aspect of the life of feeling. For example, a people can collectively feel a particular affinity for a particular body of artwork or poetry indigenous to that people's history and culture. I think here of, for example, the meaning of the Group of Seven for Canadians or Florentine Renaissance Art for Italians.

A doubleness appears in Stein's description of the elements of *Gemeinschaftserlebnisse*. This doubleness is grounded in the singularity of the human individual and his/her universality as a human person. The human individual is a member of a species that possesses certain universal structures or elements. These universal elements enable the human being, in his or her individual being, to experience communal experiences. This coincidence of universality and particularity permits a coincidence and simultaneous noncoincidence between both the individual and the community in their respective *Erlebnisströme*. In a noncoincidence between the individual and the superindividual, the individual is able to retain his or her individuality and is not reduced to a "we." Yet, a multiplicity of subjects who dwell with one another in solidarity can nonetheless experience *Gemeinschaftserlebnisse* as a "we," in a coincidence between the individual and the superindividual. This doubleness echoes both the Husserlian and Steinian claims of the originary givenness of the ego to itself concomitant with the givenness of the other. The other is not constituted as a community, but as an alter ego—an ego similar to but different from me. Thus far, the goal of the discussion has been to show that the originary co-givenness of ego and alter ego implies (read *im-plicare:* to fold in) an *überindividuelle Realität*, a reality that reveals both the particular and the universal structures of *Erlebnis*. Intentionality, sensation, and categorial and dispositional acts are understood as capacities, logical and psychic, that facilitate higher acts of communalization or solidarity.

How, exactly, are communal lived experiences experienced? Stein maintains that they are experienced similarly to those of the individual ego, discussed previously. Because they are grounded in the individual ego, and because individual subjects concomitantly experience a certain we-ness, lived experiences can be experienced through this very we-ness. Moreover, they are experienced in a flow that connects one experience to another (*Komplexbildung*), much like the lived experiences of an individual consciousness.

Stein identifies four ways in which individual lived experiences of the community are connected: by association, motivation, causality, and the activity of the will (*Willenswirkung*). Association and causality belong to the psychic realm, whereas motivation and will belong to the life of the spirit. Association—the process whereby complex relations of various *Gemeinschaftserlebnisse* are built—is a weaker kind of connection between one lived experience and another (*PP* 123–24). Like associations triggered by words within the individual psyche, individual experiences may trigger associative experiences in other individuals, thereby affecting the community; indeed, certain lived experiences are constructed from these associations. To return to the previous example, the death of a military leader and the subsequent communal experience of grief may call to mind other communal experiences of grief over other fallen comrades. The individual will feel his/her own experience of sadness as well as the sadness of the group, both at that moment and through the recollections of past grief. In this way, one lived experience, through a process of association on both the individual and superindividual levels, draws out another: one communal experience can draw out another.

The motivations of an individual can be understood by another subject if, and only if, there is a presupposed communal, reciprocal understanding or intelligibility (*Wechselverständigung*). The register of understanding is a communal given rooted in *Gemeinschaftserlebnisse*.

I can better understand the motives of someone from my own culture than those of someone from a foreign culture because of our shared cultural understanding. Stein uses the purchase of a book as an example. I am motivated to buy a book for someone because I know that she needs it for her studies but cannot afford it. My motivation for buying the book is predicated on an understanding of a communally lived experience of two basic human needs: the need for education and economic resources. My motivation toward the other is not immediate; it is mediated by an underlying knowledge of needs and the desire to help the other fulfill her needs. Hence, the motivations of one individual can connect one to another in a community, thereby reinforcing the solidarity that exists between members of the community. The recipient is grateful for the book and for the other's motivation to help her fulfill her needs (*PP* 165–66).

Stein distinguishes two principal categories of communal lived experiences that motivate us to respond to other individuals: practical and theoretical interests. The communally shared lived experience of economic deprivation and the longing to be educated are viewed under the rubric of interests that move us to respond to individual cases—in this case, the student in need of a book (*PP* 171). Here, in this discussion of motivation and interest, Stein refers directly to Husserl's concept of rational motivation. Theoretical interest strives for truth in intellectual activity, whereas practical interest strives toward more pragmatic goods. The expression of Stein's position is not identical to Husserl's, but the concepts are the same. Communal lived experiences connect with one another through motivation, understood in terms of either practical or theoretical interest. "We" can all appreciate what it means to be motivated by an interest, even though its content may be different. An interest is like Kant's moral categorial imperative, which itself is empty but can be replete with a variety of content. In the case of the purchase of the book for the needy student, the motivation is grounded in a practical consideration, namely, helping to fulfill the economic lack of an other. Theoretical interest would involve a communal interest related to intellectual activities. The extent to which the connection between various motivated communal lived experiences is shared is grounded in a common intellectual understanding. Therefore, to claim that the intellectual performance of the operation 6 − 3 = 3 is a common experience means not only that each individual can perform this act, but that a common understanding permits the community of human beings to experience the capability of performing such mathematical operations (*Allgemeinheit*). Moreover, it is this operation of logical understanding that produces the common understanding that when 3 is subtracted from 6, one is necessarily and logically left with a remainder of 3. A rational series of certain consequences can be grasped in a communal sense through the universal capacity of human beings to understand numbers and certain mathematical functions.

Stein's discussion of interest recalls Husserl's discussion of interest in *Experience and Judgment*.[18] There, Husserl describes an interest that motivates or causes one's attention to turn toward an object. One can be attracted to or by an object, and may respond by becoming interested in the object, turning his or her attention toward the object of interest.[19] Distinguished from acts of willing, interest is connected to the act of striving.[20] Interest in an object causes one to turn their attention to it in order to gain more adequate lived experiences of it. Stein advances Husserl's discussion by considering interest within the realm of *Gemeinschaftserlebnisse*. Husserl, however, realizes the communal implications of his treatment of interest, for he posits a broader conception of interest as an *inter esse*, but this conception does not directly affect *Gemeinschaftserlebnisse*. According to Husserl, in acts of interest, the ego is not alone, but finds itself "being" with or among other beings. "We can form a broader concept of interest, or acts of interest. Among such acts are to be understood not only those in which I am turned thematically toward an object, perceiving it, perhaps, and then examining it thoroughly, but in general every act of turning-toward of the ego, whether transitory or continuous, every act of the ego's being-with (*inter-esse*)."[21]

In association, a passive kind of link connects one individual's experience with another's. Motivation is marked by an understanding of a certain state of affairs and the response of one individual to another. Both association and motivation can also connect individual lived experiences and thereby form communal lived experiences. Stein identifies causality as a third way in which communal lived experiences connect the individual to the community and bind the community to itself. Causality follows the pattern set out in the first work of the *Beiträge*. It explains how certain things or events produce reactions and responses in the individual and the community (*PP* 190). Unlike motivation, causality does not deal with the spiritual or intentional life of the human being. In psychic causality, the emphasis is placed on affectivity. Accordingly, the timbre of a person's voice may cause me to react psychically in a certain way. I may feel enlivened or irritated by its quality. The voice effects in me a certain psychic response. More generally, external objects may cause interior reactions. Likewise, in communal experiences, various external experiences may cause certain internal reactions. For example, my neighbors and I witness the death of a dog caused by a careless driver. "We" all feel angry with the driver and sad for the animal. The state of affairs we observe causes us to react in this way. Broader communal experiences may be caused in a similar fashion. For example, the name "Hitler" may cause universal sadness and anger within the Jewish community; the lived experience of pain and loss is communally lived.

Stein describes another form of causality that she calls psychic "infection" (*Ansteckung*) (*PP* 173–75). Invoking the example of the herd, she notes that in a herd "mentality," one is carried away or infected by the impulse of the moment without necessarily being conscious of the reason; there is a group reaction or response to something. A "contamination" or "contagion" of sorts infects others, causing them to behave in a certain way *en masse*. In mass hysteria, the community is affected in the same way as individuals. The threat of the imminent arrival of a "killer virus" can cause the members of a community to develop symptoms like those of the virus even though the virus has not yet arrived in the local area. The virus may be remote and the chance of infection low, but in mass hysteria, fear causes people to develop the very symptoms they fear without actually being contaminated by the virus.

Finally, we come to a further Steinian description of how communal lived experiences are themselves connected, namely, through the activity of the will. Stein returns here to the discussion of freedom. The central concern revolves around the fact that individuals have the freedom to will certain acts, and these acts connect them to, or affect, others. If I choose to carry out a certain act, my intention may affect the life of another individual, and even the community at large. Stein develops this idea in "Psychic Causality," the first part of the *Beiträge*. What does it mean, then, to speak of willed *Gemeinschaftserlebnisse?* In order to clarify what this might mean, Stein appeals to the example of a parliamentary vote (*PP* 194). The will of a political party may be to vote for a certain piece of legislation. Since the party members will to vote for such legislation, the individual member who supports the legislation experiences the communal will of parliament. This communal will is concretized in the proceedings of the vote when all members of the party rise and declare their "yeas" to the Speaker of the House.

As we saw earlier in Husserl, freedom and freely willed acts have responsibility as their corollary. Stein introduces responsibility in the discussion of communally lived experiences (*PP* 193). Returning to the previous example, if the communal experience of the will of the party is experienced individually, to the extent that each member of the party feels personally responsible for a given vote on a piece of legislation, are not the individual members of the party, rather than the party itself, responsible? Stein affirms this individual responsibility, but the question remains whether there is such a thing as communal responsibility. Stein affirms that there is, for there exists a *Gemeinschaftserlebnis* of co-responsibility. As a member of a party proposing a piece of legislation, I may choose not to vote for it because of the harm it would cause to the environment. I may not, therefore, be personally responsible, by means of my individual vote, for the legislation, but insofar as I remain a member of the party that proposed it, I am co-responsible (*mitverantwortlich*) with all party members for its passing into law. Stein relies on Scheler's concept of solidarity[22] in order to make her point, albeit Stein's notion of collective responsibility is not as extreme as Scheler's view. Solidarity implies an intimate sharing not only of goods, but of fault, errors, and other negative things (*PP* 193–95). Hence, one can argue that, in communal experience, which is marked by solidarity, responsibility is relevant to the discussion of *Gemeinschaftserlebnisse*.

The discussion of responsibility for one's actions is vital. The solidarity that typifies the relations (i.e., "we") of community members is directly connected to the bearing out of responsibility. Failing to be accountable for one's acts may erode the solidarity of the community. Likewise, the experience of solidarity of the community also relates to individual responsibility. Ultimately, the discussion of freedom and responsibility as a communal lived experience reveals the inherent link between the individual and the superindividual; the freedom and responsibility of the former implies the freedom and responsibility of the latter, and vice versa—a true *mitgeteilte Wechselverständigung*.

There is one final aspect that Stein mentions in her analyses of the psychic and logical structures of individuals that permit or condition communal consciousness that is worth noting, namely, her notion of the *Erfahrungsschatz* or treasure house of experiences. She does not develop this concept at any great length, but she does mention it a few times in the *Beiträge* (*PP* 146–48). One is reminded here of Augustine's notions of the belly of memory that collects past experiences and is crucial for their reactivation at various points in one's own life. Every individual possesses a treasure house of experiences that inform lived experiences. One could also read into this concept and say that there are collective experiences, and we have seen numerous Steinian examples, that can be stored and called upon when we experience other things or when they might prove useful for understanding present lived experiences. A Steinian *Erfahrungsschatz* would help us account for phenomena like collective memories that affect both the life of a specific community or individuals in that community. I think here of the collective memories of violence that inform various communities or peoples, for example, acts of systematic brutality and violence against First Nations communities.

Stein's treatment of *Gemeinschaftserlebnisse* is remarkable for a number of reasons. First, she provides a phenomenological description of the basic elements of communal lived experiences, along with a description of how the contents of such lived experiences interrelate. The phenomenology of the communal consciousness of lived experiences is unique within the field of phenomenology, for it systematically attempts to lay the philosophical groundwork for an understanding of the psychology of community in its elemental form, albeit always from a phenomenological perspective and not an empirical one. Moreover, this work is significant because it shows the individuality and originality of Stein's thought, which, although inspired by Husserl, elevates Husserlian phenomenology to a new realm. Second, *Individual and Community*, the second book of the *Beiträge*, provides the reader with another *Abschattungen* of the discussion of intersubjectivity. Often in phenomenology, the discussion of intersubjectivity revolves around the ego—an ego that, of course, is experienced as universal in that every person is an ego. Stein's work tries to grasp what it means to experience the ego not so much in its individuality, but in a more encompassing sense, as something that shares in the experience of others as a "we."

Third, not only does Stein affirm the integrity of the ego as inhabiting its own personal sphere of experience, but she also realizes that the ego belongs to a superindividual reality. In her reading of the nature of *Gemeinschaftserlebnisse,* she extends the ramifications of Husserl's insight, namely, the coincidence and noncoincidence of the ego and the other. In communal lived experiences, the ego is never lost, or fused (*verschmelzt*). The ego and the other come to share in a "we" experience (coincidence), but the integrity of both the ego and the communal experience of the "we" remain distinguishable. They do not coincide so far that they become indistinguishable.

Finally, the discussion of communal lived experience does not fail to take into account the force and value of pre-givens, which constitute the conditions for the ego, the other, and the "we" to coincide and not coincide. These conditions include the world and certain insights into human nature, such as the assumption of human freedom, the capacity for sensation in terms of *Allgemeinheit* and *Erfahrungsscahtz*, the ability of reason as implied in foundational *Denkakten*, etc. These elements of human essence are seen as universally given and are presupposed in order for the more particular lives of the ego, alter ego, and the "we" to come to fullness. Phenomenological analysis reveals that these pre-givens exist.

The Ontic Structure of the Community

Thus far, Stein has focused on lived experience from the perspective of consciousness experienced communally. The second part of *Individual and Community* is devoted to an analysis of the ontic structure of the community. Here, Stein moves from a description of the relation between the individual and the community in terms of consciousness to their existential relation as a community. In other words, she considers what it means to exist as a community of individuals.

We encounter many kinds of communities in reality: families, religious communities, peoples (*Völker*), etc. Recall that, for Stein, communities are the most intense form of superindividual reality. In life, we find communities external to us and communities that dwell within us (*PP* 197). For example, I observe different religious communities external to me—Muslim, Jewish, Catholic, Anglican, etc. Communities such as family, the local church, and so on, also dwell within me. Furthermore, like the individual psyche, which is animated by a certain life-force or life-power (*Lebenskraft*), the community, too, has a life-force, which stems from the life-force of its individual members (*PP* 201). The communal life-force, however, is not identical to that of its members; it can be weaker or stronger despite the quality of the life-force of its individual members. Members of a community must give or share their life-force with the community. They must choose to do so, but they may also refuse. The life-force of certain individuals may be strong, but unless they agree to share it on a more communal level, the life-force of the community will be weak (*PP* 201). For example, an individual may feel an impassioned love for politics. Such a person may be full of ideas, energy, and intense commitment, but if they do not share this passion in a communal setting such as a political party, the community will not profit from the intensity of the force that drives them. So, too, a person animated by such a life-force may choose not to ally with the force of the community. An example of this is the conscientious objector.

The notion of the *Lebenskraft der Gemeinschaft* is slightly puzzling. What does it mean, to what does it refer? The life-force of the individual, understood as the soul or psychic principle of movement, is understandable to the extent that it is a traditional concept that has pervaded Western philosophy from the beginning. The life-force of the community is the force that empowers life in general, the energy that empowers the life of the world. This is to be understood not in religious terms, but rather in terms of physics. It is a basic fact, confirmed by the laws of thermal dynamics, that the universe consists of vast sources of energy that are inherent in nature. Hence, when one speaks of the life-force of a community, one can understand this to refer to the energy that produces it. But is Stein's life-force simply a principle of animation or movement? It is more than just an account of the foundation of movement and human energy.

What are the concrete sources that motivate the energy or life-force of the community? From whence does the life-force of the community draw its strength? First, from the individuals' life-forces. The community is essentially grounded in individuals but not merely reducible to them. The character of the community changes when the character of its individual members changes. The character of a community is determined by how deeply the life of the community is anchored in its individual members and by the relationship between the community and its individual members. There is an intimate relationship between individuals and communities. Ultimately, one cannot speak of a community if it is not "embodied" or "incarnated" within the lives of individuals. The individuals must choose to participate in the community and must be open (*geöffnet sein*) to each other in order for there to be solidarity (*PP* 206–7). Community is not automatically produced; it must be assented to and worked upon by the individual members. In fact, the genesis of a community is based upon open communication and mutual exchange between its members. In communal solidarity, there is mutual dependence, one upon another—a *"wechselseitige Abhängigkeit"* (*PP* 206).

The fact that individuals are reciprocally dependent upon one another in community does not, however, imply that all communities are necessarily related. Communities can be external to, or excluding of, other communities. For example, Stein maintains that the scientific community to which she belongs has no relation to the community of her family. The two are separate, yet she belongs to both. If there is a "reciprocal dependence" between the individual and the community, one might assume, then, that Stein would be the point at which the two communities naturally converge. This convergence, however, does not imply that one community experiences the other as part of its own. Communities may overlap, but though they share members, they remain external to each other. The only way that one community can come to share in the "we"-ness of another community is through the mediation of individuals. Hence, if Stein chose to bring the world of Auguste Stein into contact with the world of the Göttingen Circle, these two overlapping but separate worlds might somehow share a common "we" experience through the mediation of an individual I (*PP* 208–9). Mediation, then, is one way in which communities might come together and thereby create new communities. One community can also mediate between others; mediation is not always dependent on a single individual.

Another way of bringing communities together (or dividing them) is through *soziale Stellungnahmen,* or taking up certain social positions or stands. Adopting certain reciprocal positions in life can be a source of connection for communities. Stein offers the example of particular social acts, such as love, hate, thankfulness, etc. (*PP* 210–11). In acts of love, others are drawn into a community. The one who loves attributes an inestimable value to the other and the other is confirmed in that value (*PP* 215). They share a reciprocal love. But by extending their love and loving others, they can form a community of love. Families, through the reciprocal love of their members, have their source in such love. Likewise, families can disintegrate if their members take up a stand of hatred toward one another. By adopting certain positions in life, one can influence others, thereby producing the energy or force that, in turn, can animate the life of a community. This is especially the case where an experience of solidarity binds the individual members of the community to one another (*PP* 214). If we recall Stein's treatment of love and empathy in the first chapter, where empathy encounters its limit in love, we find in her discussion of love and community a place for love that is situated outside the discussion of other minds and the general essence of human being. Stein situates love within the rubric of the experience of community understood as solidarity.

The final source of the life-force of the community is objective. Objectivity is understood in two particular senses. First is the objectivity that is the content of a given lived experience. Second, there is a spiritual objectivity. With respect to the former, the object of lived experience may very well inspire a community. Using the example of a rainy day or a sunny, beautiful day, Stein comments that the experience of each kind of day in its objectivity will dispose the members of a community to adopt a similar attitude; they will either be glum or cheerful (*PP* 216).

Spiritual objectivities, understood as objectifications of spirit, can also bring about a communal experience (*PP* 216–17). Works of art and poetry are examples of spiritual objectivities because they make concrete the spiritual musings of the artist or poet. Certain types of art and writing may inspire a communal or national vision. Certain religious values may inspire a particular political and social vision of a community. The Reformation and Counter-Reformation are concrete examples of how the community translated spiritual values into objects such as art, poetry, architecture, moral and social codes, political conventions, etc. Such objectivities arose from a communal experience and inspired communal experience. It must be noted, however, that the sources of the life-force of a community—including mediation, the adoption of certain stands and objectivity—do not necessarily or always serve as sources of a community (*PP* 219–20); they can also serve as forces that undermine or destroy community. As an example, Stein suggests the death of a communal culture in which the legacy of great works of art is replaced by an emphasis on commerce. Here, this interest in commerce, itself a communal objectivity, is viewed as destroying the previous life that valued and promoted high culture—a culture of great works of art (*PP* 220–21). Communities, then, can have both generative and degenerative sources.

The individual's psyche has a double nature: it is both a monad unto itself and simultaneously a correlate of its surrounding world (*PP* 212). Hence, one can speak not only of the psychic capacities and intellectual characteristics of an individual, but also of the psychic capacities and intellectual character of the surrounding community. Stein identifies the community as having three particular psychic capacities: *Aufnehmen, Bewegtwerden,* and *Handeln* (*PP* 223). The community is receptive (*Aufnehmen*) because it is capable of sensation (*sinnliches Vermögen*), and it can therefore receive data from the outside world through perceptions. When one speaks of the community, one must always keep in mind that it is composed of individuals. Hence, when the community is said to be capable of receiving data, this must be understood in an analogous sense to the individual experience of receptivity or affectivity. Hence, a community is capable of being affected by the data it receives from its surrounding world. For example, an ethnic community can sense when it is being persecuted. A community is also capable of being moved by certain events (*PP* 224). For example, the earthquake that struck southern Italy in 1980 moved (*Bewegtwerden*) the Italian diaspora to send aid and funds. Finally, a community is capable of acting or responding to (*Handeln*) particular situations and events. By carrying out certain acts and doing things, diasporic Italian communities were not only moved by the calamitous news of death and destruction, but also responded by handling numerous requests for information about loved ones in the afflicted zones of the Campania and Basilicata; they also sent money and aid.

In addition to its psychic capacities, Stein notes that a community has a certain intellectual character, marked by its capacity for understanding or comprehension, what she terms *Auffassungsvermögen*

(*PP* 225). Like the individual in whose consciousness things become constituted, the community can experience an analogous type of constitutive process of comprehension. Anti-Semitic hatred will certainly come to be felt in the collective or communal lived experience of a Jewish community. For example, the Bible recounts the Hebrew experience of being hated and persecuted. This hatred was constituted in individual Hebrew members' consciousness concomitant with the shared experience of this hatred because it affected the Hebrew people as a whole. An example of a community's understanding is seen in acts of identification. A people (*Volk*) can come to identify its individual members through certain spiritual and physical qualities, thereby identifying the essential traits of a particular people or culture. For example, I might identify an Italian by means of certain physical qualities and "spiritual" traits such as warmth, laughter, a proclivity for melodrama, and a flare for theatricality. I recognize Italians through these qualities. Likewise, a community recognizes and understands these individuals as "Italian" because of their similarities to the qualities associated with the group. Such identifications may run the risk of becoming stereotypical. Nonetheless, Stein argues for our capacity to define and understand types: she has a robust notion of typology that runs through the course of her work. We find, for example, in her writings on woman, a breakdown of types of women and personalities. Stein is not alone in this kind of typologization: we find it in thinkers like Dilthey as well as in Simone de Beauvoir with her types of human beings in the *Ethics of Ambiguity*.

The final part of *Individual and Community* is devoted to an analysis of the fundamental comportment of the individual toward the community. The unity (*Gemeinsamkeit*) of the structure of lived experience serves as the ground for all social ties (*soziale Verbände*) (*PP* 239–40). In order for social ties to exist, one must assume a basic connectedness or togetherness of all lived experience. Social ties must not be understood as necessarily implying that individuals are bound in a community. Rather, they indicate a sort of "open plurality of individuals" (*PP* 240). The community is essentially founded in individuals, and the character of the community changes as the individuals in the community change. One can assume the opposite as well, such that the community may sometimes change an individual. For example, a faith community's decision to establish a hospice for the terminally ill may significantly alter an individual's comportment toward the community. Moved by such an activity, the individual may decide to become more deeply involved in the project and may subsequently feel a stronger tie to the community.

Stein concludes her treatment of the community with a recapitulation of Simmel's and Scheler's distinctions between mass, society, and community in order to highlight that there are various grades of social unities in addition to community. In a mass relation, individuals do not focus on one another and do not see one another as objects. Nor do they perceive themselves as given to one another in the same way as communal living subjects. There is here no communal understanding, merely an occupation of common space wherein everyone behaves in a similar fashion (*PP* 241). The unity between individuals in a mass is a basic psychic unity in which exchange is characterized by stimulus and response; in turn, this relation of stimulus-response can be seen as a collective objectivity. Only basic affectivity and response, not spirituality, are assumed in such a basic structure (*PP* 242–43). Because of the basic psychic mechanism of stimulus and response, one can easily understand how psychic *Ansteckung* occurs, especially in the case of herd mentality. Depending on their respective intensity, different events can "infect" masses to varying degrees, thereby producing different effects.

The opposite of the mass is society (*Gesellschaft*) (*PP* 255). The tie between individual members of a society is more spiritual and personal. Characteristic of a society is its orientation toward a common goal or purpose. A society is usually founded in order to achieve a certain goal or serve a particular purpose; to this end, it is referred to as a *Zweckverband*. As the founding purpose may change over time, the society itself may change and develop in order to accommodate different goals, especially if an earlier goal has been achieved. Furthermore, the number of individuals in a society is not limited to a particular number; societies can be as large or small as their specific purposes or goals dictate. The individuals in a society are joined in a relation aimed at satisfying a certain purpose, and there are as many types of societies as there are purposes and goals. Members of various societies can belong to multiple societies, and while many societies may have similar ends, the means to achieve those ends is "personalized" by each community. Hence, the Society of St. Vincent de Paul and the Salvation Army share the same end of alleviating poverty and loneliness, and, though their methods may be similar, their spiritual visions and founding histories may not be.

The highest unity, a community is not characterized by willed, decisive acts to fulfill (or not fulfill) a certain goal or purpose, nor is it founded on a desire to follow a common goal. Rather, it grows and dies in much the same fashion as life. The purpose of a society is determined from outside. For example, the Göttingen Philosophical Society had as its goal the study and discussion of phenomenological and philosophical questions. This goal is an "outer" goal, something that exists outside of each individual and to which each tries to conform in his or her interiority (*PP* 261).

The character of a community is determined by those traits or properties that typify the individual bearers of the community living in solidarity with one another. It is not created and determined from an outside goal or purpose, but naturally marks the interiority of individual persons who share similar characteristics (*PP* 261–62). For example, one can speak of a certain vivacity, passion, and generosity of spirit in certain groups of people. The group's character further emerges when the members of the community work toward a common purpose; the community's character informs the communal purpose and the actions undertaken to achieve it.[23] One community may differ from another in the way it handles a similar problem; the handling of the problem reflects various characteristics typical of the community in question.

Thus far, Stein has affirmed the reciprocal dependence between the individual and the community (*wechselseitige Abhängigkeit*) (*PP* 262) and the way in which this relation builds character for both. She also established the essence of the community as a togetherness in which the individual members live in one another not as object and subjects, *"sondern mit ihm lebt, von seinen Motiven getrieben wird usw"* (*PP* 262). But this is a static description of community, so Stein proceeds to consider the genesis of a community, asking from whence it arises (*PP* 262–63). She posits three answers to this question. First, the community arises naturally because relations among people cause a deeper and wider reciprocal exchange to occur on a more personal level, that is, because the personhood of one comes to live within the personhood of another. Love relationships are an example of this deeper personal exchange, which fertilizes the possibility of the existence of communities. If one individual loves another, a larger community ensues in the sense that two individuals live more deeply in one another vis-à-vis their experience of one another. Second, an object may cause a community to arise or to deepen in unity. For example, when the French won the FIFA World Cup in 1998, the unity of French people from different ethnic backgrounds was deepened. I recall listening to Radio France Internationale (RFI) and hearing that France's World Cup victory helped to heal the racial divisions that had plagued France for so many years. The community of individuals, whether Arab, French, or African, felt united in this victory; the community experienced a deepening of the sense of itself as "French." The victory of the World Cup (the object) was the source of a (re)new(ed) sense of the French community wherein racial divisions were temporarily "overcome." The experience of being French and being world champion lived in the consciousness of each individual celebrating the victory. We see this often with important victories in sport. Finally, the origin of a community must be principally rooted in freedom—the freedom to be open to others and to open oneself, one to the other and vice versa. This *Bejahung*[24] of oneself to the other is not like the freedom to perform an ego act or to work toward a common societal goal. The *fiat* uttered in this case is deeply personal, and it stamps or impresses itself on the other in a veritable seizing of the other. In this seizing of one another in each other's personhood, there is, however, no loss of individual identity in a communal fusion. Rather, there is a communal living of each in the other within each person's individuality. The unity of the members of a society is not as deeply personal, even though the personhood of each individual comes through in societal interactions. The goal or purpose, however, serves as the unifying force in societies, whereas in communal unities, the unity originates in one person saying "yes" to the other.

Communal unity arises out of the general possibility of human freedom, through a general recognition of freedom as freedom and the possibilities it lays open (*PP* 265–66). Hence, one has the specific freedom to say "yes" to the other, and vice versa, but all recognize the general condition for the possibility of community, namely, that it is freedom in general that underpins our individual beings in the first place and makes it possible for us to incarnate our freedom in specific situations and relations. This freedom also and necessarily implies responsibility. In community, because one feels concomitantly responsible for the community in a deeply personal way, one feels responsible for the other as for oneself (*PP* 276–77). In a society, its members feel responsible for achieving a specified common goal; this is an external responsibility because a society's members feel responsible for achieving that which is understood as an aim or purpose. In community, however, the responsibility is more internalized and lived more deeply and personally, one in the other, etc. The responsibility is felt toward the other person rather than toward an explicit external purpose or goal. In community, one individual "bears," or is a "bearer" (*Träger*) of, the freedom and responsibility, indeed the personhood, of the other without usurping these elements. Elements of the *Persönlichkeitskern* nevertheless remain deeply individualized. Community never implies the complete abandonment of the self to the other, for that would merely be an instance of psychic contagion.

Critical Commentary

Stein's analysis of community highlights two important features. First, there is such a thing as communal lived experiences within the realm of the psycho-spiritual. The psycho-spiritual is not merely individualized, but also takes into account the psycho-spiritual life of a plurality of subjects, the "we" of a community. In her analysis of communal lived experience, association, causality, motivation, and the activity of the will, Stein describes the communal lived experience as psycho-spiritual. Second, community carries with it existential import. Not merely an ideal that exists only within our interiority, community exists outside our subjectivity. It is something in which we choose either negatively or affirmatively to participate. In her description of the ontological structure of community, Stein presents its ontic foundations. These foundational elements, which include a relation of openness and communication, personality or personhood, character and life-force, profoundly affect our unique and communal beings in the world.

Stein's analysis of the community is interesting for several reasons. First, the community is grounded in the concrete individual and is ultimately analogous to the individual person. The community is incarnate in the life of all of its members, each of whom uniquely bears the life experience of the community to varying degrees. Furthermore, Stein makes a conscious attempt to accommodate individual personality as well as unity. Her analysis of the relation between individual and community is true to her own, and Husserl's, insight into the fundamental structure of coincidence and noncoincidence that marks the discussion of intersubjectivity in the work of both thinkers.

To describe the relation between the individual and the community in analogous terms is significant. Analogy allows for the relation of the differences and similarities between individuals and the community of individuals to be more fluid and plastic. This fluidity is important. The logic of analogy serves as a prophylactic against the possible absolutization or mutual exclusivity of the individual or the community. In fact, analogy guarantees that the individual is not reducible to the community, and vice versa. Furthermore, it prevents one from thinking that they can exist apart from one another; there can be no such thing as an absolute individual or an absolute community. Moreover, the ego is always seen in some relation to the other, whether in relation to mass, society, or community.

Second, Stein describes not only community's ontological structures but also how community is experienced in consciousness. Given the time at which Stein wrote the *Beiträge*—prior to the publication of *Ideas II* and before the publication of Husserl's lectures on phenomenological psychology—one can read Stein's work as a positive contribution to both phenomenology and psychology. Psychology at that time was deeply positivistic. Stein challenges these deterministic conceptions of the human person by introducing the discussion of consciousness, freedom, and will as fundamental to psychological anthropology.[25]

Third, Stein's work on the individual and community carries out Husserl's scientific intention to use phenomenological philosophy to ground all other sciences. Stein achieves this by applying phenomenology to psychology. Through her phenomenological psychology of the person and community, Stein challenges the then-current empirical, scientific view of the human being as merely a "piece of nature" (*PP* 305). She reveals the individual and community to be deeply personal and spiritual.

Fourth, Stein applies Husserl's original insight about the dynamic between freedom and responsibility to her phenomenology of the individual and community. In its deepest sense, community implies a responsibility for the self and other. Since freedom and responsibility come into play, one cannot divorce the discussion of intersubjectivity from its ethical ramifications.

Finally, Stein's analysis poignantly reminds the philosopher that when discussing intersubjectivity, the relation between the self and other, ego and alter ego, takes a plethora of forms and incarnations. The concrete relation between the self and other can take the general forms of mass, society, and community, and in any of these forms, it can incarnate itself in many specific ways. A society may be religious, political, artistic, libertine, etc. So, too, a community may take many forms, including family, nation, a people, etc. There is no limit to the number of possible incarnations. Moreover, an overlap occurs in the three basic forms of intersubjectivity. This overlap implies affectivity since each form can affect the relation that exists between individuals.

Stein's phenomenology of community, for all its ingenuity, nonetheless leaves certain questions unresolved. If community is conceived in such personalistic terms—one individual living within another individual via experience—can one speak of community as other than personal? For example, do animals live in communities? Some simian species dwell in communal relations that are clearly analogous to human communities. Moreover, can a community exist between an individual or a group of individuals and nonpersonal entities, like companion animals? What would it mean, for example, for there to be community between an individual and a pantheon of nonpersonal gods? Or, one can easily imagine a person who sees himself living in a community with a number of dogs. Stein might recognize these as definite possibilities, but they are not personal communities. They are, rather, communities of a different order. Stein might identify the community with its pantheon of impersonal gods not so much as a community, but as a communion of another sort insofar as the individual feels herself in communion with these higher entities. Obviously, the way in which they dwell in each other in this case would be different from that in a community of persons.

Second, with respect to the lived experiences of community (*Gemeinschaftserlebnisse*) in consciousness, might not an unconscious experience of community be possible? Jung designated the collective unconscious as a sort of treasure house of symbols, myths, and reasonings that inform the individual lives of the members of a society. Furthermore, one can definitely speak of collective repressions in the unconscious that inform individual members of a community as well as the community as a whole. For example, at the turn of the twentieth century, women in bourgeois communities in England and Germany suffered similar bouts of hysteria and fainting. The source of the hysteria was not somatic. It was later determined[26] that it was caused by a repressed desire for affection, attention, and sexual intimacy—things that Victorian society collectively shunned and repressed. The communal unconscious desire for affection, love, and intimacy, which had been repressed, was unleashed as hysteria within the *bürgerliche Gemeinschaften* of Victorian society. As awareness of the phenomenon of hysteria became more public, the greater became the number of cases. It is likely that *psychische Ansteckung* was a contributing factor to the increasing prevalence of hysteria.

Finally, both Stein and Husserl address the originality of the ego and alter ego, as well as the inherent link between individual and community. It is difficult to conceive of an individual apart from some kind of superindividual reality. Or is it? Are there not individuals who have been so traumatized in their relations with others that they choose not to interact at all with other individuals? Admittedly, it is hard to imagine such people living absolutely alone, for they, like everyone else, must nevertheless depend on others for the raw materials of life—food, energy, and water—unless, of course, they choose to live as hermits in a remote, isolated location. Such traumatized individuals usually remain in the world, and, in a certain if limited sense, deal with other people. They may feel so fundamentally and spiritually disconnected from everyone that they may be incapable of feeling the other dwelling in them; moreover, they may lack the desire to live in someone else. It might be argued that such people live in a mass relation in which no spiritual affectivity obtains. However, these individuals do, in fact, live in a spiritual relationship with others, namely, a relation of fear, distrust, and perhaps even hatred; they inhabit a negative spiritual state. One might ask, therefore, whether or not such a conscious, free decision to refuse to interact with other individuals, whether those of a mass, a society, or a community, for reasons of past suffering or trauma constitutes an example of an individual living in some kind of superindividual reality, yet failing to experience unity with others in a relation of mass, community, or society. This example opens up the possibility of an ambiguous category of relations between individuals—a category in which a person may live within a mass, society, and/or community, but feel disconnected or disassociated from any individual other than the self—a kind of privative or even apophatic community.[27] Such a person continues to be minimally connected to others through the necessary relations required for subsistence, but, in a profoundly spiritual sense, a person may be motivated to use their freedom to refuse all other relations; such an individual is profoundly disconnected from other individuals. Ultimately, the question remains: Can one choose in freedom to live apart from a superindividual world, and to what degree?

Chapter 4

Edith Stein's Political Philosophy

The previous chapters demonstrated how Stein moved from self-knowledge and understanding of ourselves as human persons through empathy to larger, more complex social structures, including community and society. I would now like to turn to another social objectivity, to borrow an expression from Husserl, namely, the state. The state, in Stein's understanding, achieves its highest, thickest sense through communal relations rooted in sovereignty and law. In this chapter, I argue for two essential claims about Stein's political philosophy. First, Stein's political philosophy must not be read in strict phenomenological terms, as one finds in the text her own liberal political sentiments. Second, we can extract from Stein's theory of the state, not only an essence of the state, but a broader notion of her own concept of the political, especially as it can be distinguished from her understanding of social relations.

Situating Stein's Treatise on the State

In 1925, Edmund Husserl published Edith Stein's treatise *Eine Untersuchung über den Staat* (*An Investigation concerning the State*) in his *Jahrbuch für Philosophie und phänomenologische Forschung*.[1] This text was written after Stein had completed her work as Husserl's assistant at the University of Freiburg. Though the text was complete in 1924, as indicated by various letters (*US* ix), it was not published until 1925. Recent German scholarship[2] views the period between

1920 and 1924 as a unique period in Stein's philosophical development, marked by intense philosophical dialogue with early phenomenologists such as Roman Ingarden, Theodor Conrad, and Hedwig Conrad-Martius, teaching, and various attempts to secure a university post. While it is true that this period of Stein's philosophical itinerary has not largely been taken up by scholars, and that work has only now begun to examine more intensely this part of Stein's oeuvre, it would be a mistake to claim that no significant work on her treatment of the state was done prior to the recent burst of scholarship that appeared with the Herder publication of the new critical edition of Stein's collected works.[3]

In this scholarship, by and large, Stein's political text is seen to be a continuation of ideas developed in her earlier phenomenological works on empathy, community, and the human person.[4] Though connections to her earlier work can be drawn, especially to the notion of community marked by one living in the experience of the other in solidarity, I argue that Stein's text on the state does not wholly fit with her earlier work. Considerable gaps exist, and a significant lacuna in Stein's phenomenological logic is the lack of a particular form of awareness that would mark one's living through an experience of the state. In her earlier works, empathy and the three forms of sociality are all accompanied by a particular mental state. While she does assert a lived experience of community (*Gemeinschaftserlebnis*), she does not offer an eidetic description of what it is for us to live through *together* an experience of the state;[5] there is no *Staatsgemeinschaftserlebnis*. No unique mental state accompanies the experience of political life. Rather, Stein's political ontology presents the state as an object of consciousness, whose meaning we, as a collectivity living within the state, can share and understand as lived experience of community, which draws upon empathy, as we have seen earlier. Though analogous to a person, the state is an ontic object, like any other object, that a community experiences together, but it reveals no particular form of subjective state consciousness, as it does in the thinking of other philosophers—for example, Hegel in his *Elements of the Philosophy of Right* or more recent Anglo-American philosophers like

Margaret Gilbert and Philip Pettit.[6] Gilbert, for example, following a similar line to that of Raimo Tuomela, argues that social reality requires some kind of conscious commitment and obligation in order for agents to collectively bring about certain political ends. Stein refrains from using the language of political commitment and obligation, preferring to discuss solidarity as the chief motivator behind political objectivities like the state.

There are also other aspects of Stein's political work that do not allow for an easy connection to her earlier writings. I wish to focus on one in particular, namely, Stein's phenomenological method. Whereas in her earlier texts Stein's methodology was very clearly Reinachian-Husserlian, seeking through eidetic variation to capture the ideal essence of an object as it appeared in consciousness, her description of the state does not quite follow the methodology of her earlier work. Once she obtained an accurate phenomenological essence, part of Stein's phenomenological methodology was to engage the theories of other philosophers, psychologists, or scientists relative to the object under investigation. So, for example, once Stein secures the description of empathy, she examines and criticizes various theories put forward by thinkers such as Lipps in psychology and Scheler in phenomenology. Scholars including Angela Ales Bello and Philibert Secretan[7] read Stein's text on the state as a classical phenomenological description of the essence of the state, and thus as consistent with her earlier writings. Having obtained her phenomenological description, Stein might then be expected, following the method of her earlier texts, to go on to criticize other communitarian state models; she only discusses the sovereignty-based one. But Stein's treatment does not really proceed in this way. She notes that there are various theories of the state and observes that the dominant ones of her day tend to be grounded in a sociality that Tönnies called "society," which Stein further defines as having a mostly contractarian structure (*US* 3–5). Though it is true that a state can be grounded in a societal structure, Stein argues that a state can also have a communal structure. It is at this point that Stein's traditional phenomenological approach begins to take on her own particular personality. Her text on the state draws upon the phenomenological method, but it is also more polemical, more argumentative, more "political." Advocating the viability and validity of a certain kind of state, namely, the sovereign model of the state as opposed to, say, a republican model, Stein remarks that though states can be societal or communal, she wishes to look at the highest form of the state, namely, the communal one. She makes an explicit value judgment that the highest form of states is communal as opposed to ones rooted in societal, contractual structures.[8]

On what grounds can I justify my foregoing claim? I would like to put forward four reasons. First, there is the historical period in which Stein found herself, Weimar Germany. Second, the tone and style of the text indicate a more pleading and argumentative style than that of her earlier, more sober phenomenology. Third, her critique of liberal contract theory is most unphenomenological, as is her rejection of the state as a religious or ethical entity. It would be naïve to think of Edith Stein as a philosopher and phenomenologist like that of Aristophanes' Socrates in *The Clouds*. She was a deeply political person who fought for various political causes, including the right of women to habilitate and hold professorships at the university; she was actively committed to serving the Prussian State during World War I (Stein was a nurse at a lazaretto near the front); and she campaigned for educational reform and against Hitler and National Socialism (as various letters of appeal and her autobiography, *Life in a Jewish Family*, testify).[9] I read her text on the state, in part, as a deep extension of her political agency and activism.

Let us examine the argument in its historical context. Ilona Riedel-Spangenberger notes that, early on, while studying history with Max Lehmann at Göttingen, Stein became deeply critical of politics (*US* xi). In 1918, she recounted in a letter to Roman Ingarden that she had undertaken various political activities, including joining the German Democratic Party (*US* xi–xii). The defeat of Germany in the First World War had resulted in extremely punitive and taxing living conditions for the German people. The nationalist belief in the supremacy of the German Reich had been dealt a fatal blow. After the war, many interest groups sought to articulate a new German ideal of the state. Philosophers and social theorists were no strangers to these debates. Thinkers such as Scheler recanted their earlier nationalist positions, while others were more critical, but all of them were trying to make sense of what had happened and offer new possibilities.[10] Riedel-Spangenberger remarks that Stein saw her text as "corrective."

Alert and interested, Edith Stein followed the efforts of the Weimar Republic. But because of the struggle of radical interest groups and their differing political theories, Stein saw the state as severely jeopardized and determined to fall. She posits, therefore, a structured theory of the state as a guiding ideal through which the State, ruled by law, employs the force of reason in the best interest of the people. She remarks, "A corrective to all of the destructive influences of these political theories lies in the power of good reasoning (*ratio*), which carries its very own real relations. Any domain or order of law that is in violation of this *ratio,* instead of carrying through its own propositions, must be prepared for the fact that it lies in opposition to this reality and is continuously breaking away from the given order of law."[11]

Given the reality of postwar Germany and Stein's political nature, it is no wonder that she threw herself into the debate. One even wonders whether Stein's treatise on the state can be read as an expression of her German Democratic Party allegiance. Staunchly opposed to the Treaty of Versailles, the GDP championed a left-leaning, liberal form of republican government. It wanted strong international ties and a place for various kinds of minorities. Many of the party's sentiments are echoed in Stein's treatment of the state. Stein regarded her treatise as a corrective to prevalent theories of the state that she found faulty or unsound, which not only suggests that she was attentive to the events and politics of her day, but demonstrates her efforts to ensure that certain forms of politics, especially nationalist ones, would not prevail.

My second claim is that the tone and form of argumentation here are different from those found in her earlier texts, and this results in a more polemical treatise. She freely uses such forms of personal address as "we hold" (*US* 9), without giving an objective phenomenological description of that which she rejects, namely, her view of contractarian theory; she also compares her view to other views that she holds to be undeveloped, especially the contractarian view. But, again, she never describes or elucidates the phenomenological essences of these opposing views, especially the various contractarian positions. Wolfgang Rieß maintains that Stein *does* undertake a rigorous phenomenological description, and he thereby links Stein's political text to her earlier work.[12] But Stein's position is very clear: she introduces an argumentative claim and employs phenomenology to prove her point. On page seven of the new German text on the state, Stein reiterates the distinction between a community and the state that she developed in her earlier *Beiträge*. She moves on to describe her project in her political work, and she makes a comparative claim: even though one finds both societal and communal forms of the state, she will try to determine which form of sociality is best. Ultimately, Stein will argue for the superiority of the communal over the societal form.[13]

Stein declares that the question of the sociality of the state cannot be an either-or question; that is, it can be resolved neither into a solely societal, contractarian view nor into an exclusively communal view. But she then goes on to say that she will consider the communal view while criticizing the contractarian, societal view. Stein unequivocally prefers the communal view of the state to the societal, contractarian one. This preference is clear; her tone and words confirm it. The *epoché* so apparent in her first two works never appears in her treatise on the state. Also missing is a sustained discussion of the eidetic variation that could result in a discussion of different kinds of communal states that are possible, other than the sovereign view. There is also no discussion of types, which was so common in her earlier works, including her *Einführung in die Philosophie*, and which could have helped her discussion along. Why does Stein privilege a communal account that sees the state as sovereign, as opposed to some other standard of communal togetherness that typifies the law of the state, for example, American republicanism? This question will be addressed later.

We come now to my third argument concerning the not-so-smooth transition from Stein's earlier texts to her political treatise: her critique of society and of contract theories of the state. Though Stein tells us that a state can have, in principle, both a societal and communal structure (recall that she says it is not an either-or [*aut-aut*] situation) (*US* 8), she never really develops the former model. In fact, despite failing to do so, she is highly critical of it. I find it most telling that a phenomenologist who admits the possibility of a societal or contractual view of the state only explains certain aspects of the contractarian view—all of which she dismisses as largely deficient. Stein offers three significant critiques of the contract theory of the state: (1) the assumption that all people within a state, including those conquered by the state, have made an original contract; (2) the state is experienced as an object like any other object, resulting in the possible personal alienation of its members from the state; and (3) in contractarian theories, the state's free acts of decision-making imply that all legitimately recognized members of the state act freely by sanctioning certain choices—this, of course, is achieved through representation, etc. Certainly, as we begin to unpack Stein's critiques, it is easy to imagine the ripostes that contract theorists might make in response to her claims. Though I am sympathetic to many of these possible counterarguments, I cannot take them up here. Moreover, it seems that Stein was not particularly interested in hearing the counterarguments, which reinforces my own claim about the polemical and argumentative nature of Stein's text.

I would like to pause briefly, however, in order to discuss Stein's critiques of the societal or contract theory of the state. First, although there is a deep connection between societal and contractarian theories, one must be careful never to reduce the sociality implied in contract theories of the state to Stein's notion (always drawing from Tönnies's sociological theory) of contractarian views of the state as rooted in what she calls society. It is not clear that all contractarian theories are marked by a societal form of sociality in which the state is seen as an end toward which we must work. For thinkers such as Rousseau in his *Social Contract* and others who speak of "the people" and of "citizens," the members of a society work together not for the state, but for a pleasurable and happy life together based on equality. There is no sustained discussion of equality in Stein's treatise, and this also marks her as different from other contractarian thinkers. Furthermore, her discussion of the people, as opposed to the seventeenth century French view, is steeped in a framework of race and ethnic identity.

Stein's first critique of contract theory is that it assumes that all people living in such a state have assented to the contract. She declares that the "origin" of the contract, understood as some kind of tacit assent to the laws of the state, is naïvely posited. Foreshadowing many postcolonial critiques of contemporary politics, Stein remarks that, historically speaking, many people that find themselves within a contract state never assented to anything; rather, they were forced into the state by conquest. Stein has in mind many of the minorities that dwell within contract states without ever having been given any real choice. She also has in mind the plight of many minority groups, Jews included, who dwell within contract states but have limited say or no say at all (*IS* 5–6).

Second, Stein views contract theories of the state as subjectively alienating insofar as they construct the sociality between its members in a subject-object form. The state is an object, an instrument through which people relate to one another. The state is not lived communally in solidarity (*IS* 28–31); rather, it is an object that exists outside of each individual but helps manage and articulate aspects necessary for communal life, including law, the distribution of resources, security, and so on. Stein argues that if people comport themselves toward the state as an object that lies outside of them, in addition to having deleterious effects on individuals, the very stability of the state may be undermined. In this formulation, the state can easily become a superstructure that subjects individual people to its own will. This is the case, for example, in Hegel's *Rechtsphilosophie*, where individual conscience is superseded by the larger consciousness of the right of the state and the awareness of state consciousness. In contractual democracies, individuals may become alienated from the state as the state may not be seen to be relevant or meaningful in any way. According to Stein, because the state occupies no internal space in the lives of individuals, democratic "*Atomisierung*" may result (*US* 29). Stein maintains that if the state is to be meaningful to a group of individuals, it must be experienced in a communal form, which is marked by a communal awareness (*Gemeinschaftsbewußtseins*) (*US* 18) of solidarity—what she calls in her earlier work *ineinandergreifen*. In a communal understanding of the state, one's comportment toward the state becomes more deeply internalized, one lives more deeply the reality of the state, which is not seen as a kind of object external to oneself; rather, the state becomes better incorporated into one's living as a community. I will say more about this when I discuss further my argument concerning the relation between sovereignty and community.

Stein's third critique of contractarian states revolves around the notion of freedom and the free acts they posit. Contract theory, says Stein, presupposes that everyone freely agrees to form a state. This is to explain, at least theoretically, the origin of the state. Stein doubts this genetic account for reasons already mentioned in my discussion of her first critique. She focuses, rather, on the presupposed freedom with which all members of the state make decisions. Traditional contract theory states that individuals alienate their freedom so that others can make decisions on their behalf. For example, wives do so, according to Locke, when they yield their freedom to their husbands, who make decisions for the family, their wives, and, ultimately, the state.[14] Stein queries this alienation of freedom, especially as it deals with rights. Contractarians maintain that the freedom alienated by individuals in the contract for the sake of society and the state is natural. They give up a freedom that is naturally theirs by right. Stein argues that there is no natural right. There are "pure rights," valued regardless of differences among peoples or institutions, and there are "posited rights," usually articulated through laws and other conventions. The alienation of one's freedom is a free choice made by a free individual, but the individual in a contractarian state is only as free as the state prescribes. In essence, because the contractarian state assumes that the members of the state were originally free to alienate their freedom for the sake of the state, Stein wonders how free one really is—one wonders how true contractarian terms can be for those who are conquered and forced into the conqueror's state (*IS* 46–52). It is evident from her assessment of contract theory (and she never specifies which kind of contract theory she is criticizing) that Stein does not take a supportive view of it as a legitimate form of statehood. She is largely dismissive, although she recognizes certain aspects, especially the insistence on certain legal principles, as valid. The fact that she does not engage the possibility of a societal contractarian view in any sustained or focused way, except by way of critique, suggests a polemical, argumentative treatise rather than traditional, rigorous phenomenology.

I will now turn to my final justification for claiming that Stein's treatise on the state is more her own political theory than a strictly phenomenological investigation of the state, namely, her critique of the state in relation to ethics and religion. In the last sections of her work on the state, Stein briefly develops her positions on religion and morality (*IS* 184–93 and 172–78, respectively). Contrary to what she alleges is Dietrich von Hildebrand's view, the state must not be an ethical entity; neither must it be religious or theocratic. Her argumentation is straightforward, but it presupposes that we accept her view of the state as communal, ruled by law and sovereignty. Once we accept this view and the premises on which it rests, religious or ethical views of the state are excluded. Why? Because they undermine the very sovereignty of the state to define and determine itself; the state's autarchy is subordinated to the outside demands of morality or religion. The state, as an independent, sovereign "person," loses its very essence. The state can very well help to foster or hinder the development of various ethical and religious positions, but it is not in and of itself religious or ethical *per definitionem*. In terms of my own argument that Stein's text is more political and polemical than strictly phenomenological (though it certainly employs insights gleaned from her earlier work on phenomenology), her treatment of ethics and religion is significant because it assumes that her analysis of the sovereign state as communal is accurate and, therefore, limits what religion and ethics can do, especially in terms of the values they wish to define, instill, and promote. Stein argues that, while religion and ethics may have a place in the structure of the state, they cannot be primary. Sovereignty is principal. No phenomenology of the religious or the ethical is developed in any sustained way; rather, Stein simply asserts what they can and cannot do in light of her phenomenological description of sovereignty, which is what she feels the state ought to be.

Interpreting Stein's Concept of the Political

If we concede that Stein's treatment of the state, though marked by key phenomenological concepts that she elaborates in her earlier work, including the notions of community and the person, is also deeply influenced by her own political proclivities, one has to ask: How ought one interpret Stein's political philosophy, while being mindful of the need to bring together her own phenomenology with her political sensibilities? I venture that Stein offers us a concept of the political that includes but is not limited to a discussion of the state. I see the following elements as constituting a Steinian concept of the political:

1. The locus of politics is the sovereign state. Sovereignty is understood as the capacity of the state to self-legislate as expressed by the will of a community of state lawmakers.

2. Politics is an extension of the life of a community and, therefore, the political can be social, but one must not reduce the political to the social and vice versa. These two realms are not identical; they are related but distinct.

3. Given 2, there is no lived experience or consciousness that is peculiar to the political.

4. Stein espouses a form of liberalism that one can call personalist and communitarian.

Again, I hesitate calling Stein's political philosophy a strict phenomenology, and I see no reason why we have to limit her political theory to a phenomenological framework; after all, as she is writing this treatise her own philosophy is developing in different directions. It is expanding beyond phenomenology: she is beginning to be influenced by a formalism through her readings of Scholastic philosophy and encounters with the Bergzabern Circle, and by her own move toward a Christian-inspired philosophy.

Let us move on to the first element mentioned above. Stein identifies the state as a particular form of community between two other kinds of communities. The lowest forms of community are those that are seen to be self-enclosed or self-contained (*IS* 7). Members in such communities need no one other than their own community members and their experience of community is not derived from others, although they may be impacted by decisions of other communities. Stein has in mind here such communities as families and friendships. These can coexist with other, larger structures such as "the people" or religious communities. The highest form of community is "the one all-encompassing community of all individuals" (*US* 10). All communities are ordered within this largest sense of a spiritual community.[15] Stein describes, for example, a "people" as a larger spiritual community. A larger spiritual community might also be something like the community of humanity or the kingdom of ends, as Kant understood it, or, perhaps, the human community that is contained in God.

The state falls between these narrower and more encompassing senses of community. The state, Stein claims, is not an absolute; rather, it may both include the narrower forms of community and be part of the larger sense of community. But the state also possesses a specific character, what Stein calls a certain limit of affectability or limit to its being conditioned (*eine Grenze für die Bedingtheit*) (*US* 10), namely, what Aristotle calls *autarkia* or sovereignty (*IS* 9). Whereas Aristotle conceives of autarchy largely as the safeguarding of internal freedom and security by ensuring that one's enemies were kept at bay or that perceived threats were eliminated, Stein's modern notion of sovereignty focuses not so much on possible external threats to security and freedom (although she was not remiss in acknowledging this very important aspect). Rather, by "sovereignty" she means that the state is defined by its very capacity or power to determine itself through its own law and act of self-legislation. Another way to understand Steinian sovereignty is as the power to self-rule (*IS* 10–12). Stein understands the state power to legislate as the capacity to constrain and to allow. Deeply influenced by a nation-state understanding of sovereignty, which stems from the Westphalian notion of sovereignty, Stein sees the state as being a unique, objective entity, constituted by a community that recognizes the objective nature of the state to legislate and rule. The state is not an extension of the will of the people, nor is it a contract between people, as we saw earlier.

Stein believes that sovereignty and the right inherent in it are powerful only insofar as they are consciously recognized. But this recognition takes on a double form for Stein. First, those that claim to belong to the state community must recognize the authority and legitimacy of the state. Second, the state must recognize itself as the source of its own sovereignty. If the state depends on other states for its recognition, its very essence is compromised and it can hardly be said to be a state. Citing Samuel von Püfendorf, Stein says that such states become "*incredibile quoddam et monstro simili,*" "something akin to a monster or unbelievable" (*US* 15). What makes the state a community, according to Stein, is the conscious awareness that one lives with others, the very recognition that the state has a right to legislate, and that this right is self-identical with the origin and nature of the state.

How does the state express its sovereignty? It does so through its right to make laws. The law becomes the central and highest expression of the essence of the state. Stein's theory of law *grosso modo* consists of a doctrine of right as well as a description of certain functions of laws. Drawing from the work of Adolf Reinach,[16] Stein maintains that there is pure right as well as positive right (*IS* 38–42). Pure right refers to the capacity of the state to enact its lawmaking capacities in order to articulate rights that are applicable to all peoples at all times, regardless of circumstances and particular differences. Usually, these are expressed very generally as the right to life, freedom of movement and speech, etc. These kinds of pure rights, which are a priori for Reinach and for Stein, are akin to the universal rights declared by the French revolutionaries in the *Declaration of the Rights of Man and of the Citizen*. Positive rights are specific rights that apply to certain groups and citizens. They are articulated by a particular state in a particular time and space, and are applicable to all or some of its citizens. Pure rights are not dependent upon their declaration by the state; they are seen to exist prior to the very foundation of a particular state and as belonging to all humans a priori. Stein does not justify the theory of pure right. She simply adopts it from Reinach and declares that these rights belong to the very constitution of a person. Pure rights must be part of any state structure as they are fundamental for the very sustenance and well-being of all persons and, in the long term, for the sustenance and well-being of the whole community. Needless to say, the a priori grounding of rights is contentious, especially given Stein's reluctance to speak of natural rights. I cannot take up the matter of Stein's adoption of a priori rights here, but I do wish to signal that this easy adoption on her part is interesting, if not problematic. In essence, she wishes to secure for members of a community certain universal rights that are not contingent upon the character of a particular state or its constitutive community members. In her discussion of the a priori reality of the state as legislating, Stein also establishes a distinction, and not an identity, between the state and the people: the state is not a tool or extension of the will of the collective, for it has its own a priori objective reality. Given the horror of World War I and that Stein was to perish in a concentration camp during World War II, one can see why Stein might wish to assert an a priori theory of pure right. Alas, these rights are one of the first things that totalitarian regimes seek to eliminate or from which they seek to exempt themselves, very much as Carl Schmitt's famous "state of exception" lays out.[17]

In terms of *Rechtseztung*, or the establishment or positing of laws, Stein draws once again from Adolf Reinach's work on the a priori foundations of civil law. Reinach draws the distinction between a command, order, or ordinance (*Befehl*) and a regulation (*Bestimmung*) (*US* 41–46). Both of these are social acts. A state can command and issue orders, but for Stein, these acts are not as deeply structured as are regulations. A command addresses a particular situation and a particular object. Thus a state may pass a specific ordinance for a certain neighborhood to respect a new waste-removal protocol. Here, the structure of the act is such that a prescription is uttered and followed, it is performed. Following Reinach's logic, this is a classic performative: The act achieves its fulfillment in its being carried out by the follower of the command. But regulations are deeper structures and imply a recognition of the authority of the state, which stems both from the state itself and from the community members that live in the state (*IS* 51–52). The state can not only pass laws that are specific commands in particular situations, but it can also, through its regulations, determine the "character" of the community as well as that of the state. These regulations, and the conventions and laws that are incarnated through them, bespeak a certain disposition of the state toward its own lawmaking, its own view of and respect (or disregard) for rights, etc. Regulations are so fundamental because they are intimately linked to recognition (*Anerkennung*), whereas commands are marked by utterance and performance. This recognition is linked to one's conscious living-through of the state as lawmaker. For example, the state's recognition that it needs to establish and regulate human rights tribunals, as well as the recognition by community members that such tribunals are legitimate and belong to the very essence of the state, and the laws passed to establish the authority of such tribunals, all of these are part and parcel of a regulation. The use and abuse of regulations speak to the state's valuing of justice and right.

Given this briefly sketched notion of Steinian sovereignty, how, then, does the community embody and live this essential sovereignty? In short, the answer is freedom. Stein insists that the state produces no spiritual products of its own; it requires human persons to carry out its life and is thus considered to be an extension of the person. When Stein speaks of the state as a person, she does not mean a human person. Insofar as the state requires a personal community to animate and ground it, it can be seen to possess similar qualities. The state grows out of the life of free individuals—free because they have the capacity to freely carry out social acts—and insofar as it can determine itself, it is seen to be free from constraint. Stein makes it very clear that the state is neither necessarily identical with the people (as in Rousseau's social contract, for example) nor dependent upon the life of a certain ethnicity or ethnic group—it is not a nation or *natio*. The state can certainly overlap and coincide with these traditional political structures, but according to Stein, they are not essential to the state. Furthermore, not all members of the state community are required to be fully conscious of the solidarity that marks the life of the state. All that is minimally required is a solidarity or community-consciousness among those who are appointed to represent or carry out the work of the state (*IS* 46–47, 66–68). Stein argues that the degree of consciousness wavers in intensity and need not be seen as always having to be present before us.

The community and the state grow out of a special bond and a particular consciousness that accompanies the living of that bond. Like any communal bond, for Stein, it is marked by a solidarity in which one lives in the experience of the other, where one seizes the life of the other in a feeling of solidarity. In terms of the state, there is a special form of consciousness in which the members live in solidarity the experience of the state as having the freedom to autodetermine itself and its inhabitants. The inhabitants of the state community become an organ of the state and its freedom to legislate and enact its sovereignty.[18]

Persons in the state community give their own free *placet* or assent to the sovereignty of the state. The state only has sense if it lives within the togetherness of its subjects. We thus arrive at a strange political claim: On one hand, the state is sovereign, and must absolutely be so; yet it is rooted in the conscious recognition of the solidarity of a particular, living lawmaking, law-abiding, and law-enforcing community. Moreover, the community of state dwellers must give their own *placet* in order for the state to exist. The state is free a priori, but, on the other hand, the state is dependent upon its constituent free subjects. Once the subjects assent to give their *placet,* the state assumes its sovereign right to legislate and autodetermine itself. One can assume, rightly I think, that once this *placet* is rescinded, the sense and very existence of the state ceases. Stein regards the communal form of the state as superior to the societal form because the bond between the inhabitants of the state is more intimate and unifying, thus securing the continuation and force of the state, even its force of law (*IS* 50–51). The problem here stems from the identification of the essence of the state as a priori, which comes into conflict with the a posteriori or practical existence of the community that needs to recognize not only the practical existence of the state but also its a priori essence as a sovereign law-giver, which exists as a real thing in itself. In short, in establishing the objectivity of the state as sovereignty, it becomes difficult to negotiate the relation of the sovereign state, which has the right to exist in itself, with the will of community members who are in time and space, even if they are all in solidarity.

At this point, I would like to advance two critiques of Stein's political theory. First, the state may not be constituted by a priori sovereignty as Stein understands it, for it is still dependent upon the *placet* of its constituents. The self-positing and absolute sovereignty that Stein propounds is compromised. This is the case because the state, insofar as it is an arm of the community's freedom, is an extension of the life of the community that forms it. Moreover, the state is dependent upon the recognition and acceptance of the unique sovereign status within the shared life of community members. The state is dependent upon the solidarity of recognition that stems from the community. Second, even if we were to concede that the state has an absolute right to determine itself, it could do so only in relation to other states, much like Aristotle's sense of sovereignty. Internally, it could not carry out its own free acts without the *placet* of community members. One might even question to what extent its external sovereignty might be possible without the recognition of its own inhabitants.

Furthermore, one could argue that the sovereignty of the state is identical with the *placet* of the community, and if this is the case, we have a fusion of state and community, especially if it is lived and experienced as a solidarity of one's living and seizing the experience of the other. Given history, what makes this claim chillingly ironic is that the state community becomes an absolute end in itself, especially if, to use contractarian terms, "all people" or "the whole people" or the "general will" do not concede or assent to the (absolute?) sovereign objectivity of the state. What seems to be lacking here is some inherent opposition or, in the spirit of Montesquieu, important checks and balances. There is always the risk, in Stein's account of the state and the state community, that, unchecked, they can become fused, even totalitarian. It could be argued, then, that Stein's notion of sovereignty is deeply colored by the legacy of absolutist notions of sovereignty common in the states of her day.

The second element constitutive of the Steinian concept of the political focuses on the relation between the social and the political. In order to understand this relation, we need to discuss her notion of the person vis-à-vis the state. In Stein's view, the state is analogically similar to the person. Stein refrains here from using the classic liberal discourse of the individual and individuality that is conceived as property. What, then, could it mean to think of the state as a person? Stein is aware that her claim is very problematic, for example, the state has no body, psyche, and spirit as in the discussion of personhood and empathy. She first makes it very clear that person is not to be understood as an object, that is, as some kind of superstructure or superindividual, much like Hobbes's *Leviathan,* which will ensure the sovereignty or autarchy of the state. It is also evidently clear that if Stein simply means here that the state is to be conceived as having similar traits or as being grounded in persons, paralleling the work of Püfendorf or Grotius, then there is nothing new about her claim. Stein indeed draws upon traditional European political theory and sees the value of such notions as the juridical and moral person. These certainly belong to the rich thesaurus of Enlightenment politics (*IS* 54–58, 86–89).

The specific introjection of phenomenology into Stein's concept of the political, however, occurs precisely within the framework of her discussion of person. The last part of Stein's text on the state deals with the ethicality and religious dimension of the state. Here, we see the conviction that both ethics and religion are the constitutive layers where one most emblematically sees the personal nature of the state manifest itself. The values that arise within the phenomenological analysis of religion and ethics are not the same values that one will find when one deals with matters that relate to feelings or the body. There is a hierarchy of values that cannot be merely reduced to those of economic exchange (Adam Smith), contractual obligations (Rousseau, Locke) or duties (Kant), or mere feelings or sympathy (Hume). The state is an extension of the personal because it is a bearer (*Träger*) of the subjective values of both individuals and the community. It is in ethical and religious values that we see the life or "character" of the state emerge, especially if it is a community of people as opposed merely to a society.

A specific phenomenological contribution of Stein's concept of the state draws from Max Scheler's *Wertlehre*.[19] Scheler maintains that a hierarchy of values exists, which incarnates itself in different layers of the person. The hierarchy moves from the bodily and the material to the psychological to the spiritual (*geistlich*). There are five value-ranks: the bodily or tactile, the useful, life-values, mental and cultural, holy and unholy. The last two orders of values are uniquely personal in that they are not merely rooted in the bodily or the useful; they bring to the fore the higher structures of the person, especially the person as she or he dwells in the social and political life-world. Examples of higher-order values include such things as the lived experience of such values as "good," "bad," "ugly," "beautiful," or the value of the "cognition of truth" or "justice and injustice." The experiencing or living through of such values does not necessarily occur only at the levels of feelings—a higher-order structure is needed to localize such experiences as they are complex and cross all three human realms of body, psyche, and spirit (*Geist*). This is what Stein, Scheler, and phenomenology in general mean by "person." Stein's extensive treatment of religion, history, and ethics at the end of her work on the state testifies to the priority she assigns to these domains as helping to foster and preserve these higher-order layers of the person (*IS* 134–39). I see Stein's treatment of the state as developing a concept of relation. The state is defined as a personal relation, and it is the relation of persons that determines the values, from higher to lower, as well as the objective and material structure of the state. The state, then, becomes the extension of the life of the social relations of its members, including its values. Also, insofar as the state is defined as a bearer or *Träger*, it can be viewed as a kind of retainer or holder of such relations.

If the state is described as a form of social relation among persons, two questions then arise. First, why are not traditional forms of statehood—including democracy, tyranny, theocracy, republics, aristocracy, etc.—not identified as essential to the nature of the state? Second, what is to distinguish the state relation from other communal or societal relations in general? In other words, what makes the state a specific form of social relation that is not reducible to the three forms of sociality mentioned earlier? Concerning the first question, Stein gives many examples of social relations under various forms of government, including democracy, theocracy, and even aristocracy. But she does not confuse these forms of government with the essence of the state itself. The claim here is that at the core of any form or concept of the political is personal, social relations; they are considered to be constitutive. The state is not to be identified merely by its form of rule or power structure. To do so would be to rip power out of its essential source, namely, the person. Given the brilliant analyses of power as embodied and executed through an institutional state apparatus, especially in the work of Michel Foucault and Louis Althusser, for example, the Steinian claim here seems either deeply misguided or lacking. In her defense, Stein would readily acknowledge the objective forms of power present in social structures or, to borrow from Husserl's terminology, higher social objectivities. In the end, however, all institutions are still extensions of human persons. Power at its core is a deeply subjective and personal phenomenon, rooted in the body, psyche, and spirit. This is what is meant by the motivational power of the *Ich kann*.

Is Stein's account adequate? Yes and no. At the heart of any politics is a social relation. One can look at every political system and see that, either explicitly or implicitly, it is the organization of social relations that is key to achieving a certain political vision. If Stein is correct, we then have to deal with our second question, which cuts more directly to a potential philosophical problem. What distinguishes Stein's analysis of the state from her analysis of social relations carried out in her earlier work? Is not the state in its highest form just a particular form of community? Stein would have to agree that the state can be a particular form of community—for example, the community of a certain people—but it is not only and necessarily this. In the state, we do find three general types of social relations. What, then, makes Stein's treatment of the state political and not social? The political character of the state is located in the claim that the state has its essence in autarchy or sovereignty, that is, its own being as free, from within and from without. The specific forms of societies and communities, which have as their unifying (*Solidarität*) essence the collective autonomy of the persons in the community, as well the masses coexist in a state; the state is defined by its very freedom to shape and live the relations of its member-persons in the way it chooses through lawmaking capacities (*IS* 2–7). This is the very condition for the possibility of the state. Just as Husserl conceives the *Ich kann* as deeply constitutive of the spiritual motivation that marks the higher layers of the person, so too can Steinian sovereignty be thought of as the extension of the Husserlian *Ich kann*. She speaks of the "[State] *kann*" (*US* 7). Stein even redefines autonomy by rooting it in the personal-phenomenological language of the Husserlian "I can." The peculiar essence of the state is the preservation and actualisation of the "I can" on a collective level or for the community. Other forms of community presuppose some kind of autonomy, but do not have autonomy itself as their constitutive essence. For example, a community of friends may enjoy each other's company for various reasons, and this is a social relation, but this community then becomes fundamentally political when questions of autonomy or sovereignty and all that it implies, structurally and materially, arise.

If the state is conceived as a social relation with autonomy being its peculiar political defining determination, then one can rightly say that the social is intimately connected to the political. But on Stein's account, again, what is peculiar is the relation between the social and the political. It would appear that the social serves as the foundation for the political as the life of the state is primarily defined in communal terms (*IS* 17–25). Given that autonomy is a *sine qua non* of the state community of lawmakers, one could rightly assume that the state is pivotal in securing autonomy for all social relations in general. It is at this point where Stein wishes to maintain a relation between the social and the political, but at the same time she will make them very distinct and separate. She argues that the relations of the state are not reducible to social relations in general because these social relations can exist outside of the objective structures of the state; the state is not the sole guarantor of autonomy. Stein believes that individual persons embody the *Ich kann* of phenomenological freedom and responsibility. If we are to speak of the state *Ich kann*, then we do so in a different frame of reference, that is, a collective autonomy geared at expressing the chosen, desired, and sometimes coerced sum of human relations. The state always exists in relation to this very individual and personal reality. Though related, one cannot reduce the social to the political, as do more contemporary thinkers like Foucault. For Stein, following Scheler, an example of the non-political, profound human relations can exist in communities of love that can be deeply altruistic.

Stein's desire to preserve the distinction and relation between the political and the social now brings me to my third claim made at the outset of this section regarding the impossibility of what I call a lived experience of the political. Though Stein develops a phenomenological language and theory to account for community through the employment of her concept of the *Gemeinschaftserlebnis,* she refrains from extending this analysis to developing a particular lived experience of the political, a *Politischeserlebnis* or *Staatserlebnis*. In other words, though Stein develops a whole concept of the political through her treatment of the state, she refrains from discussing a particular form of consciousness that is uniquely political or stately. The state is grasped within the rubric of the communal or the social, even though it has its own objectivity. Perhaps this weakens the force of Stein's phenomenological concept of the political. At this point, I would simply say that the lack of the aforesaid analysis should not be read as a weakness but more as a phenomenological claim that acknowledges the profound link between the political and the social while keeping them distinct. I also believe that the lack of a *Staatserlebnis* is faithful to the phenomenological fact that communities and societies can exist outside of the political, that is, not all societies and states are reducible to the political. Of course, we have to question whether the Steinian claim that the political manifests itself within the rubric of internal and external sovereignty or autarchy is adequate enough, but this is another question that lies beyond our immediate focus.

I can see two reasons why Stein would not want to argue for the possibility of a lived experience of the state proper. First, there are historical reasons. Second, to argue for a lived experience of the state[20] and to link it with state politics proper is to render the state an abstract, objective entity insofar as it need not be identified with the personal, thereby resulting in various potential problems like alienation.

Let us turn first to an analysis of history. The Germany that Stein grew up in and lived in was a nation-state. Political identity and the state were determined in large part by ethnic categories. To be German was to have certain rights and privileges, a shared history, personality, culture, education, language, and belief system. The state was identified with the nation or the *Volk*. To be German or Prussian was identical with what it was to be a state. The state was not primarily identified by its type of government or its economic policy or its alliances, etc. The politics of nation-states and the accompanying chauvinism and desire for larger territories to sustain economic growth and standards of living all had large roles to play in the carnage and vicious disaster that was World War I. State, community, and nation (people or *Volk*) had all become synonymous. Writing her text on the state after World War I and living through the results where consciousness of one's ethnic identity was equivalent to state consciousness certainly would have made Stein reluctant to want to speak of lived experience of the state proper. Think of Scheler's turn from a very nationalist politics prior to World War I and his renunciation of his previous views after the First World War.[21]

Also, their defeat in the war plunged Germany into a political identity crisis. How could one think of the state without totalizing it as an ethnic or German project? This became all the more relevant, especially if one thinks of what happened in World War II. Stein's proposal to think of the state as a communal experience that is not exclusively defined by nationalist/ethnic consciousness and that could include a multiplicity of experiences grounded in various types of community, including religious, ethical, linguistic, history, cultural, ethnic types, etc., has a double significance. First, there is a shifting away from a state politics of the nation-state. Second, state identity becomes determined not from a grand totalizing or absolutizing narrative of ethnic identity, but becomes localized in various senses within the respective lives of a multiplicity of communities. Ultimately, Stein's silence about a *Staatserlebnis* addresses the disaster of a previous generation of thinkers and politicians that identified the state with an ethnic community by separating the two. She also posits a politics of smaller communities wherein the state can be localized and experienced, and *not* a politics of the state where all communities are localized and ultimately find their *raison d'être*. In her silence and in her description of communities where states dwell within the mental life of the person as well as externally Stein has undermined a political legacy of chauvinism and totalitarianism.

The second reason why I venture that Stein does not posit a *Staatserlebnis* or a lived experience of the state proper is because it would result in political depersonalization. We saw how Stein's description of the state is personalist in that she conceives of the state as essentially analogous to a person.[22] The state does not exist in and of itself; it is not an end in and to itself. It is an extension of persons and their lives; it exists within people as well as being defined by people, especially with regard to external limits like national boundaries, economic rights, and international recognition. Stein describes members of the state as "carriers" of the life of the state.[23] Arguing that the state is experienced principally but not exclusively[24] within the life and being of various communities means that the experience of the state is intimately linked with individual and personal experience. It is something that can be experienced as superindividual and as communalizing, but it need not be totalizing and need not become a thing in and of itself, lying outside or abstracted from the personalist sphere. That is, it need not become an object to which all persons and subjects must adhere or work toward, as was the case with Hegelian and nation-state visions of the state. If the state becomes a superindividual object or reality it can easily alienate or become detached from the realm of human experience. It becomes a thing like any other thing, but perhaps with greater or lesser value, depending on the situation in which we find ourselves. One can feel more attached or unified to the state within the various communal experiences of it, if it is experienced as something personal rather than objective. Not only is there a different kind of relation, but it is lived with a different kind of intensity as well. The objectivity and intensity of living with and through a nation-state and its absolutist tendencies to negate individuality and consciousness (think of World Wars I and II) are quite different from living through the experience of communal solidarity that is not exclusively defined by national interests, but which may include other interests and experiences like religion, language, history, culture, etc. Whereas the totalitarian view of the nation-state stresses a political narrative of unity and identity that transcends individuality, the Steinian view of the state as communal makes possible the coincidence of individuality and community, unity and difference.[25] Recall that the individual is never lost, but one can experience in one's own individuality the experience of a community, including a state community. The individual need not be alienated from the state as the state dwells within the individual person and the communities of persons. Hence, Stein's famous line that there is no individual person proper. There exists only a community of persons.[26] Despite this argument, one must also be mindful of the earlier argument that noted a certain tension between the a priori sovereignty of the state and its possible identification with a community of lawgivers. Undoubtedly, in the end, the reader is left with a problem of how to interpret Steinian sovereignty.

Stein offers us, however, an insight into political thinking. She follows and, ultimately, is critical of a tradition of political thought that gave the political a special place in consciousness. Stein's silence about a lived experience of the state proper could be read as correcting the past view that gave to the state its own absolute inner and outer structure, inevitably depersonalizing and alienating individuals from both the possibility of a legitimate personal self-hood and the experience of community outside of the determinations of the state. In this way, Stein's text may be read not only as an alternative or corrective of a past nationalist politics but also as a blueprint for a future political view of the state that describes it as an extension of a personalist community where both individual and community properly coincide.

I will now turn to my fourth claim. Given Stein's emphasis on community, I believe that we can rightly claim that the distinct flavor of her concept of the political is personal and communitarian. She draws upon certain liberal principles, especially autonomy, but she also develops a communitarian theory of the state that is deeply rooted in the phenomenological notion of person, understood both as an eidetic structure of a mind-psyche-spiritual unity as well as in terms of the person as a bearer of values. In this respect, we can call Stein a personal communitarian who sets her discussion of personhood and community within a certain kind of liberal framework.

We end where we started in this chapter by looking at how Stein's phenomenology intersects with liberalism. While it is true that Edith Stein articulated various critiques of liberalism, especially of the contractarian sort, one must not dismiss liberalism altogether from her theory of the state in favor of a strict communitarian or personalist vision of the state.[27] I argue here that Stein does not outright reject liberalism. Again, while there is a general consensus that Stein drew inspiration from liberal ideals, scholars tend to focus on the phenomenological roots of Stein's political theory.[28] In fact, her theory of the state, including her arguments for the primacy of the rule of law, draws heavily from certain liberal precepts based on her own philosophical and personal political convictions. Stein's unique contribution to political theory lies in her interweaving of insights gleaned from her phenomenology of community, her Prussian liberal convictions about the primacy of freedom and the law, and her own reworkings of certain key tenets of German Idealist political philosophy, especially those of Hegel and Fichte. A failed nationalism and defeated nation-state, a collapsed monarchy, and the desiccated ideals of Otto von Bismarck, all of which came crashing to a halt after the First World War—these marks of political orders that once deeply influenced Stein, both negatively and positively, and pushed her to join the German Democratic Party, form part of what she had to contend with in her own political philosophy. One could conjecture, perhaps, that Stein was hoping to avoid the errors of the past and that she wanted to argue for a future political possibility for her own country and perhaps even for countries around the world. Part of that future wish and hope lay in a reworked liberalism.

It would be terribly naïve to speak of liberalism as if the term denoted a clear and distinct political concept. Liberalism is a movement marked by certain shared convictions, but it is in no way a univocal term. We have a plethora of senses, always embedded within specific cultural frameworks, of a liberal form of political rule. For our purposes here, I would like to define the concept of liberalism in the following way. First, as the name suggests, liberalism denotes a project of emancipation. It demarcates a political movement that seeks to give to its adherents freedom from autocratic, tyrannical, oligarchic, or plutocratic rule: in this sense, liberalism is associated with a *liberation from* a state of rule conceived as oppressive. This is what is called "negative freedom." But liberalism also seeks to establish a positive sense of freedom, whereby individuals should, once free from constraint, express their freedom through acts and decisions rooted in their own deliberative processes and conscious actions. When I think of positive and negative freedom, I have in mind the distinction made by Sir Isaiah Berlin.[29] Ideally, in a liberal state, *all*, not some or a few, legitimate members would possess the free agency to express their political desires. One does so, of course, through mutually agreed-upon conventions such as referenda, elections, votes, etc. When one chooses to abide by such means of free expression and agency, one also becomes alienated from one's complete freedom. One submits oneself to mutually agreed-upon mechanisms whereby the results of procedures such as elections have force. So, for example, one submits to the will of the majority, even though one may not hold the majority view.

Also constituent of liberal theory *grosso modo* are a developed sense of individuation, a respect for the rule of law, a system of checks and balances in government, an economic system deeply rooted in a sense of property and, often, free trade animated by a largely capitalist framework, a just distribution of goods, and, finally, a highly articulated and developed sense of rights, privileges, freedoms, and responsibilities. With the exception of free-trade capitalism, I would say that Edith Stein mentions or discusses all of these elements in her political philosophy. This being said, there is also a firm materialism in Stein's account of the state, especially as the state requires a territory, understood in the foundational sense developed by Rudolf Kjellén.[30] It would be fair to say that a liberal lineage looms large in her work on the state. This might be largely attributable to her connection to the German Democratic Party after World War I, as well as to her Prussian sensibilities. Let us not forget that, at the end of her doctoral dissertation on empathy, she identified herself as Prussian in her brief biographical sketch. It was the Prussian state that advanced various reforms that made larger Germany not only economically viable, but also granted greater participation to groups and individuals that had traditionally been considered outsiders, such as the Jews.[31] Stein certainly admired the strong centralization of the Prussian state, as well as its strong sense of identity and Enlightenment thinking.

Edith Stein's political philosophy can be defined as liberal, but, as is so often the case with Stein, with a twist. Her particular twist lies in the insertion of her theory of community into a traditional liberal framework. Three critical elements mark Stein's project as liberal, namely, a robust sense of freedom and autonomy that is grounded in the state community, an insistence on the primacy of law, and her arguments for both a priori civil rights as well as positive ones, understood from both the perspective of the state and that of the subjects of the state. We have discussed these elements above.

Furthermore, as a liberal, Stein never exclusively grounds the formal reality of the state in the life of a people, race, nation, or leader. The more traditional and then-timely categories of, first, "a people" (*Volk*)—defined by belonging to a certain ethnic, religious, or racial group—and second, a "nation," as in the concept of the nation-state, are limiting. A state can include various peoples, ethnicities, religious groups, races, etc., living within its domain, and though a common ethnic legacy among its subjects may, for example, help the state to act in a unified fashion, it can also be quite dangerous, as the outcome of the First World War demonstrated. Stein was all too familiar with the deadly results that can ensue from nationalist visions of the nation-state, especially such as those of Max Scheler (*US* 23n59). Stein preferred to see the state as not being confined to a specific group other than legislators, though differing communities could dwell within the state (*US* 24–25). Why? She argues that the very sovereignty of the state, its essential structure, can be easily compromised or undermined if the state becomes subject to the will of a specific group. The state can never absorb the lives of private individuals (*IS* 16–19), and it would seem that if the state were to identify with a nation or people, the autonomy of the state itself, understood as autolegislating and autodetermining, would be severely compromised.

In the end, for Stein, a state community is preferable because the bonds between its members would be stronger, as community is the most intense kind of sociality. One can certainly have societal types of associative relations (*Zusammenlebens*) in the state (*US* 5), but this kind of relationship or bond is not strong enough for Stein; the state is not fully or intensely lived within the lives of the members of the state. Here, one would live the state simply as a task to be achieved, a job to be carried out, etc. Stein claims that the state requires a deeper kind of bond, a bond that is not purely functional and externally directed; this she calls community. One is reminded of Aristotle's claim that, in order for the life of the polis to thrive, *philia* is stronger and more essential than *diké* or justice.

We come now to that which makes the state liveable, understood in a rich phenomenological sense, as a state—namely, the community. For Stein, the state should be "lived in common" as "companions in existence" (*US* 6). Community is a relation among persons marked by a certain kind of conscious lived experience, that of solidarity. Solidarity (and not love, as was the case for Aristotle) is marked by one's living in the experience of the other in a deeply felt and unified way. There is an *ineinandergreifen* and a *miteinandergreifen* that define solidarity as opposed to the relations of the masses or those of society. A consciousness of community must be manifest in the members of the state for the state relation to be lived most intensely.[32] So communal consciousness, as a living in and with the other in solidarity, marks a community as a community, and, in particular, as a state-community.

Here, we are also reminded of the German Idealist tradition, especially of Fichte and Hegel, who speak of the importance of state consciousness for understanding the structure or moment of the state. Stein is aware of this legacy, but she rejects the teleological development of Hegel's concept of the state and the Fichtean notion of property and appropriation rooted in a self-positing ego as primary.

CRITICAL ASSESSMENT

On one hand, Stein's view of the state is infused with modern characteristics: sovereignty, freedom, rights, rule of law, and room for a multiplicity of ethical and religious traditions to come to full expression. On the other hand, the bond between members of the state is communal: the state requires members to live together in some kind of solidarity. But this solidarity, for Stein, consists in recognizing the sovereignty of the state. It is precisely the nature of Steinian sovereignty that I find problematic for her claims about solidarity and community. In essence, I maintain that Stein's view of sovereignty is so ideal and absolute, so a priori, that it runs the risk of creating strong opposition within the state-community and in relation to other communities dwelling within the state. How can I justify my claim that Steinian sovereignty is too pure, too absolute?

First, although Stein admits that only a few people are required to live the experience of solidarity in relation to state sovereignty, she argues for a strong separation of private life and state life (*IS* 35–36). Though members of the state-community have private lives, the state has primacy of place (*IS* 37). When Stein argues against the state being constituted by a people or nation, she is seeking to prevent the subordination of the state to the particular wishes and wills of specific interests rooted in the identity of peoples and nations (which include things such as views on blood and race, certain values and ethical views, and religious tenets). Stein regarded such interests as compromising the right of the state to autolegislate. In the case of rule by nations or peoples, law and right become subject to desire, situation, and context. We must not forget Stein's acceptance of a priori right and the *conditio sine qua non* of such a priori right, namely, the right to self-legislate or autarchy. It is this a priori demand on the part of Stein's *Staatslehre* that I find difficult. It bespeaks a supposed universality, yet wishes to ignore the very source of such universality—the diverse multiplicities of peoples and nations that constitute all states. The primacy of Steinian sovereignty and her unmitigated defense of a formal, unconditioned view of sovereignty as legislative run the same risk as Hegel's *Rechtsphilosophie*, in which the ideal, under which all is subsumed, has its own life.

One can object, rightly I think, to my position and argue that, even though Stein stresses an a priori or pure, abstract view of sovereignty, she makes room for the differences and personalities that constitute the state. Indeed, inclusion of these differences is evident in her treatment of the necessity and role of diverse ethical and religious values within the life of the state. Her treatment of positive rights also suggests room for the personalities and individual desires of various groups to come to the fore in the life of the state. There is nothing to say that the state could not legislate laws that would protect, say, specific minority rights, which may be specific to a particular group, people, or even nation. I maintain, however, that such laws and reforms come neither from the will of the people nor from the experience of an oppressed minority. It remains the state, as distinct from any or all of the people, which concedes these rights. The state is not the people; rather, it is its own organic, self-sufficient, or sovereign power. The state chooses to respond to various events and requests, but there is no direct democracy here. Just as the state may choose to listen to the concerns of some or all of its citizens, it may equally and rightfully choose to ignore its citizens, and it is this possibility, lodged within the conceptual purity of Steinian sovereignty, that I find potentially dangerous.

My second argument revolves around Stein's notion of "people." It is clear from her text that she understands "people" in terms of "a people," or *Volk*. Traditionally, the German notion of "a people" has had definite racial, ethnic, and even religious connotations attached to it. But if we understand "people" more broadly as, for example, the people of Rousseau's *la volonté générale,* or in terms of the U.S. Constitution's "We the People...," then perhaps a more encompassing and more intensely lived notion of sovereignty, directly attached to the *placet* and wills of the broader state-community, might be possible. But Stein's notion of sovereignty, understood as the *conditio sine qua non* and the very essence of the state, cannot be seen as an extension of the will of such a people. The state is not an instrument of the will of the people; rather, it has its own proper ontological status. In contractarian theory, the state may be sovereign. But one chooses to alienate one's freedom in order to live in the state. Stein has no room for such a move. Jerome Kohn, Hannah Arendt's student, editor, and one of her literary executors, remarks that Arendt was highly critical of politics based on sovereignty: to Arendt, "perhaps the greatest American innovation in politics...was the consistent abolition of sovereignty within the body politic of the Republic, the insight that in the realm of human affairs sovereignty and tyranny are the same. The lack of sovereignty of the republic meant that it was not a national state in the European sense; its power did arise from the people, from the increasing diversity of the people and opinions it incorporated."[33] This powerful critique cuts right to the core of Edith Stein's political philosophy.

Why does Stein insist on such a strong sense of legislative sovereignty? In part, I think she wishes to avoid the excesses of past regimes that resulted in unimaginable violence, terrible defeats, and crushing human losses. Second, given her Prussian sensibilities and the chaos of her times, Stein believed that a strong centralizing power was essential to help navigate the factioned German political landscape. If the state, however, is distinguished and separated from its constituents, as Stein's view of communal solidarity vis-à-vis a sovereign state contends, then the state can turn against its own people and even refuse to identify itself with its people. The state risks becoming its own community, cut off from the other communities that make the state possible. One also wonders whether the state, as conceived by Stein, will necessarily heed or give voice to critical opposition, that is, opposition that might call for the state to compromise some of its privileged and prized sovereignty. If Stein had developed her treatment of the role of other communities in the state, perhaps she could have produced a tempered and more viable doctrine of the state.

Finally, the invocation of sovereign solidarity as constituent of the state gives us momentary pause. Though it is the most intense form of community ascribed to the state, I wonder if it is the most viable. If we were to employ a more societal model, though the state would become more functional and less intimate for us, it might better serve us in achieving a good life together. Given that so few of the members of the state can experience the sovereign solidarity that Stein invokes (as she admits when she argues that only a few are necessary for the state-community to actualize itself), the state runs the risk of becoming oligarchic. History has shown us the many difficulties that arise with such an order. A societal view of the state would create a greater distance between the state and its members, and the comportment of the latter toward the being of the state would certainly change. The state would become the *Funktionsorgan* or the means by which needs could be satisfied and goods and services delivered for the well-being of its members. One would thus live or experience the state as a means to an end. Stein, I speculate, would argue that this model has been tried before and that it resulted in the alienation of people from the state, as was the case in modern Europe, especially in its so-called empires. There, the direct consequence of this alienation was Marxism, which Stein neither fully embraced nor dismissed. She remained committed to liberalism, but with the twist of reworking the social relations within traditional liberalism as a communal relationship to the law on the part of certain members of the state.

Obviously, I cannot delineate the pros and cons of a societal model in Steinian terms as this was not Stein's focus. What I can do, however, is raise the possibility of such a model vis-à-vis her views of community. In the end, Stein's view is understandable, especially given historical events and her own political interests, but one wonders whether such a view can accommodate the radical personalism that she developed in her later philosophy, where the person and God became primary and where the state was no longer taken up as a theme of sustained inquiry.

Conclusion

Edith Stein's early work in philosophy and phenomenology are rich sources of social and political insight. Her particular focus on consciousness and the senses it affords for our understanding of self, others, and superindividual realities, including the masses, society, community, and the state, provide us with a comprehensive account of a particular aspect of reality. It would be a mistake to claim that her account is exhaustive and can be employed to explain all aspects of social and political reality. In fact, her account is quite specific: she is focused on how we understand and live, always from within our interiorities, the phenomenal experiences of self, others, the masses, society, community, and the state. One question that plagues ego-based philosophies concerns transcendence, that is, how can we move our own consciousness to experience other minds or realities outside of ourselves? This problem has persistently plagued philosophers like Descartes and Husserl. Stein's answer to this question, given what I have argued here in this book, is that one can never completely transcend one's own ego. One's experience is always still one's own experience, but I-consciousness has the capacity to experience different objects or experiences, and what is experienced objectively is not simply reducible to the I's own fashioning or projection. For Stein, social objectivities, including the essence of the human person, the other, the masses, society, community, and the state admit their own sense and have their own *Inhalt* or content, to borrow an expression from Husserl.

Stein is firmly convinced, like her teacher Husserl, that one can know and understand the meaning of objects outside of our own conscious experience. Objects, including social and political ones, are independent realities and they communicate their sense to our minds; they have meaning for us. This is an important point because it is vital for understanding how we can view Stein's social and political philosophy in a more comprehensive, unified fashion. The text on empathy reveals that an individual I comes to understand that she participates in and shares a common essence, namely, all Is are human persons. The I can confirm this knowledge through empathy, which grants access to other minds and helps confirm our shared essence. The I and the other I or alter ego are co-given to one another, that is, they are not deductions or projections; they are primordially co-present. Human persons, Stein observes, exist in social relations: mass, society, community, and the state. These relations can be explored from different angles, including sociology, psychology, geography, economics, political science, etc. Stein certainly draws from these sciences in her own analyses. But she also claims that they can be explored from the perspective of our own lived experience, how we live and experience such phenomena. These social and political realities have meaning or sense "for us," in our own interior lives. It is at the level of sense that we must read Stein's particular contribution.

Sense can constantly thicken, become more robust, granting us fuller understanding. Husserl used to speak of sense as saturation or an object being "pregnant," full, of sense. Indeed, this is what was so exciting for Stein and Husserl: philosophy and phenomenology can probe the essence of reality, and reality reveals that it has profound layers of sense, which it can yield to anyone who is willing to pay attention; reality can give to both mind and existence great possibilities of complexity and depth of comprehension. Husserl claims that consciousness is the wonder of all wonders because it is the gateway that allows us to marvel at the richness of things. Stein shares this conviction. Her early social and political philosophy unpacks what she thought was rich about our experience of ourselves, others, and the social and political realities we dwell in; we can read this work as a contribution to what she later calls the science or study of subjectivity. In order not to reduce her thinking to a static Platonic essence, it is our task to think and rethink her claims. This is what I tried to do, not in order to give a definitive interpretation, but to open up the discussion of her claims. My hope is that future scholars and philosophers will carry on the work of interrogating and pondering Edith Stein's profound and far-reaching philosophical legacy.

Notes

Notes to Chapter 1

1. Angela Ales Bello, "Edmund Husserl and Edith Stein: The Question of the Human Subject," trans. Antonio Calcagno, *American Catholic Philosophical Quarterly* 82, no. 1 (Winter 2008), 143–60; Angela Ales Bello, "Ontology, Metaphysics, and Life in Edith Stein," in *Contemplating Edith Stein*, ed. J. A. Berkman (Notre Dame, IN: University of Notre Dame Press, 2006), 271–82; Angela Ales Bello, "The Study of the Soul between Psychology and Phenomenology in Edith Stein," in *Cultura: International Journal of Philosophy of Culture and Axiology* 8 (2007): 90–108; Prudence Allen, "Edith Stein: The Human Person as Male and Female," in *Images of the Human: The Philosophy of the Human Person in a Religious Context*, ed. Prudence Allen (Chicago: Loyola Press, 1995), 399–432; Sarah Borden Sharkey, *Thine Own Self: Individuality in Edith Stein's Later Writings* (Washington, DC: Catholic University of America Press, 2009); Joyce Avrech Berkman, "Edith Stein: A Life Veiled and Unveiled," *American Catholic Philosophical Quarterly* 82, no. 1 (Winter 2008): 5–30; Joyce Avrech Berkman, ed., *Contemplating Edith Stein* (Notre Dame, IN: University of Notre Dame Press, 2006).

2. Alasdair MacIntyre, *Edith Stein: A Philosophical Prologue, 1913–1922* (Lanham, MD: Rowman and Littlefield, 2006).

3. "Homily of John Paul II for the Canonization of Edith Stein," Oct. 11, 1998, St. Peter's Basilica, Rome, www.vatican.va/holy_father/john_paul_ii/homilies/1998/documents/hf_jp-ii_hom_11101998_stein_en.html (accessed Aug. 20, 2014).

4. Marianne Sawicki, *Body, Text and Science: The Literacy of Investigative Practices and the Phenomenology of Edith Stein* (Boston: Kluwer Academic Press, 1997); MacIntyre, *Edith Stein: A Philosophical Prologue;* Reuben Guilead, *De la phénoménologie à la science de la croix: L'itinéraire d'Edith Stein* (Leuven, Belgium: Éditions Nauwelaerts, 1974).

5. See, for example, Sarah Borden Sharkey, "What Makes You You?: Edith Stein on Individual Form," in *Contemplating Edith Stein*, ed. J. A. Berkman (Notre Dame, IN: University of Notre Dame Press, 2006), 283–300; Sharkey, *Thine Own Self;* Patrizia Manganaro, *Verso l'altro. L'esperienza mistica tra interiorità e trascendenza* (Rome: Città Nuova, 2002); Peter Schulz, "Toward the

Subjectivity of the Human Person: Edith Stein's Contribution to the Theory of Identity," *American Catholic Philosophical Quarterly* 82, no. 1 (Winter 2008): 161–76.

6. Edith Stein, letter to Roman Ingarden, Feb. 19, 1918, in *Edith Stein: Self-Portrait in Letters (1916–1942)*, trans. Josephine Koeppel (Washington, DC: ICS Publications, 1994), 19.

7. Edmund Husserl, *Ideas Pertaining to a Pure Phenomenology and to a Phenomenological Philosophy*, trans. R. Rojcewicz and A. Schuwer, vol. 2 (The Hague: Springer, 1990); Edmund Husserl, *Ideas Pertaining to a Pure Phenomenology and to a Phenomenological Philosophy*, trans. T. E. Klein and W. E. Pohl, vol. 3 (The Hague: Springer, 2001); Edmund Husserl, *On the Phenomenology of the Consciousness of Internal Time (1893–1917)*, trans. J. B. Brough (The Hague: Springer, 1992); Antonio Calcagno, "Assistant and/or Collaborator? Edith Stein's Relationship to Edmund Husserl's *Ideas II*," in *Contemplating Edith Stein*, ed. J. A. Berkman (Notre Dame, IN: University of Notre Dame Press, 2006), 243–70.

8. Edith Stein, *Potency and Act*, trans. W. Redmond (Washington, DC: ICS Publications, 2009); *Finite and Eternal Being*, trans. K. F. Reinhardt (Washington, DC: ICS Publications, 2002); *Übersetzungen (III und IV) des Hl. Thomas von Aquino Untersuchungen über die Wahrheit—Quaestiones disputatae de veritate 1 und 2*, in *Edith Stein Gesamtausgabe*, ed. H. B. Gerl-Falkovitz (Freiburg: Herder Verlag, 2008).

9. Edith Stein, letter to Hedwig Conrad-Martius, Nov. 17, 1935, in *Self-Portrait in Letters*, 219–20.

10. Edith Stein, *Was ist der Mensch?*, in *Edith Stein Gesamtausgabe*, vol. 15, ed. B. Beckmann-Zöller (Freiburg: Herder, 2005); Edith Stein, *Der Aufbau der menschlichen Person*, in *Edith Stein Gesamtausgabe*, vol. 14, ed. B. Beckmann-Zöller (Freiburg: Herder, 2010); Edith Stein, *Einführung in die Philosophie*, ed. H. B. Gerl-Falkovitz and C. M. Wulf (Freiburg: Herder, 2004).

11. Jean-Luc Marion, *God without Being* (Chicago: University of Chicago Press, 1991), and *Being Given: Toward a Phenomenology of Givenness* (Palo Alto, CA: Stanford University Press, 2002).

12. For feminism examples, see Linda Lopez McAlister, "Edith Stein: Essential Differences," *Philosophy Today* 37 (Spring 1993): 70–77; and her "Edith Stein: Essential Differences," in *Contemplating Edith Stein*, ed. J. A. Berkman (Notre Dame, IN: University of Notre Dame Press, 2006), 201–11. For anthropology examples, see Anna Maria Pezzella, *L'Antropologia filosofica di Edith Stein: Indagine fenomenologica della persona umana* (Rome: Città Nuova, 2003).

13. See John Paul II's encyclical *Fides et ratio: On the Relationship between Faith and Reason: Encyclical Letter of John Paul II* (Washington, DC: Pauline Media Books, 2000), 74. Also available at www.vatican.va/holy_father/john_paul_ii/encyclicals/documents/hf_jp-ii_enc_15101998_fides-et-ratio_en.html.

14. Herbert Spiegelberg, *The Phenomenological Movement: A Historical Introduction* (The Hague: Nijhoff, 1960). See also Mary Catherine Baseheart, *Person in the World: Introduction to the Philosophy of Edith Stein* (Dordrecht, Netherlands: Springer, 2010).
15. Edmund Husserl, *Logical Investigations*, ed. Dermot Moran, trans. J. N. Findlay (London: Routledge, 2001).
16. Edith Stein, *On the Problem of Empathy*, trans. W. Stein (Washington, DC: ICS Publications, 1988).
17. Edmund Husserl, "Philosophy as a Rigorous Science," trans. in *Phenomenology and the Crisis of Philosophy*, ed. P. Lauer, 71–148 (New York: Harper, 1965). The essay was originally published in 1910.
18. This position was revised in later editions of *Ideas I*.
19. Edith Stein, letter to Roman Ingarden, Feb. 20, 1917, in *Self-Portrait in Letters*, 8.
20. Edmund Husserl, *On the Phenomenology of the Consciousness of Internal Time (1893–1917)*, trans. J. B. Barnett Brough (Dordrecht, Netherlands: Springer, 2008).
21. "Vorlesungen zur Phänomenologie des inneren Zeitbewusstseins," ed. Martin Heidegger, in *Jahrbuch für Philosophie und phänomenologische Forschung*, vol. 9 (Halle, Germany: Max Niemeyer, 1928), 367–498.
22. Edmund Husserl, *Texte zur Phänomenologie des inneren Zeitbewußtseins: 1893–1917*, ed. R. Bernet (Frankfurt: Meiner Verlag, 1985). See Bernet's introduction (*Einleitung*).
23. Calcagno, "Assistant and/or Collaborator?"
24. Edmund Husserl, "Brief an Von den Driesch, 4, XI. 1930 (Entwurf), Freiburg," in *Edmund Husserl: Briefwechsel*, vol. 8, *Institutionelle Schreiben*, ed. Karl and Elizabeth Schuhmann (Dordrecht, Netherlands: Kluwer, 1994), 115.
25. Edmund Husserl, "Empfehlungsschreiben Husserls für Stein, 6.II. 1919," in *Edmund Husserl: Briefwechsel*, vol. 3, *Husserliana Dokumente*, ed. Karl and Elizabeth Schuhmann (Dordrecht, Netherlands: Kluwer, 1994), 549.
26. Emmanuel Faye, *The Introduction of Nazism into Philosophy in Light of the Unpublished Seminars, 1932–1935*, trans. M. B. Smith (New Haven, CT: Yale University Press, 2009).
27. Some of her public lectures can be found in Edith Stein, *Woman*, 2nd ed., trans. F. M. Oben (Washington, DC: ICS Publications, 1996).
28. Hanna-Barbara Gerl-Falkovitz, "Edith Stein's Little-Known Side," *American Catholic Philosophical Quarterly* 83, no. 4 (2009): 555–81; Angela Ales Bello, "Edith Stein e il male politico," in *Il male politico: La riflessione sul totalitarismo nella filosofia del Novecento*, ed. Roberto Gatto (Rome: Città Nuova, 2000), 227–41; Ilona Riedel-Spangenberger, "Einleitung," in Edith Stein, *Eine Untersuchung über den Staat*, ed. Ilona Reidel-Spangenberger, in *Edith Stein Gesamtausgabe*, vol. 7 (Freiburg, Germany: Herder, 2006), ix–xxvi; Wolfgang Rieß, *Der Weg vom Ich zum Anderen: Die philosophische Begründung*

einer Theorie von Individuum. Gemeinschaft und Statt bei Edith Stein (Dresden, Germany: Echard Richter, 2010).

29. Joyce Avrech Berkman, "The German-Jewish Symbiosis in Flux: Edith Stein's Complex National/Ethnic Identity," in *Contemplating Edith Stein*, ed. J. A. Berkman (Notre Dame, IN: University of Notre Dame Press, 2006), 170–99; Sister Josephine Koeppel, OCD, *Edith Stein: Philosopher and Mystic* (Scranton, PA: University of Scranton Press, 2006); Angela Ales Bello, "Presentazione," in Edith Stein, *Una ricerca sullo Stato* (Rome: Città Nuova, 1993), 7–17; Marianne Sawicki, "Editor's Introduction," in Edith Stein, *An Investigation concerning the State*, trans. Marianne Sawicki (Washington, DC: ICS Publications, 2006), xi–xxviii; MacIntyre, *Edith Stein*; Beate Beckmann-Zöller and Hanna-Barbara Gerl-Falkovitz, eds., *Die unbekannte Edith Stein: Phänomenologie und Sozialphilosophie* (Frankfurt: Peter Lang, 2006).

30. Edmund Husserl, *Zur Phänomenologie der Intersubjektivität. Texte aus dem Nachlaß, Erster Teil: 1905–1920*, ed. I. Kern (The Hague: Nijhoff, 1973), Husserliana 13; *Zur Phänomenologie der Intersubjektivität. Texte aus dem Nachlaß, Zweiter Teil: 1921–1928*, ed. von. I. Kern (The Hague: Nijhoff, 1973), Husserliana 14; *Zur Phänomenologie der Intersubjektivität. Texte aus dem Nachlaß, Dritter Teil: 1929–1935*, ed. von. I. Kern (The Hague: Nijhoff, 1973), Husserliana 15.

31. See Adolf Reinach, *Was ist Phänomenologie?* (Munich, Germany: Kosel, 1951).

32. Spiegelberg, *The Phenomenological Movement*.

33. Antonio Calcagno, "Edith Stein's Philosophy of Community in Her Early Work and in Her Later *Finite and Eternal Being*: Martin Heidegger's Impact," *Philosophy and Theology* 23, no. 2 (2011): 231–55.

34. Angela Ales Bello, "What Is Life? The Contributions of Hedwig Conrad-Martius and Edith Stein," *Symposium: Canadian Journal of Continental Philosophy* 16, no. 2 (Fall 2012): 20–33.

35. Adolf Reinach, *Sämtliche Werke*, ed. K. Schuhmann and B. Smith (Munich, Germany: Philosophia Verlag, 1989), and Adolf Reinach, *On the Theory of the Negative Judgment*, in *Parts and Moments: Studies in Logic and Formal Ontology*, ed. Barry Smith (Vienna: Philosophia Verlag, 1984), 285–313, ontology.buffalo.edu/smith/book/P&M/Reinach_Negative_Judgment.pdf (accessed Aug. 20, 2014).

36. Max Scheler, *Formalism in Ethics and Non-Formal Ethics of Values*, trans. Manfred Frings and Roger L. Funk (Evanston, IL: Northwestern University Press, 1973).

37. "Besides, as a consequence [of the discussion] I have experienced a breakthrough. Now I imagine I know pretty well what 'constitution' is—but with a break from Idealism. An absolutely existing physical nature on the one hand, a distinctly structured subjectivity on the other, seem to me to be prerequisites before an intuiting nature can constitute itself. I have not yet had the chance to

confess my heresy to the Master" (Edith Stein, letter to Ingarden, Feb. 3, 1917, in *Edith Stein: Self-Portrait in Letters*, 8).

38. Edith Stein, *Endliches und ewiges Sein: Versuch eines Aufstiegs zum Sinn des Sein. Anhang: Martin Heideggers Existenzphilosophie. Die Seelenburg*, ed. A. Uwe Müller, in *Edith Stein Gesamtausgabe*, vols. 11 and 12 (Freiburg im Breisgau: Herder, 2006).

39. Ferdinand Tönnies, *Die Entwicklung der sozialen Frage* (Leipzig, Germany: Goschen, 1913), and *Gemeinschaft und Gesellschaft: Grundbegriffe der reinen Soziologie* (Darmstadt, Germany: Wissenschaftliche Buchgesellschaft, 1963); Max Scheler, *Die Wissensformen und die Gesellschaft* (Bern: Francke, 1980); Georg Simmel, *Das Problem der historischen Zeit* (Berlin: Philosophische Vorträge der Kantgesellschaft, 1916).

40. Theodor Lipps, "Aesthetische Einfühlung," *Zeitschrift Psychologie* 22 (1900): 415–500.

41. Stein, *Der Aufbau der menschlichen Person*, 5–7.

42. Edith Stein, *Philosophy of Psychology and the Humanities*, trans. M. C. Baseheart and M. Sawicki (Washington, DC: ICS Publications, 2000), 121–28.

43. Hugo Münsterberg, *On the Witness Stand: Essays on Psychology and Crime* (New York: Doubleday, 1909).

44. See Alexander Pfänder, *Zur Psychologie der Gesinnungen* (Tübingen, Germany: Niemeyer, 1913), and his *Phenomenology of Willing and Motivation and Other Phaenomenologica*, trans. H. Spiegelberg (Evanston, IL: Northwestern University, 1967).

45. Antonio Calcagno, "The Problem of the Relation between the State and the Community in Edith Stein's Political Theory," *Quaestiones Disputatae* 3, no1 (Fall 2012): 185–98.

Notes to Chapter 2

1. See, for example, Mary Catherine Baseheart, *Person in the World: Introduction to the Philosophy of Edith Stein* (Dordrecht, Netherlands: Springer, 2010).

2. Edith Stein, *On the Problem of Empathy*, trans. W. Stein (Washington, DC: ICS Publications, 1988).

3. See Angela Ales Bello, "What Is Life? The Contribution of Hedwig Conrad-Martius and Edith Stein," *Symposium: Canadian Journal of Continental Philosophy* 16, no. 2 (Fall 2012): 20–33.

4. For example, John Healy, "Empathy with the Cross: A Phenomenological Approach to the 'Dark Night,'" in *Essays in Honor of Joseph P. Brennan*, ed. R. McNamara (Rochester, NY: The Seminary, 1976–77), 21–35; Ralph R. Acampora, *Corporal Compassion: Animal Ethics and Philosophy of Body* (Pittsburgh: University of Pittsburgh Press, 2006), 160.

5. Frédérique de Vignemont and Thomas Singer, "The Empathic Brain: How, When and Why?," *Trends in Cognitive Science* 10 (2006): 435–41.

6. Jonna Bornemark, "Alterity in the Philosophy of Edith Stein: Empathy and God," in *Phenomenology 2005: Selected Essays from Northern Europe, Part I*, ed. Hans Rainer Sepp and Ion Copoeru (Bucharest: Zeta Books, 2007), 121–52.

7. Angela Ales Bello, "L'antropologia fenomenologica di Edith Stein," *Agathos: An International Review of the Humanities and the Social Sciences* 2, no. 2 (2005): 23–43; Vittorio Gallese, "The Roots of Empathy: The Shared Manifold Hypothesis and the Neural Basis of Intersubjectivity," *Psychopathology* 36 (2003): 171–80; Dan Zahavi, "Empathy, Embodiment and Interpersonal Understanding: From Lipps to Schutz," *Inquiry* 53, no. 3 (2010): 285–306; Judy Miles, "Other Bodies and Other Minds in Edith Stein; or, How to Talk about Empathy," in *Husserl and Edith Stein*, ed. R. Feist and W. Sweet, 119–26 (Washington, DC: Council of Research in Values and Philosophy, 2003); Marianne Sawicki, "Personal Connections: The Phenomenology of Edith Stein," in *Yearbook of the Irish Philosophical Society: Voices of Irish Philosophy*, ed. Mette Lebech, 148–69 (Dublin: Irish Philosophical Society, 2004); Dermot Moran, "The Problem of Empathy: Lipps, Scheler, Husserl and Stein," in *Amor Amicitiae: On the Love that Is Friendship. Essays in Medieval Thought and Beyond in Honor of the Rev. Professor James McEvoy*, ed. Thomas A. Kelly and Phillip W. Rosemann (Leuven, Belgium: Peeters, 2004), 269–312.

8. Edmund Husserl, *Zur Phänomenologie der Intersubjektivität. Texte aus dem Nachlaß, Erster Teil: 1905–1920*, ed. I. Kern (The Hague: Nijhoff, 1973), Husserliana 13, 338–39.

9. Kathleen Haney, "Empathy and Otherness," *Journal of Philosophy: A Cross-Disciplinary Inquiry* 4, no. 8, (Jan. 2009): 11–19; Kathleen Haney, "Why Is the Fifth Cartesian Meditation Necessary?," *Southwest Philosophy Review: The Journal of the Southwestern Philosophical Society* 13, no. 1 (Jan. 1997): 197–204; Ernest J. McCullough, "Edith Stein and Inter-Subjectivity," in *Husserl and Edith Stein*, ed. R. Feist and W. Sweet, 127–39 (Washington, DC: Council of Research in Values and Philosophy, 2003).

10. Max Scheler, *The Nature of Sympathy*, trans. Peter Heath (Hamden, CT: Archon Books, 1970).

11. Scheler, *The Nature of Sympathy*, 12–13.

12. Ibid., 251–52.

13. Ibid., 251, 242.

14. John Stuart Mill, "Utilitarianism," in *On Liberty and Other Essays*, ed. J. Gray (Oxford: Oxford University Press, 2008), 138–39.

15. Karsten Steuber, *Rediscovering Empathy: Agency, Folk Psychology, and the Human Sciences* (Cambridge, MA: MIT Press, 2006).

16. Monika Dullstein, "Direct Perception and Simulation: Stein's Account of Empathy," *Review of Philosophy and Psychology* 4, no. 2 (2013): 333–35.

17. Alvin I. Goldman, *Simulating Minds: The Philosophy, Psychology and Neuroscience of Mindreading* (Oxford: Oxford University Press, 2008), 113.

18. Ibid., 147.
19. Dan Zahavi, "Simulation, Projection and Empathy," *Consciousness and Cognition* 17, no. 2 (2008): 519.
20. Frédérique de Vignemont and Pierre Jacob, "What Is It Like to Feel Another's Pain?," *Philosophy of Science* 79, no. 2 (Apr. 2012): 296.
21. Frédérique de Vignemont, "Drawing the Boundary between Low-Level and High-Level Mindreading," *Philosophical Studies* 144 (2009): 464.
22. Gallese, "The Roots of Empathy," 172.
23. De Vignemont and Jacob, "What Is It Like to Feel Another's Pain?," 313–14.
24. Shaun Gallagher and Dan Zahavi, *The Phenomenological Mind* (London: Routledge, 2012), and "Empathy, Simulation and Narrative," *Science in Context* 25, no. 3 (2012): 301–27. See Dan Zahavi, "Beyond Empathy: Phenomenological Approaches to Intersubjectivity," *Journal of Consciousness Studies* 8, no. 5–7 (2001): 151–67, and Dan Zahavi, *Subjectivity and Selfhood: Investigating the First-Person Perspective* (Cambridge, MA: MIT Press, 2008).
25. Zahavi, "Beyond Empathy," 153–54.
26. See my chapter on gender and empathy, "Empathy as a Feminine Structure of Phenomenological Consciousness," in *The Philosophy of Edith Stein* (Pittsburgh: Duquesne University Press, 2007), 63–85.
27. Johann Gotlieb Fichte, *Introductions to the "Wissensschaftslehre,"* ed. and trans. D. Breazeale (Indianapolis, IN: Hackett Publishing, 1994), 186.
28. Immanuel Kant, *Critique of Pure Reason*, trans. and ed. Paul Guyer and Allen W. Wood (Cambridge: Cambridge University Press, 1999), A 116, B, 131–32, B 134–35.
29. Stein takes up this other form of individuality in her analyses of the personality core or *Persönlichkeitskern*, which helps to individuate one person from another.
30. For a rich discussion of Stein's notion of life-force or *Lebenskraft*, see Christof Betschart, "Was ist Lebenskraft? Edith Steins anthropologischer Beitrag in 'Psychische Kausalität' (Teil 2)," *Edith Stein Jahrbuch* 16 (2010): 33–64, and "Was ist Lebenskraft? Edith Steins erkenntnistheoretischen Prämissen in 'Psychische Kausalität' (Teil 1)," *Edith Stein Jahrbuch* 15 (2009): 154–83.
31. Henri Bergson, *Matter and Memory*, trans. N. M. Paul and W. S. Palmer (New York: Zone Books, 1988).
32. Angela Ales Bello, "The Study of the Soul between Psychology and Phenomenology in Edith Stein," *Cultura: International Journal of Philosophy of Culture and Axiology* 8 (2007): 96.
33. David Hume, *Hume's Treatise of Human Nature*, ed. L. A. Selby Bigge (Oxford: Oxford University Press, 1888), 89.
34. Edith Stein, *Philosophy of Psychology and the Humanities*, part 1, trans. M. C. Baseheart and M. Sawicki (Washington, DC: ICS Publications, 2000).
35. Georg W. F. Hegel, *The Phenomenology of Spirit*, trans. A. V. Miller (Oxford: Oxford University Press, 1977), 58–60. Edmund Husserl, *Ideas*

Pertaining to a Pure Phenomenology and to a Phenomenological Philosophy, vol. 2, trans. R. Rojcewicz and A. Schuwer (The Hague: Springer, 1990), § 41.

36. Thinkers such as John Searle, especially in his later social ontology, would criticize such a solipsistic account of meaning. For him, the language we speak refers to a real world, which conditions the very language we employ and the meaning we intend. Searle's pragmatic and performative account of language entails the construction of a social world, whereas Stein sees language as already operating within a world that gives itself to consciousness through meaning.

37. Mette Lebech has remarked that in addition to value, one finds in Stein's early phenomenology the beginnings of the possibility of human dignity, which, here, we can understand as a value. Lebech focuses on Stein's later philosophical anthropology and her doctrine of the state to justify fully this claim that human persons are endowed with human dignity. See Mette Lebech, *On the Problem of Human Dignity: A Hermeneutical and Phenomenological Investigation* (Würzburg, Germany: Könighausen and Neumann, 2009).

NOTES TO CHAPTER 3

1. Edith Stein, *Philosophy of Psychology and the Humanities,* trans. M. C. Baseheart and M. Sawicki (Washington, DC: ICS Publications, 2000).

2. Ferdinand Tönnies, *Die Entwicklung der sozialen Frage* (Leipzig, Germany: Goschen, 1913), and *Gemeinschaft und Gesellschaft: Grundbegriffe der reinen Soziologie* (Darmstadt, Germany: Wissenschaftliche Buchgesellschaft, 1963); see also Max Scheler, *Die Wissensformen und die Gesellschaft* (Bern: Francke, 1980). Georg Simmel, *Essays in Sociology, Philosophy and Aesthetics,* ed. K. H. Wolf (New York: Harper Torchbooks, 1959), and *Das Problem der historischen Zeit* (Berlin: Philosophische Vorträge der Kantgesellschaft, 1916), vol. 12, n. 12.

3. Theodor Litt, *Individuum und Gemeinschaft. Grundfragen der sozialen Theorie und Ethik* (Berlin: B. G. Teubner, 1919).

4. Edmund Husserl, *On the Phenomenology of the Consciousness of Internal Time,* trans. J. B. Brough (Dordrecht, Netherlands: Springer, 1992).

5. Émile Durkheim, *De la division du travail social* (Paris: Presses Universitaires de France, 2007), 122–23.

6. Gerda Walther, *Ein Beitrag zur Ontologie der sozialen Gemeinschaften,* offprint from *Jahrbuch für Philosophie und phänomenologische Forschung,* vol. 6, ed. Edmund Husserl (Halle, Germany: Niemeyer, 1923).

7. Max Scheler, *The Nature of Sympathy,* trans. P. Heath (Hamden, CT: Archon Books, 1970), 12–14.

8. Antonio Calcagno, "Gerda Walther: On the Possibility of a Passive Sense of Community and the Inner Time Consciousness of a Community," in special volume dedicated to early phenomenology, ed. Jeff Mitscherling and Kimberly Baltzer-Jaray, *Symposium: Canadian Journal of Continental Philosophy/Revue canadienne de philosophie continentale* 16, no. 2 (Fall 2012) 89–105.

9. Edith Stein, *Woman,* 2nd ed., trans. F. M. Oben (Washington, DC: ICS Publications, 1996).
10. Antonio Calcagno, "Empathy as a Feminine Structure of Phenomenological Consciousness," *The Philosophy of Edith Stein* (Pittsburgh: Duquesne University Press, 2007), 63–85.
11. Ibid., chapters 4 and 5.
12. John Searle, *The Construction of Social Reality* (New York: Free Press, 1997), and *The Making of the Social World: The Structure of Human Civilization* (Oxford: Oxford University Press, 2010); Raimo Tuomela, *The Philosophy of Sociality: The Shared Point of View* (Oxford: Oxford University Press, 2010), and *Social Ontology: Collective Intentionality and Group Agents* (Oxford: Oxford University Press, 2013); Margaret Gilbert, *Sociality and Responsibility: New Essays in Plural Subject Theory* (Lanham, MD: Rowman and Littlefield, 2000), and *A Theory of Political Obligation: Membership, Commitment and the Bonds of Society* (Oxford: Oxford University Press, 2008); Philip Pettit and Christian List, *Group Agency: The Possibility, Design and Status of Corporate Agents* (Oxford: Oxford University Press, 2011); Michael Bratman, *Faces of Intention: Selected Essays on Intention and Agency* (Cambridge: Cambridge University Press, 1999).
13. Raimo Tuomela, "Acting as a Group Member and Collective Commitment," *The Philosophy of Sociality: The Shared Point of View* (Oxford: Oxford University Press, 2010, 13–45.
14. See Emanuele Caminada, "Joining the Background: Habitual Sentiments behind We-Intentionality," in *Institutions, Emotions, and Group Agents,* ed. A. Konzelmann Ziv and H. B. Schmid (Dordrecht, Netherlands: Springer, 2014), chapter 12.
15. Michel Henry, *The Essence of Manifestation,* trans. G. Etzkorn (Dordrecht, Netherlands: Springer, 1973).
16. Edmund Husserl, *Logical Investigations,* trans. J. N. Findlay, ed. Dermot Moran (London: Routledge, 2001), 817.
17. Ibid., 821.
18. Edmund Husserl, *Experience and Judgment,* trans. J. Churchill and K. Ameriks (Evanston, IL: Northwestern University Press, 1975).
19. Ibid., 85–86.
20. Ibid., 85.
21. Ibid., 86.
22. Max Scheler, *On Feeling, Knowing, and Valuing,* ed. Harold J. Bershady (Chicago: University of Chicago Press, 1992), 248.
23. Recall that a community, like a society, can have a goal or purpose, but the goal is not the community's purpose as it is for the society.
24. This is my term, not Stein's. I draw from both Heidegger and Merleau-Ponty in the use of this word in this context.
25. Mary Catherine Baseheart, *Person in the World: Introduction to the Philosophy of Edith Stein* (Dordrecht, Netherlands: Springer, 2010), 148.

26. See Nynke van Dijk and Wouter Wieling, "Fainting, Emancipation, and the 'Weak and Sensitive' Sex," *Journal Physiology* 587 (2009): 3063–64.

27. See Kathleen Haney's very informative article "Edith Stein and Autism," in *Husserl's Ideen,* ed. L. Embree and T. Nenon (Dordrecht, Netherlands: Springer, 2013), 35–54.

Notes to Chapter 4

1. Originally published in *Jarhrbuch für Philosophie und phänomenologische Forschung,* vol. 7, ed. Edmund Husserl (Halle, Germany: Niemeyer, 1925), 1–123. Republished by the same publisher in 1970, but added to it was Stein's earlier text, *Beiträge zur philosophischen Begründung der Psychologie und der Geisteswissenschaften.* The treatise on the state remained unchanged, though the pagination shifted to 285–407. A new critical edition of Stein's text on the state is Edith Stein, *Eine Untersuchung über den Staat,* ed. Ilona Reidel-Spangenberger, in *Edith Stein Gesamtausgabe,* vol. 7 (Freiburg: Herder, 2006).

2. Beate Beckmann-Zöller and Hanna-Barbara Gerl-Falkowitz, *Die unbekannte Edith Stein: Phänomenologie und Sozialphilosophie* (Frankfurt: Peter Lang, 2006); Ilona Riedel-Spangenberger, "Einleitung," in Edith Stein, *Eine Untersuchung über den Staat,* ed. Ilona Reidel-Spangenberger, in *Edith Stein Gesamtausgabe,* vol. 7, ix–xxvi (Freiburg, Germany: Herder, 2006); Wolfgang Rieß, *Der Weg vom Ich zum Anderen: Die philosophische Begründung einer Theorie von Individuum, Gemeinschaft und Staat bei Edith Stein* (Dresden, Germany: Echard Richter, 2010).

3. Paulus Lenz Médoc, "L'idée de l'État chez Edith Stein," *Les Études Philosophiques* 3 (1956): 451–57; Angela Ales Bello, "Presentazione," in Edith Stein, *Una ricerca sullo stato* (Rome: Città Nuova, 1993), 7–17; Angela Ales Bello, "Edith Stein e il male politico," in *Il male politico: La riflessione sul totalitarismo nella filosofia del Novecento,* ed. R. Gatti, 227–41 (Rome: Città Nuova, 2000); Philibert Secretan, introduction to *De l'État,* by Edith Stein, trans. Philibert Secretan, 7–29 (Fribourg, Switzerland: Cerf, 1989); Antonio Calcagno, "*Persona Politica:* Unity and Difference in Edith Stein's Political Philosophy," *International Philosophical Quarterly* 37, no. 2 (June 1997): 203–15, and "Is the State Responsible for the Immortal Soul of the Person?," in *The Philosophy of Edith Stein* (Pittsburgh: Duquesne University Press, 2007), 45–62 and 99–112, respectively; Marianne Sawicki, "Editor's Introduction," in *An Investigation concerning the State,* by Edith Stein, trans. Marianne Sawicki, x–xx (Washington, DC: ICS Publications, 2006); Alasdair MacIntyre, *Edith Stein: A Philosophical Prologue 1913–1922* (Lanham, MD: Rowman and Littlefield, 2006).

4. For example, see Mary Catherine Baseheart, *Person in the World: Introduction to the Philosophy of Edith Stein* (Dordrecht, Netherlands: Springer, 2010).

5. Antonio Calcagno, "Thinking Community and the State from Within," *American Catholic Philosophical Quarterly* 82, no. 1 (Winter 2008): 31–45.

6. Georg W. F. Hegel, *Elements of the Philosophy of Right*, ed. Allen W. Wood, trans. H. B. Nisbet (Cambridge: Cambridge University Press, 1991). Margaret Gilbert, *Joint Commitment: How We Make the Social World* (Oxford: Oxford University Press, 2013); *Sociality and Responsibility: New Essays in Plural Subject Theory* (Lanham, MD: Rowman and Littlefield, 2000), and *A Theory of Political Obligation: Membership, Commitment and the Bonds of Society* (Oxford: Oxford University Press, 2008). Philip Pettit and Christian List, *Group Agency: The Possibility, Design and Status of Corporate Agents* (Oxford: Oxford University Press, 2011).

7. Ales Bello, "Presentazione," and Secretan, introduction.

8. "Zunächst halten wir fest: Staaten können sowohl auf gemeinschaftlicher wer auf gesellschaftlicher Grundlage ruhen. Die nähere Untersuchung dürfte zeigen, da es sich um gesellschaftliche Organisation immer erst auf einer höheren Stufe staatlicher Entwicklung handelt (d.h. das Gegenteil dessen, was die Vertragstheorie—als Ursprungshypothese verstanden—lehrt).... Vorläufig halten wir uns an die durch die empirische Anschauung illustrierte Möglichkeit, daß sich Staaten auf der Grundlage eines Gemeinschaftslebens erheben können, und fragen nach der Eigentümlichkeit der staatlichen Gemeinschaft—d.h. der Gemeinschaft der im Staat lebenden Individuen—gegenüber anderen Gemeinschaften" (*US* 9). "But right now we stress this point: States can have just as viable a basis in community as in association. Further investigation should indicate that the associational kind of organization never comes about until a state reaches a high level of development. (This is the opposite of what is taught by contract theory, understood as a hypothesis of origin.)...Meanwhile we're sticking with the possibility illustrated by a glance at the facts: states can arise on the basis of communal living. And we are inquiring into the distinctiveness of the state community—which means the community of individuals living in the state—as opposed to other communities" (*IS* 6). I have cited both the German original and the English translation. There are slight differences in the two versions. My reading is based on the German original and I quote the English translation when appropriate.

9. Edith Stein, *Life in a Jewish Family: Her Unfinished Autobiographical Account*, trans. Josephine Koeppel, OCD (Washington, DC: ICS Publications, 1986); Edith Stein, *Self-Portrait in Letters 1916–1942*, trans. Josephine Koeppel (Washington, DC: ICS Publications, 1994).

10. Hanna-Barbara Gerl-Falkowitz does an excellent job chronicling such responses and social theorizations. See her "Edith Stein's Little-Known Side," *American Catholic Philosophical Quarterly* 83, no. 4 (2009): 555–81.

11. "Wachsam und interessiert verfolgt Edith Stein die Bemühungen der Weimarer Republik. Aber angesichts des Kampfes radikaler Interessengruppen und ihrer jeweils verschiedenen politischen Theorien sieht Edith Stein den

Staat massiv gefährdet und letzlich zum Untergang bestimmt. Dagegen fordert sie eine einzige ausgebildete Staatstheorie als leitendes Ideal und einen durch das Recht geordneten Staat, in dem die Kraft der Vernunft zugunsten der Volksgemeinschaft zum Zuge kommt. Sie stellt fest: 'Ein Korrektiv gegen all diese möglichen zerstörischen Einflüsse politischer Theorien liegt in der Kraft der ratio, die die realen Verhältnisse selbst in sich tragen. Jede Rechtsordnung, die gegen diese ratio verstößt, statt ihr Rechnung zu tragen, muß gewärtig sein, dass die Wirklichkeit sich ihr widersetzt und mit ständigen Durchbrechungen der Rechtsordnung ihren Gang geht'" (*US* xiii). All translations mine unless otherwise specified.

12. "Die phänomenologische Untersuchung des Staates durch Stein zeigt als Ergebnis eine Erfassung des überzeitlichen Wesens des Staates, das in seiner Selbstgebung kraft eigenen Rechtes und seiner Autarkie besteht" (Rieß, *Der Weg vom Ich zum Anderen*, 531).

13. "Es ist nun die Frage, welcher Form der Sozialität wir die staatliche Organisation zuzuweisen haben. Es will mir scheinen, daß es sich nicht um ein aut-aut (Entweder-Oder) handelt...Doch scheint es, daß solche Willkürakte für die Bregründung und Fortentwicklung von Staaten nur dann Bedeutung haben, wenn sie bestehenden Gemeinschaftsverhältnissen Rechnung tragen und sie gleichsam nur sanktionieren" (*US* 7–8). "Now the issue is, to which mode of sociality do we assign the organization of the state? It seems to me that this need not be an either-or question. Obviously if you're a proponent of the *contract theory*, the dominant European theory, and you regard the state as being grounded in a pact among the individuals belonging to it, our question is already decided in favour of association. You take it for granted that there was a purely rational emergence, a creation by virtue of an act of will. But this theory neglects obvious phenomena of state formation, and of the life of the state, that don't fit it in with its scheme" (*IS* 4–5).

14. John Locke, *Second Treatise on Civil Government*, ed. Peter Laslett (Cambridge: Cambridge University Press, 1988), chap. 7.

15. "Ihre jeweilige Ausgestaltung ist von der Art und Zahl und der mannigfaltigen Wechselbeziehung der ihr eingeordneten Gemeinschaften abhängig. Insofern als das Bewßtsein der Zugehörigkeit zu dieser allumfassenden Gemeinschaft je nach dem Geist der engeren Gemeinschaften und der Beschaffenheit der ihnen angehörigen Individuen ein mehr oder weniger ausgebildetes und die Stellungnahme zu ihr verschieden sein kann" (*US* 10). "As for consciousness of belonging to this all-encompassing community, it may be more or less developed, according to the mentality of the closer communities and the qualities of the individuals who belong to them; and the attitude toward this community may vary" (*IS* 7–8).

16. Adolf Reinach, *Über den Ursachenbegriff im geltenden Strafrecht* (Leipzig, Germany: Verlag von Johann Ambrosius Barth, 1905); and his "Die apriorischen Grundlagen des bürgerlichen Rechtes," in *Jahrbuch für Philosophie und phänomenologische Forschung*, vol. 1 (Tübingen, Germany: Niemeyer, 1913), 685–847.

17. Carl Schmitt, *Political Theology: Four Chapters on the Concept of Sovereignty,* trans. George Schwab (Chicago: University of Chicago Press, 2005), 5–9.

18. "Spontane Akte sind *freies geistiges Tun,* und das Subjekt solchen Tuns nennen wir eine *Person.* Wie freie Akte andere Erlebnisse zum Fundament haben, so weist auch die Personalität noch andere Konstituentien auf als die Freiheit... Wir haben den Staat als souverän bezeichnet und damit ausgedrückt, daß er selbst Urheber seines Rechts ist.... Der Staat als Einheit ist nur möglich, wenn es einen Sinn gibt, ihn als *Ganzes* als Urheber seiner Akte in Anspruch zu nehmen; und eine andere als die absolute Staatsform nur, wenn es einen gemeinschaftlichen Vollzug von freien Akten gibt, wenn ein Personenverband ihr Subjekt sein kann.... Darüber hinaus aber und evetuell in einem Vollzuge damit erklärt jeder *mit den anderen gemeinsam und für alle* den Bund als bestehend, und eben dadurch konstituiert der Bund sich selbst und beginnt sein Dasein. Jeder seiner ferneren Beschlüsse hat denselben Charakter: der Bund beschließt, indem seine Glieder miteinander und für ihnen beschließen und jedes von sich aus sein Plazet erteilt. Dieses "von sich" unterscheidet die freien Akte von anderen Gemeinschaftserlebnissen, bei denen es nicht erforderlich ist. Aber es ändert nichts daran, daß die Gemeinschaft selbst das Subjekt solcher Akte ist" (*US* 37). "Spontaneous acts are *free mental deeds,* and we call the subject of such deeds a *person.* Just as free acts have other experiences for [their] foundation, so also the personality exhibits other constituents besides freedom.... The state as a unity is only possible only if there's a sense to claiming the state as *a whole* to be executor of its acts. That unity would be something other than the absolute mode of statehood only if there's a communal realization of free acts, [that is,] if a federation of persons can be the subject of them.... But from then on, and in one [act of] realization, each one *with the others in common and for all* declares the alliance as subsisting, and precisely by doing so constitutes the alliance for herself and inaugurates its existence. Each of its subsequent decisions has the same character: The alliance decides, inasmuch as its members decide with one another and for it, and each grants her *placet* on her own initiative. This 'on her own' distinguishes the free acts from other communal experiences, for which it is unnecessary. Yet that does not alter the fact that the community itself is the subject of such acts" (*IS* 46–47).

19. Max Scheler, *Der Formalismus in der Ethik und die materiale Wertethik: Neuer Versuch der Grundlegung eines ethischen Personalismus* (Boston: Adamant Media Corporation, 2004); see also Scheler's *Das Ressentiment im Aufbau der Moralen,* ed. M. Frings (Frankfurt: Klostermann, 2004).

20. Recall that for Stein solidarity and living in and for the other are mental states that are proper to the community and not the state.

21. Max Scheler, "Vom kulturellen Wiederaufbau Europas. Ein Vortrag," in *Vom Ewigen im Menschen* (1921), Gesammelte Werke 5, ed. Maria Scheler (Bern, Switzerland: Franke Verlag, 1968), 405.

22. Stein, *An Investigation concerning the State,* 3.

23. Ibid., 67.

24. "Exclusively" is understood here with reference to the experiences of soiety and the mass.

25. Calcagno, "*Persona Politica.*"

26. Edith Stein, *Martin Heideggers Existentialphilosophie,* in *Welt und Person,* Edith Stein Werke, vol. 6 (Leuven, Belgium: Nauwelaerts, 1962), 97.

27. One can find, for example, personalist and communitarian readings of Stein's political theory in Ales Bello, "Edith Stein e il male politico"; Ales Bello, "Presentazione"; Luisa Avitabile, *Per una fenomenologia del diritto nell'opera di Edith Stein* (Rome: Nuova Cultura, 2006), 53–55; Calcagno, "*Persona Politica*"; Mette Lebech, "Edith Stein's Value Theory and Its Importance for Her Conception of the State," in *Europa und seine Anderen. Emmanuel Levinas, Edith Stein, Josef Tischner,* ed. Hanna-Barbara Gerl-Falkovitz, 145–54 (Dresden, Germany: Thelem, 2010); Médoc, "L'idée de l'État chez Edith Stein"; Sawicki, "Editor's Introduction"; Secretan, introduction.

28. Scholars have commented on Stein's liberalism, especially in her education theory. See Lisa M. Dolling, "Edith Stein's Philosophy of 'Liberal Education,'" in *Contemplating Edith Stein,* ed. Joyce Berkman (South Bend, IN: Notre Dame University Press, 2006), 226–41; Rieß, *Der Weg vom Ich zum Anderen,* 465–76; Michele Nicoletti, "'Eine Untersuchung über den Staat'—eine philosophische Grundlegung der politischen Theorie," in *Die unbekannte Edith Stein: Phänomenologie und Sozialphilosophie* (Frankfurt: Peter Lang, 2006), 73–89; Claudia Mareiéle Wulf, "Freiheit und Verantwortung in Gemeinschaft—eine brisante Auseinandersetzung zwischen Edith Stein und Max Scheler," in *Die unbekannte Edith Stein: Phänomenologie und Sozialphilosophie* (Frankfurt: Peter Lang, 2006), 91–114.

29. Isaiah Berlin, "Two Concepts of Liberty," in *Four Essays on Liberty* (Oxford: Oxford University Press, 1969), 118–72.

30. Rudolf Kjellén, *Der Staat als Lebensform* (Leipzig, Germany: Hirzel, 1917).

31. Heinz Rieder, *Liberalismus als Lebensform in der Deutschen Prosa Epik des neunzehnten Jahrhunderts* (Berlin: Matthiesen Verlags, 1939); Robbie Shilliam, *German Thought and International Relations: The Rise and Fall of a Liberal Project* (New York: Palgrave-Macmillan, 2009).

32. "Zünachst muß natürlich in der weiteren Gemeinschaft alles erhalben bleiben, was Gemeinschaft als solche konstituiert: es muß *ein* Lebensstrom vorhanden sein, an dem alle ihr angehörigen Individuen teilhaben, es muß—mindestens in einem Teil ihrer Glieder—ein die ganze offene Vielheit zugehöriger Individuen der Intention nach umspannendes Gemeinschafts*bewußtsein* vorhanden sein; die mangelnde persönliche Berührung alter Glieder muß durch eine kontinuierliche Vermittlung der Solidarität zwischen den in Zeit und Raum getrennten Elementen ersetzt werden" (*US* 19–20). "In the broader community, first of all, everything that constitutes community as such must continue to hold: it needs *one* current of life to be present, of which all individuals belonging

to the community partake; it needs—at least in a portion of its members—one consciousness of community to be present, encompassing the entire open multiplicity of individuals who belong according to intention; personal contact of all members, which is lacking, must be replaced by a continual mediation of solidarity among those elements separated in time and space" (*IS* 22).

33. As quoted in Elizabeth Young-Bruehl, *Hannah Arendt: For the Love of the World*, 2nd ed. (New Haven, CT: Yale University Press, 2004), xxxiii–xxxiv.

Bibliography

Acampora, Ralph R. *Corporal Compassion: Animal Ethics and Philosophy of Body.* Pittsburgh: University of Pittsburgh Press, 2006.

Ales Bello, Angela. "Edith Stein e il male politico." In *Il male politico: La riflessione sul totalitarismo nella filosofia del Novecento,* ed. Roberto Gatto, 227–41. Rome: Città Nuova, 2000.

———. "Edmund Husserl and Edith Stein: The Question of the Human Subject." Translated by Antonio Calcagno. *American Catholic Philosophical Quarterly* 82, no. 1 (Winter 2008): 143–60.

———. "L'antropologia fenomenologica di Edith Stein." *Agathos: An International Review of the Humanities and the Social Sciences* 2, no. 2 (2005): 23–43.

———. "Ontology, Metaphysics, and Life in Edith Stein." In *Contemplating Edith Stein,* edited by J. A. Berkman, 271–82. Notre Dame, IN: University of Notre Dame Press, 2006.

———. "Presentazione." In *Una ricerca sullo Stato,* by Edith Stein, 7–17. Rome: Città Nuova, 1993.

———. "The Study of the Soul between Psychology and Phenomenology in Edith Stein." *Cultura: International Journal of Philosophy of Culture and Axiology* 8 (2007): 90–108.

———. "What Is Life? The Contributions of Hedwig Conrad-Martius and Edith Stein." *Symposium: Canadian Journal of Continental Philosophy* 16, no. 2 (Fall 2012): 20–33.

Allen, Prudence. "Edith Stein: The Human Person as Male and Female." In *Images of the Human: The Philosophy of the Human Person in a Religious Context,* edited by P. Allen, 399–432. Chicago: Loyola Press, 1995.

Avitabile, Luisa. *Per una fenomenologia del diritto nell'opera di Edith Stein.* Rome: Nuova Cultura, 2006.

Baseheart, Mary Catherine. *Person in the World: Introduction to the Philosophy of Edith Stein.* Dordrecht, Netherlands: Springer, 2010.

Beckmann-Zöller, Beate, and Hanna-Barbara Gerl-Falkovitz, eds. *Die unbekannte Edith Stein: Phänomenologie und Sozialphilosophie*. Frankfurt: Peter Lang, 2006.

Bergson, Henri. *Matter and Memory*. Translated by N. M. Paul and W. S. Palmer. New York: Zone Books, 1988.

Berkman, Joyce Avrech, ed. *Contemplating Edith Stein*. Notre Dame, IN: University of Notre Dame Press, 2006.

———. "Edith Stein: A Life Veiled and Unveiled." *American Catholic Philosophical Quarterly* 82, no. 1 (Winter 2008): 5–30.

———. "The German-Jewish Symbiosis in Flux: Edith Stein's Complex National/Ethnic identity." In *Contemplating Edith Stein*, edited by J. A. Berkman, 170–99. Notre Dame, IN: University of Notre Dame Press, 2006.

Berlin, Isaiah. "Two Concepts of Liberty." In *Four Essays on Liberty*, 118–72. Oxford: Oxford University Press, 1969.

Betschart, Christof. "Was ist Lebenskraft? Edith Steins anthropologischer Beitrag in 'Psychische Kausalität' (Teil 2)." *Edith Stein Jahrbuch* 16 (2010): 33–64.

———. "Was ist Lebenskraft? Edith Steins erkenntnistheoretischen Prämissen in 'Psychische Kausalität' (Teil 1)." *Edith Stein Jahrbuch* 15 (2009): 154–83.

Bornemark, Jonna. "Alterity in the Philosophy of Edith Stein: Empathy and God." In *Phenomenology 2005: Selected Essays from Northern Europe, Part I*, edited by Hans Rainer Sepp and Ion Copoeru, 121–52. Bucharest: Zeta Books, 2007.

Bratman, Michael. *Faces of Intention: Selected Essays on Intention and Agency*. Cambridge: Cambridge University Press, 1999.

Calcagno, Antonio. "Assistant and/or Collaborator? Edith Stein's Relationship to Edmund Husserl's *Ideas II*." In *Contemplating Edith Stein*, edited by J. A. Berkman, 243–70. Notre Dame, IN: University of Notre Dame Press, 2006.

———. "Edith Stein's Philosophy of Community in Her Early Work and in Her Later *Finite and Eternal Being*: Martin Heidegger's Impact." *Philosophy and Theology* 23, no. 2 (2011): 231–55.

———. "Empathy as a Feminine Structure of Phenomenological Consciousness." In *The Philosophy of Edith Stein*, 63–85. Pittsburgh: Duquesne University Press, 2007.

———. "Gerda Walther: On the Possibility of a Passive Sense of Community and the Inner Time Consciousness of a Community." Special issue dedicated to early phenomenology, edited by Jeff Mitscherling and Kimberly Baltzer-Jaray, *Symposium: Canadian Journal of Continental Philosophy/Revue canadienne de philosophie continentale* 16, no. 2 (Fall 2012): 89–105.

———. "Is the State Responsible for the Immortal Soul of the Person?" In *The Philosophy of Edith Stein*, 45–62, 99–112. Pittsburgh: Duquesne University Press, 2007.

———. "*Persona Politica:* Unity and Difference in Edith Stein's Political Philosophy." *International Philosophical Quarterly* 37, no. 2 (June 1997): 203–15.

———. *The Philosophy of Edith Stein.* Pittsburgh: Duquesne University Press, 2007.

———. "The Problem of the Relation between the State and the Community in Edith Stein's Political Theory." *Quaestiones Disputatae* 3, no. 1 (Fall 2012): 185–98.

———. "Thinking Community and the State from Within." *American Catholic Philosophical Quarterly* 82, no. 1 (Winter 2008): 31–45.

Caminada, Emanuele. "Joining the Background: Habitual Sentiments behind We-Intentionality." In *Institutions, Emotions, and Group Agents*, edited by A. Konzelmann Ziv and H. B. Schmid, chapter 12. Dordrecht, Netherlands: Springer, 2014.

Dijk, Nynke van, and Wouter Wieling. "Fainting, Emancipation, and the 'Weak and Sensitive' Sex." *Journal Physiology* 587 (2009): 3063–64.

Dolling, Lisa M. "Edith Stein's Philosophy of 'Liberal Education.'" In *Contemplating Edith Stein*, edited by Joyce Berkman, 226–41. South Bend, IN: Notre Dame University Press, 2006.

Dullstein, Monika. "Direct Perception and Simulation: Stein's Account of Empathy." *Review of Philosophy and Psychology* 4, no. 2 (2013): 333–50.

Durkheim, Émile. *De la division du travail social.* Paris: Presses Universitaire de France, 2007.

Faye, Emmanuel. *Heidegger: The Introduction of Nazism into Philosophy in Light of the Unpublished Seminars, 1932–1935.* Translated by M. B. Smith. New Haven, CT: Yale University Press, 2009.

Fichte, Johann Gotlieb. *Introductions to the "Wissenschaftslehre."* Translated and edited by D. Breazeale. Indianapolis, IN: Hackett, 1994.

Gallagher, Shaun, and Dan Zahavi. "Empathy, Simulation and Narrative." *Science in Context* 25, no. 3 (2012): 301–27.

———. *The Phenomenological Mind.* London: Routledge, 2012.

Gallese, Vittorio. "The Roots of Empathy: The Shared Manifold Hypothesis and the Neural Basis of Intersubjectivity." *Psychopathology* 36 (2003): 171–80.

Gerl-Falkovitz, Hanna-Barbara. "Edith Stein's Little-Known Side." *American Catholic Philosophical Quarterly* 83, no. 4 (2009): 555–81.

Gilbert, Margaret. *Joint Commitment: How We Make the Social World*. Oxford: Oxford University Press, 2013.

———. *Sociality and Responsibility: New Essays in Plural Subject Theory*. Lanham, MD: Rowman and Littlefield, 2000.

———. *A Theory of Political Obligation: Membership, Commitment and the Bonds of Society*. Oxford: Oxford University Press, 2008.

Goldman, Alvin I. *Simulating Minds: The Philosophy, Psychology and Neuroscience of Mindreading*. Oxford: Oxford University Press, 2008.

Guilead, Reuben. *De la phénoménologie à la science de la croix: L'itinéraire d'Edith Stein*. Leuven, Belgium: Éditions Nauwelaerts, 1974.

Haney, Kathleen. "Edith Stein and Autism." In *Husserl's Ideen*, edited by L. Embree and T. Nenon, 35–54. Dordrecht, Netherlands: Springer, 2013.

———. "Empathy and Otherness." *Journal of Philosophy: A Cross-Disciplinary Inquiry* 4, no. 8 (Jan. 2009): 11–19.

———. "Why Is the Fifth Cartesian Meditation Necessary?" *Southwest Philosophy Review: The Journal of the Southwestern Philosophical Society* 13, no. 1 (Jan. 1997): 197–204.

Healy, John. "Empathy with the Cross: A Phenomenological Approach to the 'Dark Night.'" In *Essays in Honor of Joseph P. Brennan*, edited by R. McNamara, 21–35. Rochester, NY: The Seminary, 1976–77.

Hegel, Georg W. F. *Elements of the Philosophy of Right*. Edited by Allen W. Wood. Translated by H. B. Nisbet. Cambridge: Cambridge University Press, 1991.

———. *The Phenomenology of Spirit*. Translated by A. V. Miller. Oxford: Oxford University Press, 1977.

Henry, Michel. *The Essence of Manifestation*. Translated by G. Etzkorn. Dordrecht, Netherlands: Springer, 1973.

Hume, David. *Hume's Treatise of Human Nature*. Edited by L. A. Selby Bigge. Oxford: Oxford University Press, 1888.

Husserl, Edmund. *Edmund Husserl: Briefwechsel*. Vol. 8, *Institutionelle Schreiben*. Edited by Karl and Elizabeth Schuhmann. Dordrecht, Netherlands: Kluwer, 1994.

———. *Experience and Judgment*. Translated by J. Churchill and K. Ameriks. Evanston, IL: Northwestern University Press, 1975.

———. *Ideas Pertaining to a Pure Phenomenology and to a Phenomenological Philosophy*. Vol. 2. Translated by R. Rojcewicz and A. Schuwer. The Hague: Springer, 1990.

———. *Ideas Pertaining to a Pure Phenomenology and to a Phenomenological Philosophy*. Vol. 3. Translated by T. E. Klein and W. E. Pohl. The Hague: Springer, 2001.

———. *Logical Investigations*. Edited by Dermot Moran. Translated by J. N. Findlay. London: Routledge, 2001.

———. *On the Phenomenology of the Consciousness of Internal Time (1893–1917)*. Translated by J. B. Brough. The Hague: Springer, 1992. Originally published as *Texte zur Phänomenologie des inneren Zeitbewußtseins (1893–1917)*. Edited by R. Bernet. Frankfurt: Meiner Verlag, 1985.

———. "Philosophy as a Rigorous Science." 1910. Translated in *Phenomenology and the Crisis of Philosophy*, ed. P. Lauer, 71–148. New York: Harper, 1965.

———. "Vorlesungen zur Phänomenologie des inneren Zeitbewusstseins." In *Jahrbuch für Philosophie und phänomenologische Forschung*, vol. 9, edited by Martin Heidegger, 367–498. Halle, Germany: Max Niemeyer, 1928.

———. *Zur Phänomenologie der Intersubjektivität. Texte aus dem Nachlaß, Erster Teil: 1905–1920*. Husserliana 13. Edited by I. Kern. The Hague: Nijhoff, 1973.

———. *Zur Phänomenologie der Intersubjektivität. Texte aus dem Nachlaß, Zweiter Teil: 1921–1928*. Husserliana 14. Edited by I. Kern. The Hague: Nijhoff, 1973.

———. *Zur Phänomenologie der Intersubjektivität. Texte aus dem Nachlaß, Dritter Teil: 1929–1935*. Husserliana 15. Edited by I. Kern. The Hague: Nijhoff, 1973.

Kant, Immanuel. *Critique of Pure Reason*. Translated and edited by Paul Guyer and Allen W. Wood. Cambridge: Cambridge University Press, 1999.

Kjellén, Rudolf. *Der Staat als Lebensform*. Leipzig: Hirzel, 1917.

Koeppel, Josephine. *Edith Stein: Philosopher and Mystic*. Scranton, PA: University of Scranton Press, 2006.

Lebech, Mette. "Edith Stein's Value Theory and Its Importance for Her Conception of the State." In *Europa und seine Anderen: Emmanuel Levinas, Edith Stein, Josef Tischner*, edited by Hanna-Barbara Gerl-Falkovitz, 145–54. Dresden, Germany: Thelem, 2010.

———. *On the Problem of Human Dignity: A Hermeneutical and Phenomenological Investigation*. Würzburg, Germany: Königshausen and Neumann, 2009.

Lipps, Theodor. "Aesthetische Einfühlung." *Zeitschrift Psychologie* 22 (1900): 415–500.

Litt, Theodor. *Individuum und Gemeinschaft. Grundfragen der sozialen Theorie und Ethik*. Berlin: B. G. Teubner, 1919.

Locke, John. *Second Treatise on Civil Government*. Edited by Peter Laslett. Cambridge: Cambridge University Press, 1988.

MacIntyre, Alasdair. *Edith Stein: A Philosophical Prologue, 1913–1922*. Lanham, MD: Rowman and Littlefield, 2006.

Manganaro, Patrizia. *Verso l'altro. L'esperienza mistica tra interiorità e trascendenza*. Rome: Città Nuova, 2002.

Marion, Jean-Luc. *Being Given: Toward a Phenomenology of Givenness*. Palo Alto, CA: Stanford University Press, 2002.

———. *God without Being*. Chicago: University of Chicago Press, 1991.

McAlister, Linda Lopez. "Edith Stein: Essential Differences." In *Contemplating Edith Stein*, edited by J. A. Berkman, 201–11. Notre Dame, IN: University of Notre Dame Press, 2006.

McCullough, Ernest J. "Edith Stein and Inter-Subjectivity." In *Husserl and Edith Stein*, edited by R. Feist and W. Sweet, 127–39. Washington, DC: Council of Research in Values and Philosophy, 2003.

Médoc, Paulus Lenz. "L'idée de l'État chez Edith Stein." *Les Études Philosophiques* 3 (1956): 451–57.

Miles, Judy. "Other Bodies and Other Minds in Edith Stein: Or, How to Talk about Empathy." In *Husserl and Edith Stein*, edited by R. Feist and W. Sweet, 119–26. Washington, DC: Council of Research in Values and Philosophy, 2003.

Mill, John Stuart. "Utilitarianism." In *On Liberty and Other Essays*, edited by J. Gray, 131–204. Oxford: Oxford University Press, 2008.

Moran, Dermot. "The Problem of Empathy: Lipps, Scheler, Husserl and Stein." In *Amor Amicitiae: On the Love that Is Friendship. Essays in Medieval Thought and Beyond in Honor of the Rev. Professor James McEvoy*, edited by Thomas A. Kelly and Phillip W. Rosemann, 269–312. Leuven, Belgium: Peeters, 2004.

Münsterberg, Hugo. *On The Witness Stand: Essays on Psychology and Crime*. New York: Doubleday, 1909.

Nicoletti, Michele. "'Eine Untersuchung über den Staat'—eine philosophische Grundlegung der politischen Theorie." In *Die unbekannte Edith Stein: Phänomenologie und Sozialphilosophie*, edited by Hanna-Barbara Gerl-Falkovitz and Beate Beckmann-Zöller, 73–89. Frankfurt: Peter Lang, 2006.

Pettit, Philip, and Christian List. *Group Agency: The Possibility, Design and Status of Corporate Agents*. Oxford: Oxford University Press, 2011.

Pezzella, Anna Maria. *L'Antropologia filosofica di Edith Stein: Indagine fenomenologica della persona umana*. Rome: Città Nuova, 2003.

Pfänder, Alexander. *Phenomenology of Willing and Motivation and Other Phaenomenologica*. Translated by H. Spiegelberg. Evanston, IL: Northwestern University, 1967.

———. *Zur Psychologie der Gesinnungen*. Tübingen, Germany: Niemeyer, 1913.

Reinach, Adolf. "Die apriorischen Grundlagen des bürgerlichen Rechtes." In *Jahrbuch für Philosophie und phänomenologische Forschung*. Vol. 1, 685–847. Tübingen, Germany: Niemeyer, 1913.

———. On the Theory of the Negative Judgment. Translated by Barry Smith. In *Parts and Moments: Studies in Logic and Formal Ontology*, ed. Barry Smith, 285–313. Vienna: Philosophia Verlag, 1984.

———. *Sämtliche Werke*. Edited by K. Schuhmann and B. Smith. Munich, Germany: Philosophia Verlag, 1989.

———. *Über den Ursachenbegriff im geltenden Strafrecht*. Leipzig, Germany: Verlag von Johann Ambrosius Barth, 1905.

———. *Was ist Phänomenologie?* Munich, Germany: Kosel, 1951.

Riedel-Spangenberger, Ilona. "Einleitung." In *Eine Untersuchung über den Staat*, by Edith Stein, edited by Ilona Riedel-Spangenberger, ix–xxvi. In *Edith Stein Gesamtausgabe*, vol. 7. Freiburg, Germany: Herder, 2006.

Rieder, Heinz. *Liberalismus als Lebensform in der Deutschen Prosa Epik des neunzehnten Jahrhunderts*. Berlin: Matthiesen Verlags, 1939.

Rieß, Wolfgang. *Der Weg vom Ich zum Anderen: Die philosophische Begründung einer Theorie von Individuum, Gemeinschaft und Statt bei Edith Stein*. Dresden, Germany: Echard Richter, 2010.

Sawicki, Marianne. *Body, Text and Science: The Literacy of Investigative Practices and the Phenomenology of Edith Stein*. Boston: Kluwer Academic Press, 1997.

———. "Editor's Introduction." In *An Investigation Concerning the State*, by Edith Stein, translated by Marianne Sawicki, x–xx. Washington, DC: ICS Publications, 2006.

———. "Personal Connections: The Phenomenology of Edith Stein." In *Yearbook of the Irish Philosophical Society: Voices of Irish Philosophy*, 148–69. Dublin: Irish Philosophical Society, 2004.

Scheler, Max. *Das Ressentiment im Aufbau der Moralen*. Edited by M. Frings. Frankfurt: Klostermann, 2004.

———. *Die Wissensformen und die Gesellschaft*. Bern: Francke, 1980.

———. *Formalism in Ethics and Non-Formal Ethics of Values*. Translated by Manfred Frings and Roger L. Funk. Evanston, IL: Northwestern University Press, 1973. German text: *Der Formalismus in der Ethik und die materiale Wertethik: Neuer Versuch der Grundlegung eines ethischen Personalismus*. Boston: Adamant Media Corporation, 2004.

———. *The Nature of Sympathy*. Translated by Peter Heath. Hamden, CT: Archon Books, 1970.

———. *On Feeling, Knowing, and Valuing.* Edited by Harold J. Bershady. Chicago: University of Chicago Press, 1992.

———. "Vom kulturellen Wiederaufbau Europas. Ein Vortrag." In *Vom Ewigen im Menschen.* 1921. Gesammelte Werke 5. Edited by Maria Scheler. Bern, Switzerland: Franke Verlag, 1968.

Schmitt, Carl. *Political Theology: Four Chapters on the Concept of Sovereignty.* Translated by George Schwab. Chicago: University of Chicago Press, 2005.

Schulz, Peter. "Toward the Subjectivity of the Human Person: Edith Stein's Contribution to the Theory of Identity." *American Catholic Philosophical Quarterly* 82, no. 1 (Winter 2008): 161–76.

Searle, John. *The Construction of Social Reality.* New York: Free Press, 1997.

———. *The Making of the Social World: The Structure of Human Civilization.* Oxford: Oxford University Press, 2010.

Secretan, Philibert, trans. Introduction to *De l'État,* by Edith Stein, 7–29. Fribourg, Switzerland: Cerf, 1989.

Sharkey, Sarah Borden. *Thine Own Self: Individuality in Edith Stein's Later Writings.* Washington, DC: Catholic University of America Press, 2009.

———. "What Makes You You?: Edith Stein on Individual Form." In *Contemplating Edith Stein,* edited by J. A. Berkman, 283–300. Notre Dame, IN: University of Notre Dame Press, 2006.

Shilliam, Robbie. *German Thought and International Relations: The Rise and Fall of a Liberal Project.* New York: Palgrave-Macmillan, 2009.

Simmel, Georg. *Das Problem der historischen Zeit.* Berlin: Philosophische Vorträge der Kantgesellschaft, 1916.

———. *Essays in Sociology, Philosophy and Aesthetics.* Edited by K. H. Wolf. New York: Harper Torchbooks, 1959.

Spiegelberg, Herbert. *The Phenomenological Movement: A Historical Introduction.* The Hague: Nijhoff, 1960.

Stein, Edith. *Der Aufbau der menschlichen Person.* In *Edith Stein Gesamtausgabe.* Vol. 14. Edited by B. Beckmann-Zöller. Freiburg, Germany: Herder, 2010.

———. *Edith Stein: Self-Portrait in Letters (1916–1942).* Translated by Josephine Koeppel. Washington, DC: ICS Publications, 1994.

———. *Einführung in die Philosophie.* Edited by H. B. Gerl-Falkovitz and C. M. Wulf. Freiburg, Germany: Herder, 2004.

———. *Endliches und ewiges Sein: Versuch eines Aufstiegs zum Sinn des Sein. Anhang: Martin Heideggers Existenzphilosophie. Die Seelenburg.* Edited by A. Uwe Müller. In *Edith Stein Gesamtausgabe.* Vols. 11 and 12. Freiburg im Breisgau, Germany: Herder, 2006. English translation published as *Finite and Eternal Being*. Translated by K. F. Reinhardt. Washington, DC: ICS Publications, 2002.

———. *An Investigation concerning the State*. Translated by Marianne Sawicki. Washington, DC: ICS Publications, 2006. Originally published as *Eine Untersuchung über den Staat*. In *Jarhrbuch für Philosophie und phänomenologische Forschung*. Vol. 7. Edited by Edmund Husserl, 1–123. Halle, Germany: Niemeyer, 1925. Republished by the same publisher in 1970, but added to it was Stein's earlier text, *Beiträge zur philosophischen Begründung der Psychologie und der Geisteswissenschaften*. The treatise on the state remained unchanged, though the pagination shifted to 285–407. A new critical edition of Stein's text on the state is Edith Stein, *Eine Untersuchung über den Staat*. Edited by Ilona Riedel-Spangenberger. In *Edith Stein Gesamtausgabe*. Vol. 7. Freiburg, Germany: Herder, 2006.

———. *Life in a Jewish Family: Her Unfinished Autobiographical Account*. Translated by Josephine Koeppel. Washington, DC: ICS Publications, 1986.

———. *Martin Heideggers Existentialphilosophie*. In *Welt und Person*. Vol. 6. Leuven, Belgium: Nauwelaerts, 1962.

———. *On the Problem of Empathy*. Translated by W. Stein. Washington, DC: ICS Publications, 1988.

———. *Philosophy of Psychology and the Humanities*. Translated by M. C. Baseheart and M. Sawicki. Washington, DC: ICS Publications, 2000. Originally published as *Beiträge zur philosophischen Begründung der Psychologie und der Geisteswissenschaften*. In *Jahrbuch für Philosophie und phänomenologische Forschung*. Vol. 5. Edited by E. Husserl. Halle, Germany: Max Niemeyer, 1922. Republished by Niemeyer, Tübingen, Germany, 1979. There is also a new German critical edition: *Edith Stein Gesamtausgabe*. Vol. 6. Edited by B. Beckmann-Zöller. Freiburg, Germany: Herder, 2010.

———. *Potency and Act*. Translated by W. Redmond. Washington, DC: ICS Publications, 2009.

———. *Übersetzungen (III und IV) des Hl. Thomas von Aquino Untersuchungen über die Wahrheit—Quaestiones disputatae de veritate 1 und 2*. In *Edith Stein Gesamtausgabe*, edited by H. B. Gerl-Falkovitz. Freiburg, Germany: Herder Verlag, 2008.

———. *Was ist der Mensch?* In *Edith Stein Gesamtausgabe*. Vol. 15. Edited by B. Beckmann-Zöller. Freiburg, Germany: Herder, 2005.

———. *Woman*. 2nd ed. Translated by F. M. Oben. Washington, DC: ICS Publications, 1996.

Steuber, Karsten. *Rediscovering Empathy: Agency, Folk Psychology, and the Human Sciences*. Cambridge, MA: MIT Press, 2006.

Tönnies, Ferdinand. *Die Entwicklung der sozialen Frage.* Leipzig, Germany: Goschen, 1913.

———. *Gemeinschaft und Gesellschaft: Grundbegriffe der reinen Soziologie.* Darmstadt, Germany: Wissenschaftliche Buchgesellschaft, 1963.

Tuomela, Raimo. *The Philosophy of Sociality: The Shared Point of View.* Oxford: Oxford University Press, 2010.

———. *Social Ontology: Collective Intentionality and Group Agents.* Oxford: Oxford University Press, 2013.

Vignemont, Frédérique de. "Drawing the Boundary Between Low-Level and High-Level Mindreading." *Philosophical Studies* 144 (2009): 457–66.

Vignemont, Frédérique de, and Pierre Jacob. "What Is It Like to Feel Another's Pain?" *Philosophy of Science* 79, no. 2 (April 2012): 295–316.

Vignemont, Frédérique de, and Thomas Singer. "The Empathic Brain: How, When and Why?" *Trends in Cognitive Science* 10 (2006): 435–31.

Walther, Gerda. *Ein Beitrag zur Ontologie der sozialen Gemeinschaften.* Offprint from *Jahrbuch für Philosophie und phänomenologische Forschung.* Vol. 6. Edited by Edmund Husserl. Halle, Germany: Niemeyer, 1923.

Wulf, Claudia Mareiéle. "Freiheit und Verantwortung in Gemeinschaft—eine brisante Auseinandersetzung zwischen Edith Stein und Max Scheler." In *Die unbekannte Edith Stein: Phänomenologie und Sozialphilosophie,* edited by Hanna-Barbara Gerl-Falkovitz and Beate Beckmann-Zöller, 91–114. Frankfurt: Peter Lang, 2006.

Young-Bruehl, Elizabeth. *Hannah Arendt: For the Love of the World.* 2nd ed. New Haven, CT: Yale University Press, 2004.

Zahavi, Dan. "Beyond Empathy: Phenomenological Approaches to Intersubjectivity." *Journal of Consciousness Studies* 8, no. 5–7 (2001): 151–67.

———. "Empathy, Embodiment and Interpersonal Understanding: From Lipps to Schutz." *Inquiry* 53, no. 3 (2010): 285–306.

———. "Simulation, Projection and Empathy." *Consciousness and Cognition* 17, no. 2 (2008): 514–22.

———. *Subjectivity and Selfhood: Investigating the First-Person Perspective.* Cambridge, MA: MIT Press, 2008.

Index

actions, 67, 142–43, 175. *See also* categorical acts; dispositional acts
Arendt, Hannah, 193
Aristotle, 25–26, 172
association, 138–41, 210n13
autonomy, 181–82, 186, 189

being, 2, 17, 19
Beiträge zur philosophischen (Philosophy of Psychology and the Humanities), 20, 23, 91, 94, 111–12, 131; on causality, 69, 142; *Individual and Community* part of, 144–54; publication of, 208n1; on sciences, 12–14, 111
Bello, Angela Ales, 63
Bergson, Henri, 61, 82
Bernet, Rudolf, 6
body, 52, 62, 69. *See also* unity, of body, psyche, and spirit; expression through, 64–65, 84–85; inner and outer perception and, 15–16; lived, 39, 57–59, 66–67, 73, 79, 82–83; as zero point of orientation, 59–60, 73
Body, Text, and Science (Sawicki), 32
body-psyche unity, 75–76. *See also* unity
Burckhardt, Jacob, 93

Cartesian Meditations (Husserl), 5, 50
categorical acts, 135–36
causality, 60, 69, 141; psychic, 21–22, 62–64, 138, 142; structure of, 82–83
character, 87–89

Christian philosophy, Stein's, 6; phenomenology vs., 2–3, 26; shift to, 1, 5, 172
Churchland, Patricia, 47–48
cogito, 16, 58
community, 39, 129; acts in, 135–36, 138; character of, 146, 149–52; collective vs. individual responsibility in, 142–43; experience of, 119, 138; feelings in, 119–21; as form of social life, 112–13; forms of, 145, 156; foundational elements of, 130, 155; gender and, 125–26; individuals and, 142, 150–51, 155–56, 158–59; intentionality within, 133–35; life-force of, 145–49; lived experience of, 18–19, 20–21, 119–24, 130–35, 138–41, 144, 154–55; mass vs., 114; members of, 117, 146; relation of individuals to, 146–47, 152–54; relations among, 147, 172; social phenomena in, 23–24; society vs., 20, 116, 118, 166; solidarity and, 129, 211n20, 212n32; sovereignty of, 175–76; within state, 184–85, 189; state as, 172–73, 181, 190; state's relation to, 175–78, 209n8; Stein's work on, 120–21, 155–57; unconscious, 157–58; unity of, 152–54
conflict, 68
Conrad, Theodor, 162
Conrad-Martius, Hedwig, 2, 162
consciousness, 4, 15–16, 18, 33, 78, 93; body and, 60, 63, 73;

communal, 130, 134, 143, 190; community and, 150, 157, 190; empathy as act of, 36, 43, 49, 51; flow of, 53–55, 95, 111–12; foreign, 40–43; in group experience, 129–30; limitations of psychology in explaining, 21–22; objects of, 92, 98, 134; of others, 100, 130; political, 182–83; reflective, 65–66, 78; in society vs. mass, 114–15, 130; solidarity and, 18–19, 118–19; state and, 162, 168, 176, 190–91; structure of, 83–84, 124, 134; superindividual, 109, 122; valuing and, 100–01. *See also* I-consciousness

contract theory, 164, 166, 167–70, 209n8, 210n13

co-primordiality, 70–71, 74, 78

correction, 87–89

creation, 101–02

creativity, 67

deception, 87–89

de Vignemont, Frédérique, 43–44, 46–48

dignity, human, 206n37

Dilthey, Wilhelm, 93–94

dispositional acts, 135–37

distrust, in social phenomenology, 117

doubleness, 137, 149

Durkheim, Émile, 118, 190

education, 125–26, 164

ego, 73, 76, 156; alter ego and, 37, 40, 54, 70, 74, 137–38, 158; categorical acts of, 135–36; immanence of, 36, 38; pre-givens of, 144–45. *See also* I

egology, 69

Eine Untersuchung über den Staat, 161, 208n1

emotion. *See* feelings

empathy, 60, 95, 126; as act of consciousness, 43, 49, 51; as act of mind, 11, 29, 41; analogizing one's own with other's, 72–73; analytic vs. Continental interpretations of, 28–29; community and, 120–21, 123; deceptions and corrections of, 87–89; effects of, 36, 77–79, 83–85, 93–94, 106, 196; experience of, 36–38, 43–44, 72–73, 86, 92; individual vs. collective, 38–39; knowledge of others through, 27–31, 35, 78, 104; knowledge vs., 81–82; levels of, 52, 69, 71; limit of, 100–01, 106–07, 109–10, 118, 120–21; Lipps on, 37–39, 41; mirroring in, 47–48; neurological accounts of, 47; objects of, 11, 123; phenomenological account of, 48–49; placed within intersubjectivity, 31–32, 49–50; primordial and nonprimordial, 32–37, 40–41; projection in, 36, 44–45; reiterated, 75–76, 78; Scheler on, 39–41; self-awareness in, 69, 75; self-knowledge and, 13, 17, 98; self-knowledge through, 50, 53, 89–90, 105–06; sensual, 70–71; solipsism and, 45, 50; Stein's work on, 10, 14, 17, 21, 28, 32–36, 111; studies of, 29–30, 41–44; sympathy vs., 28, 39; types of pain and, 46, 48; valuing and, 101–02, 106

ethics, 170–71, 179

expectations, 34, 128

experience, 56, 62, 65, 78, 83, 132, 143; communal, 18, 125, 129–30, 134, 138; empathy and, 36, 43–44, 70–71, 86; flow of, 77, 95–97; incomplete persons lacking, 104–05; inner and outer,

16, 52–53, 114, 116; unity and, 55, 68–69; of will, 66–67
experience, lived, 42, 63, 99, 118, 144, 179; communal, 130–35, 154–55; communities in, 20–21; of community, 119–24; connections among, 138–41; of state, 183–84, 186
Experience and Judgment (Husserl), 140
expression, 84, 87, 96; bodily, 64–66, 85–86; imitation of, 113–14

families, 126
fantasy, 34, 60
feelings, 81, 99; communal, 132–33, 141; effects of, 97–98; expression and, 65–66; individual and communal, 119–21, 136–37; as internal experience, 52–53; in lived experience of community, 119–22; moods vs., 62, 97
Finite and Eternal Being, 2, 18–19, 32
form, 2
formalism, 172
freedom, 99, 156, 189; alienation of, 169–70; in communities, 153–54; positive and negative, 187–88; spirit concretized by, 90–91; in states, 169, 175–77

Gallagher, Shaun, 48–49
Gallese, Vittorio, 43, 47
gender, 125–26
German Democratic Party, Stein's membership in, 164–65, 187–88
German Idealism, 93, 187, 190–91
Germany, 183; nationalism in, 165, 184, 187; Stein's political activism in, 164–65
Gilbert, Margaret, 127, 129, 162–63
God, 2, 17
Goldman, Alvin, 44–46

Göttingen Circle, 10, 14
Guilead, Reuben, 9

Hegel, Georg W. F., 74, 192; on causality, 83–84; influence of on Stein, 25–26; on the state, 162, 168
Heidegger, Martin, 3, 5–7, 17–18
Henry, Michael, 133
herd mentality, 141, 151
history, 91, 122–23, 130–31
human beings. *See* persons
humanity, shared, 51
human persons. *See* persons
Hume, David, 30, 64
Husserl, Edmund, 52, 74, 127, 133, 139–40, 156; books by, 2, 5–6, 13–14, 25 (*see also specific titles*); on categorical acts, 135–36; differences of Stein's phenomenology from, 14–15; on empathy, 10, 49; *Ich kann* of, 180–81; influence of on Stein, 14, 53, 112; and inquiry into prerequisites for sense, 12–13; on meaning, 25, 85; moving from eidetic to transcendental phenomenology, 4–5, 14, 124; on psyche vs. spirit, 90–91; published vs. unpublished work of, 15; realism vs. idealism of, 10, 13; relations of with Heidegger and Stein, 3, 6–7; solipsism and, 29, 50; Stein's collaboration with, 2, 5–6, 10–11, 144; Stein's frustration with, 1–2, 5; as Stein's mentor, 4, 10, 27, 161; unpublished manuscripts by, 56, 112

I, 32, 66, 101; body and, 58, 60; in choosing values, 99–100; empathy and, 109, 196; feelings and, 61–62, 97–98; other and,

70, 73–74, 103; pure, 53–54, 58, 119, 122; stream of consciousness and, 54–55; will and, 67, 78. *See also* ego
Ich kann, 180–82
I-consciousness, 61–62, 69
idealism, vs. realism, 10, 13
Ideas I (Husserl), 25, 124
Ideas II (Husserl), 14
Ideas III (Husserl), 13, 14
Ideas Pertaining to a Pure Phenomenology (Husserl), 2, 4
imitation, 113–14
indexicality, 74
individuation, 32, 53–55, 58
induction, 64
inference, 41–42
Ingarden, Roman, 162
intentionality, 124, 128–29, 133–35
interests, practical vs. theoretical, 139–40
intersubjectivity, 15, 112, 144; empathy giving low-level, 109–10; empathy placed within, 28, 31–32, 49–50; multiple forms of, 156–57
Introduction to Philosophy, 8
An Investigation concerning the State, 8, 25

Jacob, Pierre, 44, 46, 48
Jarhrbuch für Philosophie und phänomenologische (Husserl), 161, 208n1
John Paul II, Pope, 1, 3

Kant, Immanuel, 83–84
Keysers, Christian, 47
Kjellén, Rudolf, 25
knowledge, 25, 43, 139; empathy vs., 81–82; by other, 89–90; of other minds, 13, 27–31, 35, 39, 42, 69, 78, 104
Kohn, Jerome, 193

language, 127, 206n36
law, 189; sovereignty of state in making of, 173–75; state to be ruled by, 165, 173–75
Lebech, Mette, 206n37
lectures, Stein's, 7
liberalism: freedom and, 187–89; Stein's, 171, 186–89
life-force, 145–49
Lipps, Theodor, 21, 30, 37–39, 41
Litt, Theodor, 112
Logical Investigations (Husserl), 4, 10, 135–36
love, 100–03, 147–48

MacIntyre, Alasdair, 1
Marion, Jean-Luc, 3
Marxism, 194
mass, 112–15, 130, 141, 151
materialism, 188
meaning, 25, 96, 132; existence and, 4–5; making, 86–87
meaning-context, 96–97, 111, 121
meaning-structures, 111, 136
memory, 34–35, 143
mental functions, 22–23
Mill, John Stuart, 30, 41–43
mindreading, 44–47
minorities, 165, 168, 192
mirroring, in empathy, 47–48
moods, 62, 97
motivation, 96–97; in communities, 138–41, 146; flow of consciousness and, 111–12; in society vs. mass, 114–16
movement, 79–80, 83, 146
Münsterberg, Hugo, 13–14, 22–23, 41
Münster lectures, Stein's, 3, 21, 32

nationalism, 164–65, 187, 189
nature, 14–15, 90–91
The Nature of Sympathy (Scheler), 39
neurology, of empathy, 44–45, 47

objectivity, 148
object(s), 91, 140, 141, 168–69
oneness, 37–38, 120
On the Phenomenology of the Consciousness of Internal Time (Husserl), 2, 5–6
On the Problem of Empathy, 4, 8, 11–12, 27
ontic structure, of community, 145
other(s), 69, 74, 92, 130; analogizing one's own experience with, 72–73, 79–80; comparisons with, 76, 106–07; ego and, 103, 137–38, 156; expressive signs of, 84–85; knowledge by, 89–90; motives for responding to, 139–40; personhood of, 100–03, 105; self and, 27–28, 76, 156

pain, 46, 48
perception: empathy and, 33–34, 40, 43, 81–82; inference in, 41–42; inner and outer, 15–16, 74, 90, 106
personality, 93–94, 100, 102, 115–16, 205n29
personhood, 8, 11, 125; as common essence, 45–46; revealed through love, 100–03; transcendental, 51–52; valuing of, 101, 105
persons, 17, 20, 56, 95, 105, 137, 196, 211n18; and constitution of human beings, 53, 79–82, 89; essence of, 29, 110–11, 144–45; knowledge of, 14, 29, 51–52; spiritual layers of, 92, 95; state and, 178–80, 184–86; state as social relation among, 180–81; as unity of body, psyche, and spirit, 51–53, 57, 68–69, 95, 104, 111, 124, 126, 179; valuing of, 100–01
Pettit, Philip, 162–63

Pfänder, Alexander, 25
phenomena of life, 80–82
phenomenology, 53–54, 56, 64, 93, 111, 117; eidetic vs. transcendental, 3–5, 11, 14, 124; on empathy, 48–49; as foundation of science, 12, 14, 156; Husserl's, 14–15, 156; influences on Stein's, 13–14, 17–18, 21, 25–26; method of, 10, 12; nature in, 14–15; Stein's, 4, 156, 171–72, 186–87; Stein's early work in, 3, 7, 16–20; Stein's method of, 18, 92, 163–67; Stein's shift to Christian philosophy from, 2–3, 5, 26; Stein's unique voice in, 11–12, 26, 42, 144; Stein's work on community and, 155–57; Stein's work on the state and, 170, 178–79
philosophy: analytic, 127; political, 25, 161, 171–90; psychology vs., 22; Scholastic, 172; Stein's, 25, 162, 171–90
Philosophy of Psychology and the Humanities, 8
politics, Stein's, 164, 171–90
positivism, 10, 92, 156
Potency and Act, 2
power, of persons and states, 180
promises, 128
psyche, 15, 63, 83, 111, 149; spirit vs., 23, 90–91. *See also* unity, of body, psyche, and spirit
psychic contagion, 120, 151, 154; between members of a mass, 113–14, 141
psychology, 10, 64, 93, 127; experimental, 22–25; limitations of, 21–22, 24–25; Stein and, 21, 24–25, 156

Quaestiones disputatae de veritate (Aquinas), 2

racism, 6–7
realism: Husserl's, 4, 10; idealism vs., 10, 13
reality, 56, 67, 75, 83, 92, 163; experiencing of, 96–97; external, 77–78; language communicating, 127–28; superindividual, 144–45, 158–59, 185
reflection, 65–66, 68, 99–100
Reinach, Adolf, 12–13, 128; influence of on Stein, 4, 10, 14, 25–26; on pure vs. positive rights, 174–76
religion, 170–71, 179
reliving, 91–95
responsibility, 142–43, 154, 156
Riedel-Spangenberger, Ilona, 164–65
Rieß, Wolfgang, 166
rights, pure vs. positive, 169, 174–75, 192
Roman Catholic Church, 1–2, 7–9, 126

sainthood, 1, 3
Sawicki, Marianne, 9, 32
Scheler, Max, 13, 21, 49–50, 80, 82, 90, 114, 179; on empathy, 39–41, 53, 69; on German nationalism, 165, 184; influence of on Stein, 14, 20, 103, 112; on society, 116–17; on solidarity, 142–43
Scholastic philosophy, 172
Schütz, Alfred, 49
science, 4, 22, 24, 64; foundations of, 11–14, 17, 51–52; Husserl and, 10, 156; self-knowledge's importance in, 27–28
sciences, 21; cultural, 91–95, 104–05
Searle, John, 127–28, 206n36
self, 31, 76, 92, 94, 103; comparing with others, 39, 42, 106–07; empathy and, 75, 95; other and, 27, 54, 62, 156. *See also* ego; I

self-knowledge, 14, 51, 53; empathy and, 13, 17, 69, 75, 98; importance of, 27–29, 98; through comparisons with others, 106–07; through empathy, 50, 89–90, 105–06
sensations, 58–60, 63; communal vs. individual, 131–33; of feelings, 61–62; own and others', 70–71, 73
senses, 12–15, 127, 149, 196
sexism, 6–7
Simmel, Georg, 20, 93, 112, 123
simulation theory, 44–46
Sixth Logical Investigation (Husserl), 22
socialities, 162, 180, 196, 210n13; comparison of types of, 166, 189; state as societal vs. communal, 166, 177; three forms of, 112–13, 151
social ontologies, 14, 127; Stein's, 8–9, 20, 25, 27
social reality, 38
social relationships, 109–10, 112–13
society, 112–18, 128, 130, 151–52, 156, 163, 166, 167
sociology, 26
solidarity, 118, 124, 137–38, 163, 190; of communal state, 169; of communities and individuals, 119–22, 146–47; in community, 119–23, 129, 177–78, 211n20, 212n32; responsibility in, 142–43; within states, 175–76, 191, 194
solipsism, 29, 45, 50, 206n36
soul, 55–56, 63, 67, 69, 146
sovereignty: of community, 175–76; of the state, 163–64, 170–78, 191–93
spatialization, 59, 61, 73–75
spirit, 23, 25, 90–95, 105, 148. *See also* unity, of body, psyche, and spirit

spontaneity, 90–91
St. Paul, 68

the state, 14, 26, 117, 125–26, 188, 210n13, 211n18; autonomy and, 181–82; communal structure of, 163–64, 168–69, 171, 185; communities within, 184–85, 189; community and, 172–73, 175–78, 181, 190, 209n8; consciousness, 190–91; contract theory of, 167–70; ethics and religion in, 170–71, 179; German ideal of, 164–65; lived experience of, 183–84, 186; as nation-state, 183–85, 189; persons and, 178–81, 184–86, 192; relation of social and political in, 180–82; as societal vs. communal sociality, 166, 177; solidarity within, 191, 194; sovereignty of, 171–77, 191–93; Stein's definition of, 186, 189; Stein's Germany as, 183–84; Stein's political activism and, 164–65; Stein's work on, 162–67, 178–79
Stern, William, 10, 25
subjectivity, 52, 68–69, 95, 97–98, 111
sympathy, vs. empathy, 28, 39

time, 54–55, 116–17, 122–23
Titchener, Edward, 30
Tönnies, Ferdinand, 20, 112, 163
Tuomela, Raimo, 127–30, 163

unconscious, 157–58
unity, 51–53, 57, 68–69, 95, 104, 111, 124, 126, 179
university, 2, 6–8, 162, 164

values, 101, 103, 105–06, 137, 148, 206n37; capacity to choose, 99–100; hierarchy of, 179–80
Vischer, Robert, 30
Volkelt, Johannes, 72
von Helmholtz, Hermann, 30

Walther, Gerda, 120, 123, 133
we-consciousness. *See* consciousness, superindividual
Weltvernichtung (annihilation of the world), 4
we-ness, 135–37, 144, 147, 155
will, 68, 95, 99, 129, 142; acts of, 41, 78, 91; motivation and, 66–67; in society vs. mass, 114–15; spirit and, 90–91, 93, 138
willing, 25
women, 164
world image, 74–75
World War I, 183–84; effects of loss in, 187, 189; Stein in, 119, 164
writing style, Stein's, changing in work on the state, 165–66. *See also* phenomenology, method of

Zahavi, Dan, 45, 48–50